Apocalyptic Politics

Apocalyptic Politics

A Tap-root of Political Radicalization and Populism

MARTYN WHITTOCK

CASCADE *Books* • Eugene, Oregon

APOCALYPTIC POLITICS
A Tap-root of Political Radicalization and Populism

Copyright © 2022 Martyn Whittock. All rights reserved. Except for brief quotations in critical publications or reviews, no part of this book may be reproduced in any manner without prior written permission from the publisher. Write: Permissions, Wipf and Stock Publishers, 199 W. 8th Ave., Suite 3, Eugene, OR 97401.

Cascade Books
An Imprint of Wipf and Stock Publishers
199 W. 8th Ave., Suite 3
Eugene, OR 97401

www.wipfandstock.com

PAPERBACK ISBN: 978-1-7252-9275-8
HARDCOVER ISBN: 978-1-7252-9276-5
EBOOK ISBN: 978-1-7252-9277-2

Cataloguing-in-Publication data:

Names: Whittock, Martyn J., author.

Title: Apocalyptic politics : a tap-root of political radicalization and populism / Martyn Whittock.

Description: Eugene, OR : Cascade Books, 2022 | Includes bibliographical references.

Identifiers: ISBN 978-1-7252-9275-8 (paperback) | ISBN 978-1-7252-9276-5 (hardcover) | ISBN 978-1-7252-9277-2 (ebook)

Subjects: LCSH: End of the world. | Religion and politics. | History—Religious aspects.

Classification: BL503 .W54 2022 (print) | BL503 .W54 (ebook)

OCTOBER 28, 2022 3:59 PM

To Ali Hull, with thanks for your friendship, suggestions, and insights over the years. They are much appreciated.

Contents

Acknowledgments | ix

CHAPTER 1
Apocalyptic Beliefs across Diverse Cultures | 1

CHAPTER 2
Political Consequences of Jewish and Early Christian Apocalyptic Thinking | 11

CHAPTER 3
An End to Jewish Apocalyptic Politics? The Jewish-Roman Wars | 24

CHAPTER 4
A Shared Hope? The Place of Apocalyptic Beliefs within Islam | 36

CHAPTER 5
Apocalyptic Politics within Early and Medieval Christianity | 47

CHAPTER 6
The Hope of a Persecuted Minority: Apocalyptic Beliefs within Medieval and Early Modern Judaism | 59

CHAPTER 7
Apocalypse Now! The Impact of the Reformation | 71

CHAPTER 8
Islamic Apocalyptic Response to Colonialism in Sudan | 83

CHAPTER 9
African Syncretistic Anticolonial Apocalypse | 95

Chapter 10
New World—New Apocalypse? | 107

Chapter 11
Apocalypse in the Philippines | 118

Chapter 12
Apocalyptic Slaughter in China | 127

Chapter 13
When the Millennium Goes Rogue:
The Thousand-Year Nazi Third Reich | 138

Chapter 14
Contested "Zionisms" | 149

Chapter 15
The View from the East: Orthodoxy, Putin,
and Russian Millenarianism | 161

Chapter 16
Apocalyptic Politics in Iran, and ISIS | 177

Chapter 17
"One Nation—*Deeply Divided*—Under God":
Apocalyptic Politics and the Modern US | 189

Afterword: The Nature of Political Apocalypse | 201

Bibliography | 205

Acknowledgments

I AM GRATEFUL TO a number of people who have assisted me in the writing of this book. Sheikh Muhammad Amin Evans offered very helpful suggestions regarding the basis of Islamic end-times beliefs. Conversations with Professor Julie Ingersoll and Professor Crawford Gribben provided valuable insights into Christian reconstructionism in the USA and its influence on the evangelical community there. Discussions regarding faith, theology, and history are a frequent part of discussions with my family. I thank them for their support and for always being willing to let me discuss my ideas with them. I also wish to thank my agent, Robert Dudley, for his friendship, advice, and encouragement over many years, and the team at Cascade Books (an imprint of Wipf and Stock Publishers) for their support. The authorial views, interpretations, and assessments within this book are my own. All errors, of course, are also my own.

CHAPTER 1

Apocalyptic Beliefs across Diverse Cultures

*A*POCALYPTIC *P*OLITICS EXPLORES the political impact of "eschatology." The Greek word *eschatos* means "last things" and is often used to describe the end of the world as we know it. It views "history as moving towards a future goal."[1] That future event will see the replacement of the current—deeply flawed—world order with one that is good and just. In particular this book examines "apocalyptic" and "millenarian" beliefs across a wide range of religious communities. It is a book about the political application and manipulation of belief, not a book of theological exploration or exegesis. However, theology certainly underpins the politics, and the connection between the two will certainly be explored and explained.

The two words that are often used to describe these beliefs—"apocalyptic" and "millenarian"—have now entered into common usage. This is certainly true of the former. One only has to think of the title of the 1979 film *Apocalypse Now*, directed and produced by Francis Coppola and based on Joseph Conrad's 1899 novella *Heart of Darkness*. In the film the setting is changed from the late-nineteenth-century Congo to the Vietnam War. The relevant point here is the title, which is enough to prompt thoughts of violence, calamity, destruction, and catastrophe. That was clearly intentional when it was chosen for the film.

1. Travis, "Eschatology," 228.

A Google search will extend the range of material currently associated with the word to the most astonishing extent. However, in its origins the word had a specific and technical meaning before it came to have this general flavor of "disaster." The Greek word *apokalupsis* (English apocalypse) literally means "an uncovering"[2] and refers to the revelation of something previously hidden. Within the Jewish and Christian Scriptures, the type of writing described as "apocalyptic" is, technically, only found in the Old Testament in the book of Daniel and in the New Testament in the book of Revelation. These are not, though, the only examples of this kind of literature in Judeo-Christianity. A number of other texts have also survived, although these did not succeed in being accepted into the official canon of Scripture. The key characteristics of this kind of writing are: revelations of heavenly mysteries; unveiling of the divine plan for history; the end-times future of the world; and the cosmic order is revealed. The word "apocalypse" is used eight times in the New Testament itself to describe the second coming of Christ.[3] Among early Christians, the word became closely associated with this longed-for event. It has continued to do so.

It is from this baseline that the word has developed and become used generally of huge events that shake the established order and bring it crashing down. However, it must always be remembered that in its original meaning it had a crucial spiritual dimension. It is about titanic conflict between good and evil; heroic action by those who side with good against the forces of evil; the triumph of good and the destruction of all that corrupts existence and opposes good; the end of the present world order and the establishment of a new order of existence characterized by holiness and harmony. This connects it with the lesser-known term that tends to now be used in a more technical and less sensational manner. This is "millenarian" and "millenarianism."

"Millenarian" does not have the same cachet when it comes to authors and those choosing the titles of films and video games. Within Christianity, millenarianism refers to the belief that the second coming of Christ will establish a literal kingdom on earth, leading to a millennium (1,000 years) of peace prior to the final judgment. There are different versions of this belief (and different suggested end-times timetables) that have developed over time, but the most dramatic one envisages a

---

2. Vine, *Expository Dictionary*, 532.
3. Vine, *Expository Dictionary*, 532.

violent end to human history that will culminate in the victorious return of Christ and the start of the millennium. It should be noted that "millennium" (the time period) is spelt with a double "n," while the phenomenon of "millenarianism" is spelled with a single "n." Although the millennium is hugely important in Christian thought, this thousand-year reign of Christ ("thousand" being *chilioi* in the original Greek, *mille* in later Latin translations and use) is only referred to once in the New Testament—in Revelation 20, where it occurs six times.

From this basis, the word has been adopted to describe movements that preach the coming of catastrophic conflict and the bringing in of a new world order. As a result, the term is often used to describe this phenomenon whenever and wherever such ideas are promulgated, whether or not they contain reference to a thousand-year-period of any kind. And this is the case whether or not they are religious in nature. For that reason, the "Thousand Year Reich" of the Nazis can be described as a millenarian phenomenon, even though it was a secular political movement, because it drew on the concept and adapted it to meet its own requirements. However, enough of its origins remained in the minds of those who did this intellectual hijacking to cause them to describe their goal as a millennium of National Socialism. The number of years that were ascribed to the Nazi vision was clearly not an arbitrary choice. While the Nazis promoted a "pick 'n' mix" form of religiosity that, if it had any religious dimension at all, referenced Norse mythology more than Christian beliefs, they still operated within a culture where outlooks were largely framed by a heritage of Christianity. The "Thousand Year Reich" was no arbitrary term; it had clear religious millenarian roots. There was a terrible irony in the fact that the Nazi antisemitic racist fantasy was rooted in Christian beliefs that were themselves derived from Jewish concepts of the "day of the Lord" and the transformation of the world and cosmic order.

At other times the millennium is absent from radical movements, but the idea of impending cataclysmic change is sufficient to cause the group to be described as "millenarian." These movements, as we shall see, exhibit much of the same general outlook, while lacking detailed similarity when it comes to specific ideology. In this book we will be mostly looking at the idea globally as a religious concept. However, we will also explore how it has been co-opted by semireligious and secular movements too. They too are part of what we might call the "apocalyptic tradition." And they are very present in the twenty-first century, just as they have been throughout history.

The political manifestations of these beliefs are often seen via grassroots mass movements driven by dominant figures who claim insights (revelations) into the nature of current and future events. In short, there is a clear link between apocalyptic political ideology and what we would now term "radicalized populism." Such a prophetic outlook is, not surprisingly, usually associated with a putative "prophet." The faith in such an insightful prophetic leader is often found among those believing in these belief systems. This suggests that, while the overall pattern of events are thought to be foretold and inevitable, human agency still plays a part. This becomes even more obvious in the more secular manifestations of the belief. Looking at this meeting point of radical religious beliefs and radical politics is the focus of this book.

A WIDESPREAD PHENOMENON

Within this book the apocalyptic beliefs and their political impact as found in Judaism, Christianity, and Islam will feature on a number of occasions. This is because each one of these "Abrahamic" world religions contains a form of this belief and, crucially, a concept of "linear history"; and through widespread dissemination of these faiths, this has influenced a very large part of the global community. This can be seen even when that legacy is not explicitly attributed by individuals or groups. Despite this lack of reference, the connection is often clear. Absence of evidence does not constitute evidence of absence when we look more deeply.

As a consequence, there are a wide range of examples throughout the history of the last two millennia where these beliefs have had a significant impact on a wide range of communities, in a number of cultural and geographical contexts. However, while Jewish Scriptures look towards a final decisive act by God to vindicate his chosen people and establish a new order of peace and justice, and while Christianity and Islam see this as being inextricably connected with the second coming of Jesus/*Isa*, other cultures too have articulated apocalyptic beliefs as a way of envisaging the destruction of the current world order and its replacement with a new system. A brief survey of this phenomenon across a range of highly diverse cultures will demonstrate the validity of this assertion across time and place.

For the Vikings, the future apocalyptic events would see the destruction of the Norse gods and goddesses by the giants and allied forces of destruction on the day of *Ragnarok*. Found in the collection of Norse myths known as the *Prose Edda*, and in a section called *The Tricking of Gylfi*, a dramatic version of this story tells of the end of the world. Traditions about this event are also found in a document known as *The Seeress' Prophecy*. *The Seeress' Prophecy* is the first and probably one of the most well-known poems contained in the *Poetic Edda*. The poem is recited by a seeress who can both look back to the beginning of the world and forward to its eventual destruction at an event termed *Ragnarok*. It is one of the most important primary sources for the study of Old Norse mythology because of this wide-ranging scope. It was almost certainly the basis for much of the work of Snorri Sturluson, the thirteenth-century Icelandic scholar who brought together so much of what we know about Norse mythology and sagas. The poem shows the god Odin questioning the seeress on what is to come at *Ragnorok* to better equip himself for the event. This is one of a number of ways in which we see Odin trying to acquire knowledge through the course of the Norse mythological corpus.[4]

Ragnarok means the "doom of the gods" in Old Norse. The Norse word *rok* (doom) has, though, sometimes been confused with the word *rokkr* (twilight) leading to the alterative name of "Twilight of the gods," or *Gotterdammerung* (as used by Richard Wagner in the name of the final part of his operatic Ring Cycle). *Ragnarok* is comprised of a series of events, including a great battle where almost all the major Norse gods will die. This is accompanied by a series of natural disasters ultimately leading to the flooding of the world. After this, the world will start anew with a younger generation of gods and goddesses; and the remaining humans who have managed to survive by hiding in *Yggdrasil* (the mythical tree that connects the nine worlds in the Norse cosmos). It is unclear whether the mythological new world is free from evil or whether the same mix of good and evil is retained.

The events of *Ragnarok* are inevitable and there is nothing the gods can do to prevent it happening. This is despite the strength of Thor and Odin's continuous quest for wisdom and knowledge. This presents the gods in a strangely vulnerable light as beings who, despite their supernatural powers, are as bound by the same power of fate (Old Norse *urthr*) as humans. The only comfort appears to be that the world will start

---

4. Whittock and Whittock, *Norse Myths*, 161–62.

anew—albeit with a new generation of deities.[5] Destruction and renewal are integral to the mythology.

Within Buddhism, several different traditions developed concerning the future state of the world. One tradition arose that the teachings of the Buddha would disappear 5,000 years after his death (AD 4600 in the Christian calendar).[6] This will be preceded by the disintegration of human society, followed by a new golden age associated with a new Buddha, named Maitreya. The preceding time of violence, greed, poverty, and social collapse will see the teaching of the Buddha forgotten in a period of declining *dharma*.[7] That which follows will be an earthly paradise. In contrast, in the *Sattasuriya Sutta* (Sermon of the Seven Suns), found in the *Anguttara Nikaya* of the *Pali Canon*, the Buddha describes the ultimate fate of the world. He does so, in this tradition, by referencing an apocalypse that will be dramatically characterized by the sequential appearance of seven suns in the sky. Each of these suns will cause progressive ruin until the Earth is finally destroyed by fire. The timescale envisaged in this tradition is vast, stretching over hundreds of thousands of years from the time of Buddha. The only ones who will survive this total conflagration and the destruction of all things will be those who have trodden the path of enlightenment.[8]

It seems that much of Buddhist eschatology—alongside many of the facets of modern Buddhist practice—developed in China. This occurred through the blending of earlier Buddhist cosmological ideas with Chinese Daoist eschatological views. This led to the formulation of a complex canon of apocalyptic beliefs. These composite beliefs, although arguably not originally part of orthodox Buddhism, nevertheless form an important collection of Chinese Buddhist traditions. These served to bridge the gap between monastic Buddhism and the local beliefs and ideologies of contemporary Imperial China.

At times these beliefs have given rise to eschatological sects within Buddhism such as the so-called White Lotus Movement, which developed in China during the twelfth century of the Christian era and preached what they considered to be a spiritually reformist creed. Some groups within this broad movement were led by laypeople who attacked

---

5. Whittock and Whittock, *Norse Myths*, 173–74.
6. Germano, *Embodying the Dharma*, 14.
7. Hooper, *End of Days*, 156.
8. Hooper, *End of Days*, 156.

what they considered to be spiritual laxness among Buddhist monks, even though these radical sects themselves rejected celibacy as a lifestyle. A similar movement arose in Japan in the thirteenth century, whose leader, Nichiren, preached that the Mongol invasions of Japan in 1274 and 1281 were apocalyptic events due to the failure to follow what he would have termed true Buddhist teaching. He argued that out of the upheaval a new order would arise due to the destruction of rival Buddhist monastic groups. The Mongol invasions failed. The expected new order did not occur.

The idea of degeneration, followed by renewal, is reminiscent of the Norse outlook and may be compared with the mounting series of cataclysmic events that lead to the battle of Armageddon and the second coming in the book of Revelation in the New Testament. This is one of several comparable motifs found within otherwise very different apocalyptic traditions.

While not uniformly accepted, some within Jainism look forward to an apocalyptic transformation of human life and world society in the transition from what is termed the sixth *ara* of the *avsarpini* cycle to the first *ara* of the *utsarpini* cycle. In the current age (*dusama*) it is believed that no additional great world religious teachers will arise. Consequently, although righteous people still exist in this stage of human history, no person can attain true *moksha* (liberation or enlightenment) without going through at least one cycle of rebirth. This state of affairs will degenerate still further. This future worsening period of time is called *dusama dusama*. However, eventually this degeneration will lead back to a golden age of existence.

Set far in the future (from a twenty-first-century perspective), the concept found in Jainism is comparable with the Hindu belief in all of creation contracting to a singularity and then again expanding at the end of the epoch of *kali yuga*. Although this event is thought to lie far in the future, this is open to more immediate interpretation through a later Hindu prophetic tradition that it will occur when the moon, sun, Venus, and Jupiter enter the same sign (not a rare event and occurring as recently as 2012). This particular date caused excitement among some who also claimed this was a significant doom-laden year in the ancient Mayan calendar, being regarded as the end-date of the 5,126-year-long cycle in the "Mesoamerican Long Count calendar" (while academics declared this was a clear misunderstanding of Mayan culture and calendrical evidence).

Regarding Hinduism,[9] while the matter is very complex, there is a widespread belief that the universe goes through four distinct phases: the *krita* or *satya yuga*, the *treta yuga*, the *dvapara yuga*, and the *kali yuga*. In total, these periods of time are thought to amount to 432,000 years.[10] In the course of these *yugas*, or ages, it is believed that human beings will become increasingly alienated from the gods and goddesses, and (consequently) from the divine principles that underpin human and cosmic existence. It is believed that over human existence so far, the god Vishnu has incarnated in order to redeem humankind. These existences constitute successive *avatars* of this god. However, the general arc of existence appears to be towards degeneration and destruction. According to this dramatic and long-term cosmology, the current world situation constitutes the fourth age: the decadent age of *kali yuga*. Many Hindus believe that the god Vishnu will appear on earth one final time as the *avatar* Kalki. However, this appearance will not be to save humanity but instead will set the scene for the inevitable final judgment of all humanity and the destruction of the existing world order.[11] As a result, the culmination of the age of *kali yuga* is the destruction of the universe. Yet this destruction is believed to be the precursor to eventual renewal. A new world order will arise following the destruction of the old, and this will culminate in a golden age of harmony and blessing.[12] Even though there are dramatic differences between Hindu end-times beliefs and those of other world religions and traditions, the idea of degeneration and destruction, followed by renewal and transformation, is comparable with key aspects of other religious traditions.

However, while religiously motivated violence is apparent within Buddhism and Hinduism (as seen in contemporary nationalist movements in Myanmar [Burma] and India), arguably the *end-times* form of it is mostly manifested in societies influenced by the Abrahamic religions, with their *linear concept of history* and *traditions of imminent apocalypse* and *millenarianism*.

There are some exceptions. The tribal revolt led by Birsa Munda, in 1898, against British rule, in the Indian state of Bihar, is a striking one. Combining local Munda and Hindu beliefs with Christian millenarian

---

9. Geitner, "End-Times in the East," 1–4.
10. Zimmer, *Myths and Symbols*, 13–16.
11. Parrinder, *World Religions*, 223.
12. Parrinder, *World Religions*, 211.

ones, he identified his contemporary context as that of *kali yuga*. The poverty and landlessness of his people he attributed to dark forces (represented by the British) that would soon be overthrown with great violence. At Dombari Hill, in February 1898, he and his followers combined the Hindu celebration of Holi with the declaration of the end of British rule. In 1900, British troops crushed the movement and Birsa died in prison later that year.[13]

Similar tribal uprisings against British rule in India (such as the Santal *hool*, or uprising) also combined pre-Hindu and Hindu beliefs with Christian millenarian concepts. It was the latter that provided messianic and apocalyptic/millenarian themes that would arguably otherwise have been absent from a solely Hindu perspective.[14]

However, the most obvious and frequent examples of explicit millenarianism (as usually understood)—translated into politics—comes from movements influenced by the Abrahamic faiths. Therefore, it is these three religions (and groups influenced by their beliefs) that will mostly feature in this study.

We will also explore its occurrence within the belief systems of indigenous peoples on the American continent: north, central, and south. This includes both belief systems closely related to (and developed from) Judeo-Christian and Islamic beliefs, and those that have looser connections (or little or no connection) with Judeo-Christian or Islamic ideas. As we shall see, a number of these indigenous movements show signs of being influenced by the messianic ideas and eschatology inherent in Judeo-Christianity due to interaction with colonizing forces. Some movements have been influenced by similar themes within Islam, because of particular, countercultural, black responses to the dominant ideology of white society, and looking to Islam for a model of spirituality and community. These movements represent energetic resistance to colonialism and to white control. But, through interaction with the religious beliefs of the colonizers, these often reveal aspects of these religious beliefs appropriated and reimagined as a form of resistance to colonial power. Similar phenomena will be observed in some African responses to colonialism, and other examples will be found in Asia. In these cases, as with those we will examine from the Americas, indigenous ideas show signs of borrowing certain aspects of belief or outlooks from the colonizers, even as

---

13. Urban, "Millenarian Elements," 373–74.
14. Urban, "Millenarian Elements," 373.

they sought to resist colonialism. It is a vivid example of both the appeal of apocalyptic beliefs and the variety and malleability of these ideas. And borrowing often took the form of taking on board millenarian themes, outlooks, or mindsets, rather than complete "packages" of beliefs.

As a result, we will examine political apocalyptic activities as diverse as the Xhosa Cattle-Killing Movement, *Mumboism*, the Satiru rebellion, the *Maji Maji* rebellion and the Chilembwe uprising in Africa; the Tepehuan revolt, the followers of Tenskwatawa the "Shawnee Prophet," the Ghost Dance, Rastafarianism, the Nation of Islam, the Nuwaubian Nation, and the Black Hebrew Israelites in the Americas; and the movement of *Cofradia de San José* and that of *Santa Iglesia*, the Taiping rebellion, and the actions of the Righteous Harmony Society in Asia. Together they represent a diverse range of responses to cultural change, stress, and threat. All have apocalyptic aspects. Many show signs of drawing on beliefs from other religious systems. But they also were deeply rooted in the belief systems of their indigenous cultures.

What is clear is that the concept of apocalypse and millenarianism is found in many religious cultures, although expressed in very different ways. What is also clear is that, at times, the belief has had discernible impacts on politics. That latter point is the main focus of this book. Apocalyptic beliefs often lead to radical politics, because when faith is radicalized it "gives moral justifications for killing and provides images of cosmic war that allow activists to believe that they are waging spiritual scenarios."[15] If this can be true of some deployments of religious faith generally, it is even more so when eschatological confidence (in identifying the imminent completion of a linear view of history) is high. This book aims to chart this characteristic and explain why this is so often the case.

---

15. Juergensmeyer, *Terror in the Mind of God*, xiv.

CHAPTER 2

Political Consequences of Jewish and Early Christian Apocalyptic Thinking

MESSIANIC AND APOCALYPTIC Old Testament Scriptures influenced the definition of later Jewish messianic kingship, the expectations regarding existing leadership, and the way that the future of the national community of Judaism was envisaged. The view of politics and power was changed by this perspective, as were the religious and political strategies geared towards its ultimate implementation. This outlook was also influenced by the changing power politics of the eastern Mediterranean, as the once-independent Jewish state passing under the control of different emerging regional superpowers. This can be seen in events such as the Maccabean Revolt and other attempts to reassert Jewish political autonomy and semiautonomy in the face of Greek and Roman power. The legacy of this for messianic-inspired political ideology, both at an official (elite) and an unofficial (radical) level, was profound, along with the way that messianic beliefs affected aspects of political revolts.

This apocalyptic tradition influenced how early Christians understood Jesus and the significance of the emerging Christian community. This colored views of, and relationships with, the Roman state and its agents. In this context, the political ramifications of the fourth-century conversion of the empire were significant. As a consequence of this later change, *Realpolitik* shifted the tone of the apocalyptic mood music, and its political radicalism reduced as a consequence. However, that is getting ahead of the story.

THE APPEARANCE OF THE JEWISH MODEL

Inherent in Jewish thought was the idea that, in the future, God will transform the flawed world order, vindicate his people's trust in him, and establish a kingdom of righteousness. At times this took the form of an expected political restoration. At other times it promised a radical transformation of the whole created order.

From the time of the exile of the Jewish people in Babylon (ca. 597–38 BC), the idea grew of a restoration of the people to their ancestral lands, over which they would exercise control. From this physical restoration developed the idea of a future cosmic transformation. Such apocalyptic elements can be identified in several Old Testament books, especially those of Joel, Zechariah, and Isaiah (especially chapters 24–27 and 33), but the book of Daniel is the clearest example of this kind of literature. None of these documents are political manifestos, although Daniel was once sometimes considered to be one. Instead, they look to God for decisive action. The hope for Israel is clearly seen in Isaiah chapters 40–46, where "Israel is the chosen people of the one God, who has plainly declared His purpose ever since the beginning. Though it is now a despised race, trodden under foot, its glorious future is certain."[1]

It has been argued that, as Jewish experience of dominant empires increasingly restricted their own room for maneuvering, a political realism caused thinkers to recognize that in the normal run of things their hopes and ambitions were unlikely to be realized. In short, they would not achieve political supremacy in relationships with their neighbors. As a direct result "the belief in an age to come, in which righteousness and the true religion should hold undisputed possession, came more and more prominently into the foreground."[2] To put it another way: contemporary political ambition became future apocalyptic hope. The Babylonian exile had already emphasized this, and it was further underlined during the period of Hellenistic (Greek) domination of the Middle East following the conquests of Alexander the Great. This reached its climax in the Maccabean Revolt, which, as we shall see, broke out in 167 BC. This combined the existing outlook on limits to Jewish political ambitions with a realization that an existential threat hung over the whole Jewish people and their religious culture. This changed the resistance to it from a war of liberation to one that had potentially cosmic implications, since some

1. Torrey, "Apocalypse," lines 240–42.
2. Torrey, "Apocalypse," lines 245–47.

understood it as playing a part within God's plan for the future of the world. Ideas concerning a crisis leading to God's judgment of the world and a transformation of the cosmic order now became apparent within Jewish understanding. It was in this crucial period of a fight for national survival (in the face of severe persecution) that "there grew of necessity the doctrine of 'the world to come' (*ha-'olam-ha-ba*); the ever-present contrast between which and 'this world' (*ha-'olam-hazeh*) is one of the fundamentals of apocalyptic literature throughout its whole history."[3]

THE IMPORTANCE OF THE MACCABEAN REVOLT

The Maccabees were a Jewish priestly family who led a rebellion against the oppressive Seleucid ruler Antiochus IV. As a result of their victories they were able to reconsecrate the Jewish temple in Jerusalem, which had been previously defiled. The name "Maccabees" means something like "hammer" or "hammerer" and was a title accorded to Judas, a hero from the family that led the revolt (167–164 BC). Later the description was extended to include his whole family. This included his father Mattathias and Judas's four brothers: John, Simon, Eleazar, and Jonathan. It was further used to include John Hyrcanus, who was son of Simon. The context to their dramatic uprising against oppressors of the Jewish religion lay in the fragmentation of the empire of Alexander the Great (died 323 BC).

At the time of the Maccabees, the Jewish cultural capital of Jerusalem (once capital of the independent kingdom of Judah) was contested between the two rival regional states of Egypt and Syria. These states are often described using the names of the dynasties ruling them: the Ptolemies in Egypt and the Seleucids in Syria. Both dynasties were descended from generals of Alexander the Great. In Syria, Antiochus IV ruled from 175 to 164/163 BC. Something of the Greek-inspired ideology associated with him can be glimpsed in his additional Greek name *Epiphanes*, meaning "god manifest." His political ambitions included detaching Judah from the sphere of influence of Egypt. Not only this but he also aimed to unite his expanded empire by imposing Greek religious beliefs on it, and this included presenting himself as a personification of the divine. Such a strategy had earlier been deployed by Alexander the Great himself. This set Antiochus on a collision course with monotheistic Judaism.

---

3. Torrey, "Apocalypse," lines 250–53.

Antiochus intervened in the appointment of the Jewish high priest and used his alliance with the new appointee to have a gymnasium built in the vicinity of the Jerusalem Temple. With its naked sports and pagan imagery, it was a flagrant and provocative display of pagan ideology in close proximity to the ideological center of Judaism. In addition, Antiochus ordered that elite Jews must take part in the activities there. This was cultural imperialism at its most extreme.

In the face of outraged Jewish opposition, he then increased the severity of his campaign against Judaism. He banned Jewish Sabbath observance and other Jewish traditional feasts and practices. This involved banning Jewish religious sacrifices, banning the reading of the law of Moses, and the destruction of Jewish Scriptures. In addition, he outlawed circumcision. In 168 BC, he seized Jerusalem, had the temple treasure removed to Antioch, and set up his political base on the hill overlooking the temple. It would lead to the desecration of the temple and city.[4] He ratcheted up the campaign and carried out pagan sacrifices in the holy of holies in the temple. His erection of a pagan idol there, to the Olympian god Zeus, was accompanied by similar actions in other Jewish settlements. Local Jews were expected to make sacrifices on pagan altars to the Greek deities. What then occurred was more than a nationalist revolt; it was a religious uprising of staggering proportions. And it was accompanied by the production of literature that would inspire both Jewish and Christian political activists for centuries.

About 17 miles (27 km) northwest of Jerusalem lay the village of Modi'im. Here resistance was led by a priest named Mattathias and his five sons: John, Simon, Judas (Maccabeus), Eleazar, and Jonathan. The dynasty that would eventually be derived from them was the "Hasmonean," named (according to the later Jewish historian Josephus) from Mattathias's great-grandfather Asamonaios. Their role in the ensuing revolt began when Mattathias hit a Jew who was preparing to offer sacrifice to the Greek gods and killed the royal official present.

Many other Jews joined the family in the hill country to which they had fled. A particularly significant group of supporters were the *Hasideans*, who were committed to strict adherence to the law of Moses. Although at first their refusal to fight on the Sabbath cost them many casualties, their belief in their cause being a fight for continued Jewish survival led them to abandon this prohibition. It was a sign of the apocalyptic conflict that

---

4. Oegema, *Anointed and His People*, 56.

was occurring between two bitterly opposed rival belief systems and the Maccabean belief that they were God's chosen warriors in this holy war.

In the end, the guerrilla war that ensued was also a civil war as those considered collaborators were ruthlessly attacked, alongside the Syrian forces. After Mattathias's death in about 166 BC, the leadership of the war against the Hellenizing Syrians fell to Judas Maccabeus, his third son. Judas saw himself as the embodiment of Jewish religious and cultural resistance. He clearly modeled himself on the great leaders of Jewish national history such as Joshua and Gideon, who had conducted successful military campaigns against the pagan Canaanites. This was both a co-opting of existing Jewish military history and an attempt to frame his campaign as comparable to theirs in terms of representing God's will as expressed through the Jewish people. And, as with these earlier traditional figures, Judas was engaged in a cultural as well as an ethnic conflict. As with them it was framed as a holy war against false gods. But unlike their wars of conquest, Judas's was a fight for national survival. It was this that gave it a particularly apocalyptic tone.

In December 164 BC, Judas recaptured Jerusalem. It was three years since Antiochus IV had defiled the holy temple. The entire city was now back in Jewish hands—that is, except for the royal citadel: the Acra. The temple area was then ritually cleansed. A new altar of unhewn stones was raised and dedicated. The sanctuary was reconsecrated on 24 December, or 25 *Kislev* in the Jewish calendar. The eight-day-long Jewish festival of *Hanukkah* (Dedication), is the Festival of Lights that still commemorates this seismic event.

Next, Judas pursued the war in Galilee and across the Jordan but was killed in battle after over five years of military leadership. He was succeeded by his brother, Jonathan, with whom the new Syrian king, Alexander Epiphanes, came to terms. In 153 or 152 BC, Jonathan became high priest in Jerusalem. This effectively consolidated religious and political leadership within the same family. It was, in effect, the beginning of the high priestly Hasmonean line. This was not without controversy since traditional Jews maintained (and were supported in this by scriptural evidence) that only a descendant of Aaron (the brother of Moses) should hold this position. What had started as an apocalyptic war had now settled down into controversial dynastic politics.

Under the Hasmonean ruler, John Hyrcanus I (died 104 BC), the dynasty brought Samaria under its control and forced the Idumeans—descendants of the ancient Edomites southeast of the Dead Sea—to convert to Judaism. It would be from this converted community that the later ruler known to history as Herod the Great would ascend. But that is part of a different story. What is important in this account is the institutionalizing of the original cause. The new ruler of the expanded kingdom was, in effect, a Sadducee—one of the conservative elite who only accepted written Jewish Law as divinely authoritative. Ironically, given the origins of the movement, by the time of Jesus in the early first century AD they had further become associated with making accommodation with the Romans, who had once more eclipsed Jewish political independence and dominated the region. The importance of the Maccabees in any history of apocalyptic or millenarian activism is in the muscular religious nature of their original revolt and in the literature that developed alongside it. In this they left a powerful legacy that would continue to reverberate in later Judaism and Christianity.

THE MACCABEAN REVOLT AND THE BOOK OF DANIEL

Jewish apocalyptic beliefs certainly did not begin under the Maccabees. They had much deeper roots than that in the belief in the future "day of the Lord." These ideas had developed during and after the Babylonian exile. However, these ideas "do not usually imply a movement of any sort"[5] and such ideas have been described as "utopian rather than revolutionist."[6] What the whole Maccabean episode did was give it a sharp political edge. It is no surprise, therefore, to learn that many biblical scholars consider that the book of Daniel was composed during this formative period of Jewish political and cultural resistance. That it combines resistance to earthly rulers (who oppose God's will) with a visionary exposition of the ultimate revealing of God's power on earth, and the vindication of his people, is highly significant.

This is particularly apparent in chapters 7–12 of Daniel. The book is traditionally attributed to a revered visionary who lived some four centuries earlier during the Babylonian exile. Indeed, this is still the position of conservative theologians and scholars. However, most modern biblical scholars consider the composition of at least these key chapters to have occurred during the initial stages of the Maccabean revolt (ca.

5. Collins, "Millenarianism," lines 65–66.
6. Collins, "Millenarianism," line 66.

167 BC).⁷ According to this interpretation the book presents a visionary succession of four terrible beasts, which clearly represent earthly kingdoms, and which culminate in a fourth kingdom, "terrifying and dreadful and exceedingly strong" (Dan 7:7).⁸ For those who consider the book a product of the second-century conflict with hellenization, this is seen as the kingdom of Antiochus IV Epiphanes, the arrogant little horn that appeared among the ten horns on the head of the fourth beast (Dan 7:8). It is following this that the "Ancient One" (or "Ancient of Days" in Aramaic) establishes his throne in the company of vast numbers of heavenly beings; judges and destroys the fourth beast; and finally gives power and authority to one who is described as "like a human being" ("one like a son of man" in Aramaic) who will have "an everlasting dominion that shall not pass away," a kingdom "that shall never be destroyed" (Dan 7:9–14). The images are vivid and dramatic. They have influenced centuries of thinking about the establishment of God's millennial kingdom.

How are we to understand this in the context of the Maccabean revolt? It has been asserted that "The book of Daniel does not speak of a messiah, and so is not strictly a witness to messianic hope."⁹ It seems clear that he did not envisage a Jewish earthly kingdom replacing that which was imposed on the Jews by the Seleucids. There is no exploration of an earthly kingdom in the prophecies. Instead, the focus appears to be on God's rule and on heavenly sovereignty. It was, it has been asserted, not designed to provide the ideology of an apocalyptic movement.¹⁰ It was fundamentally "unsupportive of activist movements."¹¹ In short, it was not the "Manifesto of the Maccabees." One finds something more like that in the apocryphal book I Maccabees (that did not make it into the Old Testament). But even then, this is more of an explanation for why the rebels had God's favor. It does not actually present them in messianic terms. A similar, if more emotional, account of the war can also be found in II Maccabees.¹²

However, it is difficult not to see this as a theological counterbalance to the war being waged by Mattathias and his sons. Clearly, both they

---

7. For example: Firestone, *Holy War in Judaism*, 26.
8. *NRSV*. All Bible quotes are from this version, unless otherwise stated.
9. Collins, "Millenarianism," lines 53–54.
10. Esler, "Social-Scientific Approaches," 128.
11. Firestone, *Holy War in Judaism*, 26.
12. Firestone, *Holy War in Judaism*, 29–32.

and the writer of Daniel saw this as a conflict on behalf of God against an existential threat to the Jewish people. Mattathias and his sons might not have framed themselves as messianic leaders but there clearly were those who saw this moment of conflict as being a key part of God's plan for the ages. One can also see how the idea of the "Son of Man" found there—and the idea that his appearing would accompany the destruction of the last world empire and the establishment of God's eternal kingdom—provided an important input into the idea of a personal messiah who would bring in both political and cosmic change.

At the very least, we can see that at the end of a series of periods of human history, "a (human) figure is expected to play a liberating role."[13] It is from this time forward that, arguably, we see messianic concepts in Judaism presented as including a royal and/or priestly figure[14]; and in which present circumstances were viewed as fulfillments of ancient prophecies and the prelude to future world and cosmic transformation. The latter was associated with the idea of idealized kingship, as exemplified by the earlier (and then reimagined) figure of King David, and prophetic verses that looked towards a restitution of David's line in future times: "A shoot shall come out from the stock of Jesse, and a branch shall grow out of his roots" (Isa 11:1). This could be read as God raising up a righteous king (in a way reminiscent of the rise of the Maccabees) but without this being miraculous in terms of the origins of that king. However, in time, Christians would read these verses as implying a more heavenly origin of the Messiah (Christ in Greek).

Here was a combination of idealized Davidic rule, worldly and cosmic transformation, and a suggestion of how radical political activism—as had been seen in the activities of the early Maccabees—might foreshadow the activities of a future messianic leader. The Maccabees were not messiahs in this developed sense (and never claimed to be), but they pointed to how radical political action might be part of such a future hope. This could lead to "urgency and enthusiasm" of a kind often associated with radical millenarian movements.[15]

---

13. Oegema, *Anointed and His People*, 57.
14. Oegema, *Anointed and His People*, 57.
15. Collins, "Millenarianism," line 70.

MESSIANIC HOPE AFTER THE MACCABEAN PERIOD

This messianic emphasis developed further during the period of increased Roman influence and then outright occupation of Judea, which takes us into the period of the life of Jesus. In this time, the hope for a personal political messiah—which had been latent in the revolt of the Maccabees and the literature composed at that time—increased dramatically. We see this in a number of failed revolts against Rome. Some have read in the Qumran texts (found in modern times near a Jewish religious settlement near the Dead Sea that was eventually destroyed by the Romans) belief in a messianic pair composed of a priestly messiah originating from the family of Aaron and a royal messiah from the family of David. Scholars continue to debate this interpretation. Among the Dead Sea Scrolls, the War Scroll (1QM) describes the *Kittim* (the Romans) as being among the followers of Belial who oppose God. The War Scroll describes an army of angels, under the leadership of the archangel Michael, coming to save the "Sons of Light." While this could be seen as a future event independent of human agency, some clearly saw it as accompanying or following a human uprising. The ground was prepared for radical action.

The hailing of Jesus as "Son of David" reflects this ideology of a looked-for rescuer from the family of the great historic king. Others saw this person in the "Son of Man" of Daniel; and it is noteworthy that this was Jesus' preferred self-designation. While Jesus almost certainly meant something different by these titles, when compared with his contemporary society, it seems clear that many of those in the crowds who used them of him had temporal-political, as well as spiritual-eschatological, hopes.

The messianic hopes of the period are mentioned within the writings of the late-first-century Jewish historian Josephus, and within the New Testament. Josephus, in his books *Antiquities of the Jews* and *The Jewish War*, mentions a rebel, called "Judas the Galilean," who led a revolt against Rome in AD 6. The basis of the revolt was a refusal to accept any authority other than that of God. Josephus described him as "a teacher of his own sect." From this, a number of scholars have assumed that it was the Zealots that Josephus had in mind, but he does not actually say this, so we cannot be specific concerning the group represented by "Judas the Galilean."[16] However, there does seem evidence that his descendants were

---

16. Brighton, *Sicarii*, 2.

active in the much-later Zealot and *Sicarii* (assassins) movements,[17] so there may have been an ideological and organizational connection with the earlier events and movement. The key thing is that a careful study of these various groups as they rose and developed through the first century AD indicates that all shared "a common, fundamentally religious and eschatological ideology that resulted in common activities and goals."[18] The way ancient writers (Jewish and Roman) labeled these groups has caused some controversy among scholars over their relationship to each other, whether they constituted distinct groups, and exactly when each group appeared and was active.[19] However, what is fundamental to this study is the assumption that apocalyptic political demands, even when not a core feature of a group's ideology, were never far away.

This meant that there was a background of increasing messianic expectation in the run-up to the outbreak of war with Rome in AD 66. It is likely that sects such as the one at Qumran, and the descendants of Judas the Galilean, saw this as the event that would trigger divine intervention. However, we do not know what the so-called "Sons of Light" there made of these events. Anyway, the community was geared more toward withdrawal from the world than action designed to overthrow the current political order. It was eventually to be destroyed by the Romans.[20] There were others, though, who were committed to radical social change that involved interaction with the world order and not withdrawal from it.

CHRISTIANS AND THE APOCALYPSE

Both John the Baptist (whom we meet in the Christian Gospels) and the inhabitants of Qumran held similar apocalyptic views that were expressed in similar terms: the impending end of the current world order, due to God's judgment. Both John and the Jewish community at Qumran drew heavily on the prophetic language and imagery found in the Old Testament book of Isaiah. They were not alone. It has been speculated that John's group was one of a number of groups operating in and around the valley of the Jordan, preaching an end-times message. The later Jerusalem Talmud (for example the text known as *Sanhedrin 29c*) claims

17. Brighton, *Sicarii*, 2–3.
18. Hengel, *Zealots*, 48.
19. See: Hengel, *Zealots*, 48, 400.
20. Collins, "Millenarianism," lines 205–9.

that twenty-four such sects were operating by the year AD 70.[21] Some of these had political aspirations to accompany these religious beliefs and this fed into the cataclysmic events that engulfed the region in the later Jewish-Roman War.

This gives us the context of the ministry of Jesus and the rise of Christianity. Two of Jesus' followers may have been members of one of the resistance groups that mixed apocalyptic beliefs with a radical political agenda. One of these was Simon, referred to variously as "Simon the Zealot" (in Luke and Acts) and also known as "Simon the Canaanite" or "Cananaean" (in Mark and Matthew). The reference in Luke 6:15 is particularly striking because it explicitly connects Simon with the extreme nationalist party of the Zealots. Even the less politically radical surname of "Canaanite" was probably derived from the Aramaic *qan'ana'*—meaning a Zealot.[22]

The second example is less certain but remains a very real possibility: Judas Iscariot, who betrayed Jesus. He possibly took his surname from the unlocated village known as Kariot or Kerioth. On the other hand, it may have been derived from *Sicarii* (knife-men, assassins). In this case he was Judas *Sicarius*, Judas the knife-man.

There is, however, a complication since the Zealots and the *Sicarii* only came to prominence in the Jewish nationalist fervor of the 60s AD. This was about thirty years after the ministry of Jesus.[23] So, the matter is undecided but it could have provided the motivation that finally led Judas to betray Jesus. Either he became disillusioned with what he regarded as Jesus' lack of political activism, or perhaps he hoped to force the pace of apocalyptic change?[24] However, the matter must be left unresolved.

What is clear is that Jesus did not embrace the radical political agenda of many of those around him. The challenge in his message was "dependent on God rather than human agency for its fulfillment."[25] Indeed, his preaching has been interpreted as a direct challenge to those of his contemporaries who sought apocalyptic conflict with Rome.[26] From

---

21. Whittock and Whittock, *Jesus*, 87.
22. France, *Gospel According to Matthew*, 177.
23. Carrington, *Early Christian Church*, 1:33.
24. Whittock and Whittock, *Jesus*, 214.
25. Whittock and Whittock, *Jesus*, 171.
26. Wright, *Jesus and the Victory of God*, 317.

this perspective, Jesus' teaching declared that Jewish nationalism would destroy the Jewish community in the resulting conflict. In other words:

> Politically radical Judaism, fixated on revolutionary nationalist fervour, would not win. It had set its sights on national liberation which would actually lead to death and destruction; rather than the community transformation which would come from embracing the good news being promulgated by Jesus.[27]

Nevertheless, he clearly looked forward to an end-times culmination of the present world order that built on existing Jewish beliefs about the day of the Lord. It was simply not one that would be triggered by political activism. Later Christians would prove to be less patient in waiting for the culmination of history and, for many of them, radical activism was very much on their agenda.

As a result, early Christians were the heirs of a complex legacy as far as their view of history and the end times were concerned. On one hand, they drew on Jewish traditions that for centuries had contained varied apocalyptic Scriptures that looked towards future decisive acts of God to vindicate his people, judge their enemies, and establish a new order of righteousness. On the other hand, they saw this as occurring both in the life, death, and resurrection of Jesus and also in his eventual return. This, they believed, was the culmination of Jewish apocalyptic hopes.

We can see the fusion of old and new ideas in the way in which, for example, prophecies from the book of Daniel can be traced through the New Testament.[28] In Matthew's Gospel, Jesus' disciples question him regarding the signs of his (future) coming and the end of the age (Matt 24:3). This follows his prediction of the complete destruction of the Jerusalem Temple (Matt 24:2). Given the destruction of the temple in AD 70 by the Romans, it would not be surprising if the compiler of Matthew and his readers thought these apocalyptic events were about to occur and this prophecy be imminently fulfilled. The book of Revelation combines Jewish and Christian imagery and concepts in an apocalyptic series of visions. As such, it stands out from the rest of the literature that was eventually accepted into the New Testament canon. It is a New Testament equivalent of the Old Testament book of Daniel, and it frequently references that book in its imagery. As in Daniel, Revelation 13 describes a ten-horned beast that symbolizes the last world power, with a second

---

27. Wright, *Jesus and the Victory of God*, 317; Whittock and Whittock, *Jesus*, 197.
28. Tabor, "Jewish and Christian Millennialism," 257.

beast demanding divine honors be paid to this ruler. References to the sea, animal imagery, and ten horns appear to link to Daniel 7. A number of other Christian apocalypses were written during the period between AD 100 and AD 400. These included the *Apocalypse of Peter*, the *Apocalypse of Paul*, the *Ascension of Isaiah*, and the *Testament of Abraham*. Written after the books and letters that were eventually accepted into the New Testament, they nevertheless reveal how apocalyptic ideas were circulating within the early Christian community.

It is not surprising that many then, and now, read the passages in Revelation as a reference to the persecuting Roman Empire. The question was: How active could, or should, Christians be in bringing prophetic events to fruition? How political should they be in opposing Rome, in order to welcome the kingdom of God?

The apocalyptic beliefs that had become increasingly politicized in Judaism under Roman rule became more spiritual in nature as they appear in early Christianity. However, it was not long before they began to be expressed in more radical political and revolutionary terms. However, before that had occurred, apocalyptic politics within Judaism had exploded into a series of wars of terrible violence. These were wars in which religious and national aspirations were intimately intertwined with apocalyptic and millenarian hopes. This brought those articulating these views into direct conflict with the Roman state—and national catastrophe.

CHAPTER 3

An End to Jewish Apocalyptic Politics?
The Jewish-Roman Wars

THERE IS DEBATE over whether apocalyptic beliefs were interwoven into the Maccabean Revolt or independently accompanied it as apocalyptic religious beliefs that were not directly political in their implications. Similarly, there is debate over the extent to which Jewish radical nationalist ideas were actively present among the followers of Jesus in the early 30s of the first century AD. There is no doubt, however, that such Jewish radical beliefs—combining religious and political ideas—exploded in the second half of the first century and then again in the first half of the second century. In this time period we witness an explosion of radicalized politics that saw Jewish hopes for national independence reach extraordinary heights, only to end in cataclysmic events that were a disaster for the Jewish people.

THE FIRST JEWISH-ROMAN WAR

In AD 66 to 73, the Jewish communities of Judea and Galilee revolted against Roman rule and maladministration in a huge national uprising. For many it had apocalyptic features at a time of heightened messianic hopes for the restoration of Israel. It finally ended in defeat and the destruction of the temple in Jerusalem. Three years later, the last center of Jewish resistance—the fortress of Masada—fell to Rome.

The years before the outbreak of open warfare had witnessed an increase in apocalyptic preaching linked to political claims. We know a fair bit about this from the writings of the Jewish historian Josephus who was initially involved (apparently reluctantly) in resistance activities in Galilee before going over to the Roman side. His work, *The Jewish War*, was written in seven books between AD 75 and 79 and looked back over the events leading up to, and during, the conflict. While Josephus's account is geared to his personal take on events and was clearly designed to promote his own personal prospects as one who had changed sides, we can still get from it some idea of the key events of the time, albeit as seen through a particular and partial lens.

Those involved in the most radical of these events leading up to the outbreak of open warfare are sometimes described as "sign prophets," as they claimed divine authority to interpret the contemporary situation and declared themselves capable (with God's aid) of actions that would establish the rule of God on earth. One of these was apparently named Theudas, who was active while Fadus was Roman governor of Judea, in about AD 45. According to the account found in Josephus's *Antiquities of the Jews*, he gained a large following and led them to the River Jordan where he claimed the waters would part at his command.[1] This was a dramatic claim that was rooted in Jewish religious history and brought to mind other occasions where Jewish faith proclaimed the direct intervention of God in the politics of the past. The first had echoes of the exodus from Egypt under the leadership of Moses, and escape from the pursuing Egyptian army. The second recalled the crossing of the Jordan, under the leader Joshua, when the Israelites began the conquest of Canaan.

The actions of Theudas remind us of the messianic and apocalyptic atmosphere that existed at the time of Jesus. We hear more about Theudas in a passage from the New Testament book of Acts. In this passage, a Jewish leader named Gamaliel is a member of the Jewish council that examines the apostle Peter and a number of other early Christian leaders who have been arrested for preaching about Jesus in the Jerusalem Temple. This is part of the very early history of the church and after the earthly ministry of Jesus. In a speech reported by the compiler of Acts, Gamaliel reminds his listeners of others who had recently caused unrest in the region:

---

1. Collins, "Millenarianism," lines 220–22.

> Some time ago Theudas rose up, claiming to be somebody, and a number of men, about four hundred, joined him; but he was killed, and all who followed him were dispersed and disappeared. After him Judas the Galilean rose up at the time of the census and got people to follow him; he also perished, and all who followed him were scattered. (Acts 5:36–37)

The chronology of this unrest is a little unclear. As Gamaliel puts it, the revolt by Theudas occurred before that of Judas the Galilean. However, we know from Josephus, in *Antiquities of the Jews*, that Judas the Galilean's revolt was in AD 6. And Gamaliel says it occurred "at the time of the census" (Acts 5:37), which was clearly the one organized by the Roman administrator Quirinius (mentioned in the Gospels in connection with the birth of Jesus in Bethlehem) and which occurred in AD 6, at the time of the imposition of Roman direct rule on Judea. The revolt of Theudas, on the other hand, occurred ca. AD 45—decades after that of Judas the Galilean. The matter is further complicated by the fact that the speech by Gamaliel would have occurred prior to AD 37, which was almost ten years before the revolt of Theudas. It is very hard to resolve the matter, and the fact that both Judas and Theudas were fairly common names may not help us, since there could have been different revolts by men with the same names. However, the revolt of Judas the Galilean does seem firmly anchored on a known date. All we can say is that there were many revolts and periods of unrest in Judea and Galilee during the first century AD. Josephus, looking back from the end of the first century, claims "ten thousand disorders," but only provides detail concerning four of them.[2]

We would like to know more about the message that was proclaimed by these preachers. How much of it was religious? How much political? We cannot answer these questions, but, from what exploded in the 60s, it is reasonable to guess that the two were almost certainly mixed.[3]

In the decade after Gamaliel's speech, another radical leader also arose and in this case the apocalyptic politics that formed part of the action are clear. This occurred when Festus headed up the Roman administration in the area (AD 52–60). Josephus has left us an account of the uprising in his work *The Jewish War*. Josephus says that the leader identified as "the Egyptian":

---

2. Williams, *Acts*, 109.
3. Brighton, *Sicarii*, 4.

made himself credible as a prophet and rallied about thirty thousand dupes and took them around through the wilderness to the Mount of Olives. From there he intended to force an entry into Jerusalem, overpower the Roman garrison and become ruler of the citizen body.[4]

It seems that "the Egyptian" expected the walls of Jerusalem to fall as those of Jericho had once done in the accounts of Joshua's conquest of Canaan. Once again we see the radicals drawing on the same common traditions of divine acts in the past history of the Jewish people. The rebels were to be disappointed. The walls did not fall and the revolt was crushed by Roman troops. However, it seems that the Egyptian responsible for it all escaped.

The event is referred to in passing in the New Testament, again in Acts. In this case, a Roman officer in Jerusalem attempts to identify the apostle Paul and to establish what is going on after a riot in the city in which Paul has been attacked by a Jewish crowd. After Paul speaks to him in Greek, "The tribune replied, 'Do you know Greek? Then you are not the Egyptian who recently stirred up a revolt and led the four thousand assassins out into the wilderness?'" (Acts 21:37b–8). This is a particularly interesting comment as it is the only time in the New Testament that we have a specific reference to the radical nationalist fighters known as the *Sicarii*. It is that word which lies behind the word "assassins" used in the English translation, which has just been quoted.[5] It should be noted that the connection between Judas Iscariot and this group (which we explored in chapter 2) is postulated, not proven.

We lack the manifestos of these people, and so we cannot definitely say whether they expected an earthly victory but one that was divinely aided (a limited millenarianism), or a supernaturally enabled victory that led to a radical and divinely empowered reordering of the world (full millenarianism). It seems clear that it was at least the former and there may have been aspects of the latter. As a consequence, it seems reasonable to describe them as "millenarian prophets" who believed they were at the epicenter of apocalyptic events.

There is good reason for interpreting Jewish revolts against the Roman Empire in this light even if some scholars challenge a political interpretation of the earlier book of Daniel and its legacy. The composite

---

4. Collins, "Millenarianism," lines 225–27.
5. Vine, *Expository Dictionary*, 42.

text 2 Esdras or Latin Ezra—not to be confused with the Greek Apocalypse of Ezra—contains sections of Jewish apocryphal thinking and was probably written between AD 90 and 96.[6] The "eagle" referred to in the fifth vision almost certainly refers to the Roman Empire and it describes this "eagle" being rebuked and destroyed by a "lion" (usually interpreted as the looked-for Messiah).[7] The sixth vision then describes a man—who is best understood as representing "one like a son of man" (Dan 7:13) referred to in Daniel—who destroys sinners and restores Israel. Now, this was clearly written after the failure of the First Jewish-Roman War and the destruction of the temple. It looks to supernatural agency, rather than human action, but it is not too large a step to assume that such views of the Roman Empire and its imminent destruction, while sharpened by the events of the war, built on existing deep antipathies towards Rome and expectations that God would soon destroy it through sending his messianic leader. It is also reasonable to assume that some people saw their own actions as, in some way, playing a part within this judgment on Rome and the ushering in of God's eternal kingdom. Leaders such as Theudas, Judas the Galilean, and "the Egyptian" are probably best understood in this light, even if we lack direct statements to this effect.

A similar outlook can be found expressed in a text known as 2 Baruch—thought to have been written at a similar time, in the same historical context, and expressing the same antipathy towards the Roman Empire. The text known as 2 Baruch is also called The Apocalypse of Baruch or The Syriac Apocalypse of Baruch (the last name to distinguish it from a text known as Greek Apocalypse of Baruch). Like 2 Esdras, 2 Baruch sees the destruction of Rome as being accomplished by the Messiah. The "prophecy" is couched as if it had occurred at the time of the historic Babylonian exile. This is a characteristic it arguably shares with the Old Testament book of Daniel and with the apocalyptic passages found in 2 Esdras. Both 2 Baruch and 2 Esdras model key aspects of their message and imagery on the book of Daniel and its succession of empires culminating in the establishment of God's kingdom. The essential point is that such a kingdom—whether contemporaries considered it temporal or eternal—"was worth fighting for" and would involve a messianic figure who was "invincible in war."[8]

---

6. Gottheil et al., "Esdras," lines 162–63.
7. Gottheil et al., "Esdras," lines 159–61.
8. Cohn, *Pursuit of the Millennium*, 22.

THE EVENTS OF THE WAR

It was in this context that events spiraled down to the First Jewish-Roman War. The war was the result of small conflicts that had occurred over a number of years in which Jewish resistance fighters struck at Roman forces and the Romans responded with characteristic extreme violence.

The conflict was rooted in a desire for national independence, combined with a determined attempt to oppose any imposition of pagan practices on the Jewish community. At times this involved violent opposition to Roman actions that had varied from the insensitive to the openly provocative. An example of the latter occurred in AD 39 when Emperor Caligula ordered his name to be placed on the temple in Jerusalem. Only his assassination in Rome prevented a major uprising. Within the temple hierarchy, those at the top, who sought accommodation with the Roman authorities, became increasingly estranged from priests lower down the hierarchy. The community leadership was splintering as radicalization increased. The mounting religious and cultural friction combined with high levels of taxation to produce an escalating crisis.

In AD 66, a Jewish revolt occurred that spread rapidly across the region. The Jewish high priest, Eleazar Ben Ananius, refused to offer sacrifices to the deified emperor (Nero) and the Roman garrison in Jerusalem was killed in the uprising that followed. Any remaining Roman military forces were expelled from Jerusalem, and an army sent to crush the uprising, under the command of Gallus the imperial legate in Syria, was defeated at the pass of Beth-Horon by the Zealot leader Eleazar Ben Simon. The pro-Roman king Herod Agrippa II (the eighth and last ruler from the Herodian dynasty) had earlier escaped from Jerusalem, together with officials of the Roman administration. It should be noted that Agrippa II ruled a patchwork of territories as a client-king of Rome, but his authority in Jerusalem (within Roman-administered Judea) was only that of *tetrarch*. However, this included the power to appoint the high priest.

In Jerusalem, a revolutionary government was established. Its rule was soon extended across the whole country. The Romans responded with predictable speed and vigor. The Emperor Nero sent an expeditionary force under an experienced general, Vespasian, to crush the rebellion. In the company of his son Titus, Roman armies entered Galilee in AD 67, where the future-historian Josephus commanded Jewish forces. They quickly smashed the Jewish resistance there, and after the fall of the fortress at Jatapata, Josephus surrendered. He would soon switch sides and provide us with a detailed, if at times self-serving, account of the war, its origins, and its aftermath. From Galilee, the Roman army moved south against Judea.

In the cultural and religious capital of Judaism the situation had become increasingly radicalized. This was in line with the way the revolt had developed since its beginning. It has been noted, on the basis of modern study, that those who followed Eleazar Ben Simon constituted "a millenarian sect who believed the final days were at hand."[9] In Jerusalem itself, those loyal to Eleazar Ben Simon and the Zealots were so radical in their antagonism to Rome and in removing the temple aristocracy (that they considered collaborators) that any peaceful settlement with Rome—never very likely—became impossible. A divisive battle for power took place within Jerusalem in AD 67 to AD 69 as power passed to the most extreme of Rome's enemies there, and rival groups were defeated and eliminated. Opponents within Jerusalem were slaughtered. Then defeated groups fought back as the alliance of those in control splintered, and roles were reversed. As the groups within Jerusalem fought each other, the Romans gathered to eliminate them, regardless of their competing agendas and plans. They fought each other, and then the Romans slaughtered them. Disunity preceded a terrible and total defeat. There are even reports that, as the Roman army had approached the city, radical groups destroyed huge stocks of food that could have supported a besieged population for several years, in order to force a desperate fight that involved everyone.[10] Apocalyptic politics were taking what would become a familiar course of extreme positions leading to disaster. The revolt against Rome was, in this way, accompanied by a bitter civil war as the rival Jewish groups battled for mastery. It was a prelude to catastrophe.

In April of AD 70, the Roman general Titus began his siege of Jerusalem. In a brutally cynical move, the Romans allowed pilgrims to enter the city for the celebration of Passover but refused to let them leave afterwards. It was a strategy to rapidly deplete the resources of the city in terms of food and water. Outside the walls the Romans crucified hundreds of Jews that had been captured or who tried to escape the siege. Within the city the bitter rivalries continued. Josephus, who had once been in command of Jewish forces in Galilee—but then changed sides

9. Fern and Sorek, *Jews against Rome*, 99
10. Goodman, *Ruling Class of Judaea*, 195.

in the face of defeat—attempted to negotiate a settlement. Distrusted by the Romans and the object of contempt for Jewish radicals, this came to nothing. Starvation mounted as the year continued into the summer.

Jerusalem finally fell to the encircling Roman armies on the ninth day of the month of *Av* or 29 August. Vast numbers of civilians were slaughtered, the temple was burned, and the city sacked. Survivors were enslaved. The (briefly independent) Jewish state collapsed. However, Jewish resistance continued at the fortress of Masada, near the Dead Sea, until April of AD 73. In the final hours the survivors there committed suicide.

What had begun as a war for national liberation had led to national catastrophe and the crushing of any hopes for a politically independent Jewish nation. Today the Western Wall of the temple is the only visible survival of the great Second Temple. For Jews it remains a place of prayer and pilgrimage. However, at the time Jerusalem ceased to be a Jewish city.

The loss of the Second Temple is still mourned by the modern Jewish community in the fast of *Tisha be-Av*. In contrast, imperial power celebrated the fall of Jerusalem by erecting the triumphal Arch of Titus in Rome and decorated it with victorious Roman soldiers carrying away the sacred treasures of the temple.

THE SECOND JEWISH-ROMAN WAR

The First Jewish-Roman War ended in national disaster, but violence between Jewish members of the empire and imperial forces and also with their non-Jewish neighbors continued. From AD 115 to AD 117 occurred the Second Jewish-Roman War, sometimes called the "Kitos War" from the name of the imperial commander who crushed it, or the "Rebellion of the Diaspora." At a time when Roman armies were engaged in warfare on the eastern border of the Roman Empire (the Parthian War), uprisings by Jews in Cyrenaica, Cyprus, and Egypt escalated and led to the destruction of the Roman garrisons in these areas and the deaths of huge numbers of non-Jewish Roman citizens. At the same time there were also uprisings by members of the Jewish population in Judea. Revolts also occurred in a number of other areas in the east where there were substantial Jewish urban populations.

Roman sources claim widespread atrocities were committed by Jewish rebels against Greek-speaking gentile civilians. While the huge death counts are open to question, it is quite clear that a vast reservoir of bitterness had been created by the events of the earlier First Jewish-Roman War. Following the end of the conflict, and the defeat of the Jews who had supported it, when the new emperor, Hadrian, visited the Eastern Mediterranean in AD 130, he decided to rebuild the ruined city of Jerusalem but rename it as the Roman colony of *Aelia Capitolina*. This was derived from his own name. A temple to Jupiter was built on the Temple Mount. These decisions accompanied other sanctions against the Jewish population of the empire and were a major contributory cause of the last major uprising of Jewish nationalists against imperial rule.

THE THIRD JEWISH-ROMAN WAR—THE WAR OF SIMON BAR KOKHBA

The catastrophe of the First Jewish-Roman War was not the end of apocalyptic nationalism. Fought between AD 132 and AD 136 was the last of the three major Jewish-Roman Wars and is known as "The Third Jewish-Roman War" or "The Bar Kokhba Revolt." The last takes its name from the title used to describe its leader—Simon ben Kosiba—by his supporters (and perhaps by himself). We will return to this shortly.

In AD 132, a revolt quickly spread from central Judea across the country and succeeded in isolating the Roman garrison in *Aelia Capitolina* (Jerusalem). There is evidence that its leader, Simon, had messianic aspects to his leadership, although historians disagree over the reliability and interpretation of the limited sources that state this.[11] There are certainly aspects that can be taken as suggesting this. His assumed surname/title *Bar Kokhba* ("son of a star") appears to have referred to a messianic Old Testament prophecy: "a star shall come out of Jacob" (Num 24:17). The Christian Apocalypse of Peter (although a very biased source regarding Jewish messianic beliefs) claims that he assumed the title of Messiah and that it was accepted by many of his followers.[12] Ariston of Pella, quoted by Eusebius in his *History of the Church*, asserted that "The Jews were led by a certain Bar Chochebas, which means Star."[13] Coins minted under his leadership included a star above a depiction of the Jerusalem Temple, with the ark of the covenant within it. Rebuilding the temple was clearly

---

11. Mor, *Second Jewish Revolt*, 139, 440.
12. Mor, *Second Jewish Revolt*, 411.
13. "Simon Ben Kosiba," line 40.

a national aim, but it was also associated at this point in time with messianic status. An Aramaic translation of Isaiah 53:5, which was written ca. AD 100, adds the words "and the Messiah will build the sanctuary."[14] This *targum* needs to be borne in mind when assessing the terminology and iconography associated with Simon and, it seems, actively promoted by him. It is clear that some thought that eschatological violence—as expressed in apocalyptic literature written before and current with the revolt—was legitimate because the messianic age had arrived in the form of Bar Kokhba.[15]

That there is reason for thinking this is revealed in the responses of those who disagreed with him. The later text of the Jewish-Palestinian Talmud refers to him as "*Bar Kozeba*," a derogatory term meaning "son of the disappointment" or "son of the lie," and indicating that he was a false messiah.[16] It was clearly a deliberate contrast with the title accorded him by his followers and throws light on that controversial claim. While the limited evidence suggests that there was disagreement among Jewish rabbis over whether he claimed this title and whether he was the Messiah, it seems a reasonable assumption that, at the very least, messianic status was attributed to Simon by a number of his supporters and that he himself may have actively embraced this. The title *Nasi* (prince of) *Israel* that he took for himself (and used in letters) was one with messianic associations and was used by some as a synonym for Messiah. This may also explain the claim by the Christian Justin Martyr that he "gave orders that Christians alone should be led away to cruel punishments, unless they should deny Jesus as the Christ."[17] Conflict over who was Messiah may have been behind this persecution of Christians, if Justin is correct in his assertion.[18] While it has been suggested that some Christians wished to explain the fate of Judaism, following the destruction of the temple, by painting Simon as one who falsely claimed and was accorded messianic status,[19] there does seem to be a significant amount of evidence to suggest that this is what he did. On the other hand, the coins and letters do

---

14. "Simon Ben Kosiba," lines 47–48.
15. Collins, *Apocalyptic Imagination*, 289.
16. "Simon Ben Kosiba," lines 16–18.
17. "Simon Ben Kosiba," lines 38–39.
18. Evans, *Jesus and His Contemporaries*, 193.
19. Mor, *Second Jewish Revolt*, 137.

not explicitly state this,[20] so there may always have been some creative ambiguity in his positioning regarding the matter.

As Roman reinforcements were rushed from Syria, Egypt, and Arabia, early rebel victories enabled the Jews to set up an independent state which controlled most of Judea for over three years. Large numbers of Jews from elsewhere made their way there to join the fight for national existence. It did not last. Nearly one-third of the entire Roman army was brought against the rebels. Perhaps as many as ten legions were eventually deployed in Judea. The Jewish strongholds fell one by one, until only Betar, in the Judean highlands, remained. It fell to Roman attack in AD 135 and Simon was killed there. By the spring of AD 136 the last resistance, in isolated pockets, had been destroyed.

According to the Roman historian Cassius Dio, about 580,000 Jews died in the war and more died of hunger and disease as a consequence of the fighting. In addition, vast numbers of Jewish war captives were sold as slaves. The same Roman source asserts that fifty fortresses and 985 villages were destroyed, suggesting that something approaching genocide occurred in central and northern Judea, impacting communities that were closely associated with the revolt.[21] This accompanied an imperial prohibition of Jewish practices that continued until Hadrian's death in AD 138. The regional name "Judea" was replaced in Roman official terminology by the descriptor *Syria Palaestina*, and Jews were banned from entering Jerusalem.

However, Jewish populations survived in Galilee, the Golan, and Beit She'an. A close examination of the literary and archaeological evidence reveals that it would not be correct to assume the total destruction of Judea. It is clear that Jewish communities continued in areas such as Lod (Lydda), south of the Hebron Mountain, and on the coast. In short, it seems that areas that were not directly connected with the revolt survived, and that, even in the most devastated areas, the destruction of Jewish communities was not as widespread as sometimes assumed.[22] Nevertheless, the loss of life and the destruction was still huge. The effect on national morale was devastating, coming on top of the previous destruction of Jerusalem during the first war.

20. Evans, *Jesus and His Contemporaries*, 183.
21. Schwartz, *Imperialism and Jewish Society*, 108n11.
22. Mor, *Second Jewish Revolt*, 484.

THE END OF APOCALYPTIC JUDAISM?

The end of the War of Simon bar Kokhba seemed to be the end of Jewish apocalyptic politics. From this point onwards Jewish messianic beliefs are often described as being highly spiritualized, with rabbinical thought and religious politics becoming conservative and wary of radicalized claims.[23] However, as we shall see, that is not entirely accurate. Aspects of apocalyptic politics have survived within Judaism. However, never again would it occur as dramatically as it did in the first and second centuries AD.

23. Mor, *Second Jewish Revolt*, 463 examines this issue, as does Sheinfeld, "Decline of Second Temple Jewish Apocalypticism," 187–210.

CHAPTER 4

A Shared Hope?
The Place of Apocalyptic Beliefs within Islam

ISLAM TEACHES THAT on the last day the world as we now know it will come to an end, the dead will be raised, and a final judgment will be pronounced on all. Many of the *surah* (chapters) in the Qur'an refer to the rewards and punishments of heaven and of hell. Within the Qur'an, terms for "punishment," "fire," "hell," "hellfire," and "blaze" appear 586 times. Those for "heaven," "Eden," "gardens," "paradise," and "reward" appear 323 times.[1] As a result, eschatology is a major part of Islamic belief. In this climactic series of events, God (*Allah* in Arabic), who has been described as caring creator, will also be experienced as the annihilating judge.[2] As with God in Judeo-Christianity, it is only *Allah* who knows the time of *yawm al-qiyamah* (the day of resurrection), *al-saʿah* (the hour), and *yawm al-din* (the day of judgment). In total, Arabic words referring to end-times events occur 157 times in the Qur'an.[3]

AN OUTLINE OF ISLAMIC ESCHATOLOGY

After human beings have been resurrected, the judgment on them will be made according to their acceptance or rejection of God's clear signs to

---

1. Dastmalchian, "Islam," 158, Table 8.1.
2. Robinson Waldman, "Eschatology," line 48.
3. Dastmalchian, "Islam," 158, Table 8.1.

them as presented by the many messengers he has sent throughout history. On the basis of this, some people will go to an eternal reward of *jannah* (heaven), also described as *firdaws* (paradise), while sinners will be consigned to the place of fiery suffering called *jahannam* (hell),[4] the last being an Arabic word that is related to the similar Hebrew term *gehenna*.

Generally, the Qur'an refers to a personal judgment. However, there are some verses that refer to the resurrection of distinct communities. These will be judged according to the revelation they have received.

> The [Muslim] believers, the Jews, the Christians, and the Sabians—all those who believe in God and the Last Day and do good—will have their rewards with their Lord. No fear for them, nor will they grieve. (Surah 2:62)[5]

Despite this Qur'anic reassurance, some extreme Islamic groups—as with Christians who have ignored the gentle humility of the Sermon on the Mount—have used forced conversion and persecution (including martyrdom) regarding members of these other faiths. This, as we shall see, is especially so when apocalyptic groups, such as ISIS, have taken power in an area and begin to execute "end-times judgments" on those considered enemies or apostates. Incidentally, "the Sabians" are rather mysterious. They are grouped in the Qur'an with Jews and Christians, as "People of the Book" (*ahl al-kitab*),[6] but it is uncertain who they were.

According to several commentaries written after the Qur'an, the day of judgment will be announced when the archangel Israfil sounds two blasts from his trumpet. At this point the souls of the dead will be reunited with their bodies in their graves; they will rise from the dead and will await the judging of their deeds. Following this, they cross a bridge over a fire, and sinners will fall into the fire. Those who are saved will cross into the garden of paradise. Some Islamic commentators have stated that each community of believers will be led there by their prophet. All will be led by Muhammad and the community of saved Muslims. This same tradition held that at the place of fire Muhammad may intercede for some of the sinners who are Muslims. While it would certainly not be accepted by most mainstream Muslims, there have been some Islamic writers who have suggested that this fire acted similar to Catholic purgatory, with

---

4. Dastmalchian, "Islam," 158; Robinson Waldman, "Eschatology," lines 48–54.
5. All quotations from the Qur'an are from: Abdel Haleem, *Qur'an*.
6. Peters, "People of the Book" provides a succinct explanation of this term.

some even suggesting that it might operate as such (with the prospect of eventual deliverance) for all in the fire, not just "Muslim sinners."[7]

Complex and dramatic though Islamic beliefs are about the broader aspects of eschatology (as they refer to death, judgment, and reward), the area that concerns us is the process through which the current world order will be ended, rather than the details of Islamic beliefs about the nature of the afterlife itself.

The various Islamic beliefs about the end times, which can be identified within the Muslim community (the *ummah*), over the years since the seventh century, are based on a number of sources: passages from the Qur'an, words of the *hadiths* (reports about the exemplary deeds, utterances, and unspoken approval of Muhammad), and the later reflections of early Muslims. Some of these converted to Islam from Judaism, Christianity, and Zoroastrianism, and these backgrounds clearly influenced areas of their thinking; it is possible to detect aspects of beliefs from these other religions in some of their writings.

SIGNS OF THE APPROACHING END TIMES

As in the Jewish and Christian Scriptures there is an emphasis on the onset of the last day taking people by surprise. As the Qur'an puts it:

> Just one blast and—lo and behold!—they will look and say, "Woe to us! This is the day of judgment." [It will be said], "This is the Day of Decision, which you used to deny." (Surah 37:19–21)

The events themselves are dramatic and have similarities to imagery found in both the Old and the New Testaments. In the Islamic tradition, people will be scattered like moths; the mountains will be plucked up like tufts of wool and turned to sand; the earth will be shaken and ground down to powder; the heavens will be split and rolled back; stars will be scattered; the seas will boil over; the sun will be darkened.[8]

The Qur'an and the hadiths describe several events happening before the day of judgment. Islamic scholars often divide these into "minor signs" and "major signs," and a number appear in the hadith collections.

"Minor signs" include:

---

7. Robinson Waldman, "Eschatology," lines 153–65.
8. Robinson Waldman, "Eschatology," lines 106–9.

> Lewd acts, working to bring about lewd acts, the cutting off of the ties of relationship and the trusting of deceivers. (*Hadith at-Tabarani*)⁹

Other "minor signs" are:

> The abundance of wealth, increasing of ignorance, numerous tribulations and widespread trading and business. (*Hadith al-Hakim*)¹⁰

Also included among the "minor signs" are strife among Muslims, the conquest of Constantinople (achieved in 1453), and the capture of Rome by Islamic armies.¹¹

"Major signs" include this account:

> Thereupon he [Muhammad] said, "It will not come until you see ten signs before it." And (in this connection) he made a mention of the smoke, *Al Dajjaal* [the Islamic equivalent of the antichrist], the beast, the rising of the sun from the west, the descent of Jesus son of Mary (peace be upon them), Gog and Magog, and landslides in three places, one in the east, one in the west and one in Arabia, at the end of which a fire would burn forth from the Yemen and drive people to the place of their assembly. (*Hadith Saheeh* or *Sahih Muslim*)¹²

These hadith traditions are very significant. The collection known as *Sahih Muslim* is regarded as one of the two most authentic hadith collections, along with the collection known as *Sahih al-Bukhari*. It is one of the six major hadith collections (*kutub al-sittah*) within Sunni Islam. Consequently, the end-times statements found in it are very influential in framing Muslim apocalyptic beliefs.

Reading the ten signs that appear in *Sahih Muslim*, the relationship to Christian apocalyptic beliefs is clear in the "descent of Jesus"; and also in the figures of *Al Dajjaal* ("antichrist"), the beast, Gog and Magog. These are highly reminiscent of the apocalyptic beliefs expressed in Revelation in the New Testament and in other Christian eschatological writings.

As in Christianity, there have been and remain major disagreements over the identification of these "signs." Given that these can be seen as

---

9. al-Din Zarabozo, "Major Signs," lines 45–47.
10. al-Din Zarabozo, "Major Signs," lines 54–55.
11. Furnish, *Holiest Wars*, 95.
12. al-Din Zarabozo, "Major Signs," lines 72–77.

signalling the imminent end times, such identifications can become very important within apocalyptic expectations and in political responses to contemporary events.

Most Muslims believe, from the hadith tradition, that the "minor signs" will occur first, then the "major signs" will take place. There is some debate among Islamic commentators about whether these latter signs will take place simultaneously or will happen at different points over an extended period. Some Islamic commentators have suggested that there is no explicit textual basis for ordering the appearance of the "major signs." Others assert that a chronology can be suggested.[13] There is, however, a hadith tradition that records Muhammad as saying: "The signs shall appear one after the other like the beads on a string follow one another" (Al-Tabarani, died 971, in *Al-Ausat*).[14] And "The signs are like beads strung on a string. If the string breaks, they [quickly] follow one after the other" (Ahmad ibn Hanbal, died 855, in *Musnad*).[15] This would seem to indicate a rapid series of events once the process has started.

LATER REFLECTIONS ON THE END TIMES

The matter of post-Qur'anic traditions reminds us of the various streams that have flowed into the eventual Muslim understanding of the end times. It has been commented that, with regard to the original Qur'anic information,

> Not every question is anticipated, and little attention is paid to the period between revelation and eschaton, even less to the time between death and resurrection, except to say that it will seem like nothing.[16]

As a result, later generations of Muslims reflected on these Qur'anic eschatological verses and, as they did so, they interpreted verses where they were specific and elaborated where the verses were not.[17] This later process of elaboration led to variations both among Islamic scholars and, even more so, within the popular imagination across the Islamic world.

---

13. al-Din Zarabozo, "Major Signs," lines 102–21.
14. al-Din Zarabozo, "Major Signs," line 22.
15. al-Din Zarabozo, "Major Signs," lines 24–25.
16. Robinson Waldman, "Eschatology," lines 109–12.
17. Robinson Waldman, "Eschatology," lines 112–13.

In the latter case it is possible to identify how aspects of existing and ancient folklore became incorporated in some later Islamic beliefs.

The evidence suggests that the Sunni majority within Islam began elaborating Qur'anic eschatological verses and ideas at the same time as the hadith tradition began to form. Hadith collections now survive, in their current written form, from the period ca. 800–1000. (Muhammad died in 632 or year 11 of the Islamic dating system.) Not all the surviving hadiths are accepted as authentic by all Islamic scholars. Today, acceptance of different collections of hadith differentiates various branches of the Islamic community.[18] This is part of the explanation for some of the differences found within Islam, although others are due to different interpretations and approaches to sources that are commonly held as authentic (as also found in differing Christian interpretations about the end times). What is clear is that significant developments continued, regarding these beliefs, for centuries after the establishment of the agreed text of the Qur'an and after the hadith collections were written. This is especially seen in a number of key areas: firstly, beliefs about the period between death and resurrection; secondly, beliefs concerning the role of end-times figures; and, finally, beliefs about the nature of judgment and the afterlife.

It is the second of these areas that is most relevant to this book since these ideas interact with some beliefs about what part Islamic believers should play in the approach to the end times. In this, attempts to identify some of these end-times figures in the contemporary world have occupied the attention of many Muslims over the centuries in the same way as the preoccupation has affected the outlook and speculations of many Christians (and, to a lesser extent, Jews). This is allied to attempts to identify "signs of the times" that appear to signal the impending end of the current world order. Again, this is common to the outlook of many believers within Christianity (and, to a lesser extent, Judaism) over the centuries.

END-TIME FIGURES IN THE ISLAMIC TRADITION

A number of end-times figures appear in the Islamic tradition and, as in Judaism and Christianity, this has at times led to believers seeking to identify some of these figures in contemporary society.

18. Brown, *Misquoting Muhammad*, 8.

Prophet *Isa* (Jesus) is seen as playing a key role. Another end-times figure is one described as *Al-Dajjal*. This person is an "antichrist" character, comparable to that person within Christian traditions. Another is the *Mahdi*, or the divinely guided one. In complex traditions, developed over many centuries, there is much variation regarding how these figures are described and interpreted.

The figure of *Al-Dajjal* appears in the hadith tradition but not in the Qur'an itself. This is reminiscent of antichrist in Christianity, where little is specifically written in the New Testament but was much developed and expanded in later history. The person *Al-Dajjal* will emerge toward the end of time, and this will be the culmination of a turbulent and extended period of societal, and also natural, decay and disturbance. He will conquer the earth until he is killed either by the returning *Isa* or by the *Mahdi*. Traditions vary regarding this fate and the one responsible for it.[19]

The role of *Isa* within Islam is striking. He is regarded as Messiah and a great prophet, but not as the Son of God or sharing the same status as God. The Qur'an does not explicitly speak of *Isa*'s return (the second coming). However, it does state that he did not die (Surah 4:157) and that he will, in some way, signal the coming of the end (Surah 43:61a). In the latter verse—"This is knowledge for the Hour"—the pronoun *hu* may refer to the Qur'an or to *Isa*.[20] Some Islamic scholars (such as Al-Tabari, died 923) interpreted this as meaning that *Isa* will unite all believers under the banner of Islam.[21] *Isa* does, though, figure prominently and explicitly in the hadith traditions, as we have already seen regarding his descent at a decisive moment within the "major signs." In hadith tradition there is also a belief that *Isa* will return to break the cross and kill the pigs.[22] Pigs, in this context, refers to an animal considered unclean by Muslims but eaten by Christians. It would seem that this hadith tradition "implies the abolition of non-Islamic religions and specifically Christianity [exemplified in the symbol of the cross]." ISIS, in the twenty-first century, claimed to be anticipating this end-times event. This hadith tradition illustrates the profound disagreement between some in Islam and Christianity over

---

19. Robinson Waldman, "Eschatology," lines 138–42.
20. Abdel Haleem, *Qur'an*, footnote b; Günther, "Eschatology and the Qur'an," 4.
21. Larson, "Jesus in Islam and Christianity," 335.
22. *Mishkat al-Masabih*, 2:1159.

this central Christian symbol and its association with Jesus in Christian faith.[23]

The *Mahdi*, like *Al-Dajjal*, is another figure who does not appear in the Qur'an. In many Islamic traditions he is regarded as being an unnamed member of the family of Muhammad. Some traditions claim that he will look like Muhammad.[24] He will restore justice and peace on earth for a period of time, before the final end of the present world order. In so doing, he will fulfil the mission of Muhammad. In this sense he is regarded as his last earthly successor (or *caliph*). He will be an inspired interpreter of the revelation of Muhammad. He will enforce Islamic law (*shari' ah*).[25] He is always described as one of the "major signs" (as with *Isa* and *Al-Dajjal*) but is sometimes described in a way that presents him as "the crucial transformative link between the two categories ["minor" and "major" signs]."[26] For those Muslims who believe this, the identification of the *Mahdi* is crucial in deciding the start of the final apocalyptic timetable. The *Mahdi* and *Isa* will cooperate (in an unspecified way) to defeat the forces of evil.[27]

Some traditions claim that the *Mahdi* will be descended from Fatimah (the daughter of Muhammad); other traditions claim his descent will be from Fatimah via Hassan (the son of Muhammad's first-cousin and son-in-law, Ali). This suggests some convergence of Sunni and Shia views (see below). But others insist that he will be a "rightly-guided caliph and *imam*" who is not Shia,[28] which clearly reflects the deep division within the Islamic community.

Some Sunni Muslims interpret the *Mahdi* less as a specific end-times figure and more as an inspired Islamic leader, sent by God at any point in history to correct and guide the Islamic community when and if it drifts away from the correct path of righteous living. The term used for such a figure is *mujaddid*. Unlike the *Mahdi*, as he is usually understood, the *mujaddid* may appear in the form of several figures and not just preceding the end of time. It should be noted that, since Muslims believe that Muhammad is the "Seal of the Prophets" (the final prophet in Islam) and

23. Whittock and Whittock, *Story of the Cross*, 142.
24. Furnish, *Holiest Wars*, 95.
25. Robinson Waldman, "Eschatology," lines 142–46.
26. Furnish, *Holiest Wars*, 95.
27. Furnish, *Holiest Wars*, 95.
28. Furnish, *Holiest Wars*, 95.

the final messenger from God, none of these other figures are believed to bring a subsequent revelation. Nevertheless, other figures are important but are always seen in the context of Muhammad's primacy as revelatory prophet.[29] This, of course, means that the role of *Isa* in Islamic belief and eschatology is not comparable to the primacy given to him in the second coming as understood within Christianity. This is a direct result of the differences between the Christology found in the Christian faith and the position of *Isa* (however much respected) within Islam.

THE SHIA PERSPECTIVE

Shia Muslims make up about 15 percent of the worldwide Islamic community.[30] This community is itself complex, and most of what follow refers to the beliefs of the largest branch ("Twelvers") because their views on the Imamate are quite different to the *Zaidis* and very different to *Isma'ilis*.

Shia believe that, by command of God, Muhammad designated Ali ibn Abi Talib as his successor. He would thus become the *imam* and *caliph*—spiritual and political leader—after him. Ali was Muhammad's first-cousin and his closest living male relative. He was also his son-in-law, as he had married Fatimah, the daughter of Muhammad. This succession is based on (disputed) interpretations of some Qur'anic verses and hadith traditions. Shia still believe that the rightful leadership of the *ummah* (the worldwide Islamic community) is vested in Ali and his successors. The name Shia is derived from "*Shiat Ali*" (Party of Ali).

However, Sunni Muslims insist that the rightful succession was decided when Muhammad's other companions appointed Abu Bakr as caliph. He thus became, in their view, the first of the "rightly guided caliphs and imams."

This disagreement contributed to profound tensions, and eventually conflict, within the early Islamic community. Ali was assassinated in 661, after being caliph for five years that were marked by civil war. His sons, Al-Hassan and Hussein, were blocked from succeeding their father by those who rejected the legitimacy of this line of succession. Al-Hassan was forced to abdicate after having earlier been recognized as caliph. Al-Hassan is believed to have been poisoned in 680 by Muawiyah, a Sunni rival and the first caliph of the Sunni dynasty known as the Umayyad.

---

29. Robinson Waldman, "Eschatology," lines 147–52.
30. Nafissi, "Shiism and Politics," 111.

It should be noted that Muawiyah's rule predated the formal establishment of the *ahl as-sunnah wa l-jama'ah* (The people of the Sunnah and the community), though he is usually now described as "Sunni." Hussein died in battle against the Umayyads in 681. These events had profound consequences for the later history of Islam. They continue to reverberate today in the Sunni-Shia tensions in the Middle East. They bequeathed to Shia Islam a strong sense of martyrdom and rituals of grieving their dead martyrs. They also had implications for Islamic apocalyptic thinking, since Shia developed very particular beliefs regarding aspects of this that are not widely shared by Sunni Muslims. Hussein's death, for example, Shia believe will finally be avenged on the day of judgment, along with all wrongs.

Members of the largest branch of Shia ("Twelvers") have a specific belief in something called the "occultation," which maintains that the twelfth imam (in the direct succession from Ali) was taken into hiding and will be revealed at the end of time. This disappearance is believed to have occurred ca. 940, and for Shia this belief assisted in their survival at a time when they were experiencing persecution under Sunni rulers. In effect, they went underground in a number of Muslim societies.

The disappearance of the twelfth imam brought to completion a number that has echoes in salvation history in other faiths: i.e., the twelve tribes of Israel and the twelve apostles of Jesus. Before *yawm al-din* (the day of judgment), Shia believe that the twelfth and absent imam, *Al-Qa'im*, will return as the *Mahdi*. In this role he will prepare the way for the end of the world. He will appoint 313 lieutenants from among the righteous, some of whom may be resurrected for a time. He will kill *Al-Dajjal* and all the enemies of the family of Muhammad.

This is often interwoven into ideas about *Isa*—described as *Al-Mas'ih* (Messiah) in the Qur'an—who also will have returned (an Islamic second coming) and will rule for a time. Following this, the *Mahdi* (and some believe Hussein himself) will reign—bringing peace and justice to the earth. This will complete the work of all the prophets who have appeared throughout history. Some Shia additionally believe that, variously, Ali or Fatimah or Hussein will impose judgment on the world as members of the family of Muhammad.[31] There is also a belief that the *Mahdi*'s death— either due to natural causes or, in some traditional accounts, killed by the opponents of God—will trigger a time of chaos which immediately

---

31. Robinson Waldman, "Eschatology," lines 193–200.

precedes the end of the world.[32] A related version of this belief is that a time of chaos will *precede* the *Mahdi*'s return to establish peace and that his death will be the end of time.

Given these specific end-times figures as presented within Shia Islam, it is not surprising that at various points in history believers have thought that particular contemporary leaders represented them or pointed the way towards their imminent appearance. From such a preoccupation has come several apocalyptic political outcomes that continue into the twenty-first century.

---

32. Günther, "Eschatology and the Qur'an," 5.

CHAPTER 5

Apocalyptic Politics within Early and Medieval Christianity

THE JEWISH BACKGROUND colored Christian views of the Roman Empire (as we saw at the end of chapter 2). This negatively affected views of the Roman state and its agents, which emerged in Christian millenarian movements before the official conversion of the empire to Christianity. The empire was viewed as the enemy of God in the last days.

Consequently, the fourth-century conversion of the empire to Christianity had profound implications for this worldview. A new *Realpolitik* shifted the tone of the apocalyptic mood music since the traditional enemy had now become a supporter of Christian belief.

However, as we shall see, this did not put an end to apocalyptic ideas or their potential impact on politics. This continued to occur at all levels of society, from government policy to radicals who challenged the system. As a result, a great many medieval political innovations and developments can be linked to an underlying millenarianism, from the iconography of late-Anglo-Saxon coinage and the honoring of key royal saints and use of national fasts, to ideologically driven representations of pagan enemies as anti-Christian "others." German imperial court ceremony and representation also developed in this context. The presentation of the crusading cause and the portrayal of its enemies developed a similar apocalyptic tone at key times, as did responses to other times of social, economic, and political stress. This was often associated with increased political radicalization.

MILLENARIAN CHRISTIANS

Most leading Christians in the first three centuries of church history subscribed to what is often described as a futurist and a "premillennialist" reading of prophecy. According to this reading, prophecies looked forward to a future date when Christ would return. At that point he would initiate a literal thousand-year reign on earth. Most early Christians thought that this would happen soon. The early church leader Clement of Rome (died AD 99) wrote:

> Of a truth, soon and suddenly shall His will be accomplished, as the Scripture also bears witness, saying, "Speedily will He come, and will not tarry."[1]

The emphasis was on the word "speedily." An additional statement, based on scriptural prophesy, promises that "The Lord shall suddenly come to His temple, even the Holy One, for whom ye look,"[2] suggesting a Jerusalem-focused expectation, even though the temple there had been destroyed by the Romans in the year AD 70. Nevertheless, the holy city remained a key point of focus.

These ideas were very popular. When another church leader, Irenaeus (died ca. AD 202), wrote his *Against Heresies* in the last decade of the second century, the final part of the work was written as something of an anthology of existing messianic and millenarian prophecies.[3] And some of these early Christians translated their theology into active revolutionary politics.

In the year AD 156 or 157, in Phrygia (now in modern-day Turkey), a preacher named Montanus revealed how a belief in the literal fulfillment of the prophecies in the book of Revelation could be combined with heretical teachings to produce a very influential and explosive mix. He declared himself to be the incarnation of the Holy Spirit, with a mandate to lead followers into "truth." A group of ecstatic followers gathered round him and their teachings even began to be described as a "Third Testament."[4] This was a direct challenge to the idea that the canon (accepted holy Scriptures) of Christianity was complete. Montanus and his followers proclaimed the imminent appearing of the New Jerusalem,

---

1. Stanton, "Doctrine of Imminency," 115.
2. Stanton, "Doctrine of Imminency," 115.
3. Mounce, *Book of Revelation*, 22.
4. Cohn, *Pursuit of the Millennium*, 25.

which would descend from heaven to Phrygia. All Christians should gather there and await the second coming. Two settlements, Pepouza and Tymion, were even designated as constituting "Jerusalem."[5] This had the potential for social upheaval.

This took place at a time of renewed persecution of Christians. Montanism spread throughout Asia Minor, south into Africa and as far west as Gaul (roughly modern France). During this process the focus on the descent of the holy city onto Phrygia was replaced by a less geographically stated hope of its appearance.[6] In this form the movement drew in more mainstream believers.

Such beliefs in a literal thousand-year reign of Christ on earth that would occur between his return (in Greek the *parousia*) and the last judgment can be traced from this early period to modern times,[7] albeit with variations (some dramatic) in the timing and ordering of events. This millennialism (or *chiliasm*, from the Greek equivalent word), giving rise to many and varied millenarian movements, became a core feature of Christian apocalyptic beliefs and remains a distinct aspect of these in the twenty-first century.

However, the situation that had given rise to Montanism changed significantly when the Roman Empire converted to Christianity in the fourth century. This was because the process—first the toleration of Christianity though the Edict of Milan (313) and then the official conversion of Constantine, followed by the increasingly prominent role of the church within the empire—meant that readings of prophecy, which had long interpreted them as indicating a persecuting imperial power, were no longer attractive. The "enemy" had converted; "them" had become "us." Not surprisingly, this was soon accompanied by a change of theology that saw prophecy as allegorical and that no longer envisaged a physical struggle with the Roman Empire. This view was particularly associated with the influential theologian Augustine of Hippo.

With no obvious successor state in view or even imaginable, late-Roman Christians were left with the experience of living in a community that was becoming increasingly Christianized and that seemed here to stay. Old views of emperors as antichrist were no longer tenable when such rulers were now considered to be the defenders of Christian faith

---

5. Court, *Approaching the Apocalypse*, 52.
6. Cohn, *Pursuit of the Millennium*, 25.
7. Porter, "Millenarian Thought," 64.

and the bulwark against heresy. Both the church and the (converted) empire were soon seen as "catholic, universal, ecumenical, orderly."[8] Not surprisingly, this accelerated ways of reading passages of prophetic Scripture that stood in marked contrast to the outlook that had once been strongly adhered to by large numbers of Christians, both clerical and lay. This encouraged the reading of prophecies as allegory, as spiritual, as symbolic, and (crucially) none-historically predictive. Such a view defused the tendency towards political radicalism that had characterized earlier movements.

This did not mean that a literal interpretation of prophecy could not be believed in. After all, the prophetic verses could still refer to a future empire or kingdom deeply antagonistic to Christianity—just not the Roman one. In time, such views would push back against the official view that prophecy was symbolic. Nevertheless, in the short term the changes in imperial religious ideology defused much of the political explosiveness inherent in traditional apocalyptic beliefs. This was because in the fourth century few envisaged the end of the newly Christianized empire. In fact, in the East the Byzantine form of imperial rule would last until 1453, when Constantinople was captured by an Islamic army.

THE RETURN OF APOCALYPTIC THINKING

In fact, the socially challenging nature of apocalyptic thinking had not actually gone away. At times of stress it would reemerge again and again. Gregory of Tours (died 594), in his *History of the Franks*, describes the activities of the so-called "False Christ of Bourges." In 591, following a terrible outbreak of disease in the old Roman province of Gaul, this peasant claimed to be the returned Christ. His claim was greeted by enthusiastic crowds. We may assume that they were desperate for the second coming to alleviate their current sufferings. Not everyone was so positive in their reaction to the news, as Gregory also refers to "those who despair at the coming end of the world."[9] The peasant preacher was eventually assassinated by killers in the pay of the bishop of Clermont.

Then, in 847, a woman named Thiota came to Mainz and announced that the world would end in 848. The unrest associated with her is recorded in the chronicle known as the *Annals of Fulda*, which refers to

---

8. Johnson, *History of Christianity*, 76.
9. Landes, "Views of Augustine," lines 65–74.

her "presumption." In a time of increasing turbulence, she attracted supporters both among the clergy and lay people. Those clerics who opposed her asserted that Jesus had been born 5,000 years after creation and that the apocalypse would not occur before the year 1000. So, Thiota had proclaimed the end about 150 years too early. Gregory of Tours (who had used a similar approach, but with different mathematics, to oppose the False Christ of Bourges) would have approved. According to Thiota's critics, as exemplified by one cleric in Paris, the release of antichrist would not occur until the year 1000. Only after that would the second coming and last judgment happen. This was, no doubt, sincerely believed—but it also had the effect of pushing apocalyptic hopes beyond the visible time-horizon and thus calming social tension. Thiota was summoned to a synod in Mainz where she confessed that she had made up her prophecies in the hope of receiving financial reward from those to whom she preached. She was punished by public flogging.

A pattern had emerged of apocalyptic ideas coming to prominence at times of societal stress. Not surprisingly, the violent upheavals of the Viking wars—from the late eighth century onwards—caused many believers to see these new invaders as signaling the approaching end of the world.

> To these Christians it seemed like an End Time event. It sent shock waves across Britain and western Europe. As established Christian centers suffered escalating destruction, the faith itself seemed under threat, and Vikings were identified as manifestations of Antichrist and their actions were read as apocalyptic signposts.[10]

The Vikings were not the only raiders who were described as being harbingers of the end of the world. In the 950s, continental writers viewed the invasions of Magyar raiders as heralding the revealing of antichrist and the events leading to the end of the world.[11] Given this interpretation, one approach could have been to accept the situation as inevitable. However, in reality, such views tended to stimulate political activity.

These ideas were often deployed by those in authority to bolster their political power and to encourage respect for the established order. This was clearly sincerely motivated and not just a manipulation of beliefs for political ends. Among the many personal sins that were preached as

---

10. Whittock and Whittock, "Vikings," lines 36–39.
11. Roach, Æthelred, 246.

being the cause of such raids and destruction can also be found the crime of disloyalty to the government, disrespect for conventions of class and social order, and regicide. In this, kings were in a particularly strong position to present themselves as defenders of Christian orthodoxy. Coins in Anglo-Saxon England, such as the *Agnus Dei* (Lamb of God) coins produced by the (infamous) Ethelred II ("the Unready"), are a case in point. These had the Lamb of God on the obverse and a dove on the reverse, and it seems likely that they were linked to the law code known as *VII Ethelred*.[12] This was an attempt to gain the mercy of God through a program of national penance, which involved fasting, alms-giving, confession, and abstinence from wrongdoing.[13] Around the same time, the cult of royal saints was heavily promoted (such as that of Ethelred's murdered half-brother, Edward the Martyr). Apocalyptic politics were not always associated with challengers to the status quo. Nowhere was this more obvious than in the Eastern Roman Empire.

THE APOCALYPSE AND IMPERIAL AND ROYAL POLITICS

The sixth century saw the emergence of some extraordinary assertions that the surviving Greek-speaking Eastern (Byzantine) Roman Empire represented the kingdom that will never be destroyed (Dan 2:44). This claim, by Kosmas Indikopleustes of Alexandria (died 550), fused the idea of the Eastern Roman Empire with that of the eternal kingdom of Christ. For Kosmas, barbarian attacks might occur as chastisements for sin, but the permanence of this imperial theocracy was not in question.[14] Apocalyptic texts could be reinvented as politically stabilizing supports.

In the West, as in the East, Christian elites recognized both the problems of lower-class unrest but also the potential inherent in the manipulation of end-times beliefs. The coronation of Charlemagne, as the newly minted emperor in the West in the year 800, caused a relocation of much of the apocalyptic expectations concerning the Roman Empire from the East (where it had been much emphasized by the Byzantines) to the West.

---

12. Keynes, "Abbot," 190.
13. Keynes, "Abbot," 178–80.
14. Sivertsev, *Judaism and Imperial Ideology*, 12.

Later imperial European rulers were ready to take on the sanctified mantle of being God's chosen ruler in the last days. This was not a claim to be a messianic figure. Rather it was a nonscriptural belief that had developed that asserted that God would raise up a leader to oppose antichrist—and then Christ would return. Emperor Otto III (died 1002) applied this outlook to defining his role as emperor. It was a thoroughly conservative and Byzantine one, and it called for obedience to those in power.

In France, the social upheavals accompanying the installation of a new ruling family (the Capetians), which replaced that of the Carolingians in 987, accompanied the arrival of the millennium, which was a year freighted with apocalyptic expectations. King Robert II the Pious (died 1031) ruled a kingdom fragmented among rival warlords, and the attendant in-fighting, upheaval, and suffering reminded many that the Carolingians had once been considered to be the force restraining the appearance of antichrist, found in 2 Thessalonians 2:6–7. Now this restraining force had been removed. This led to a whole range of grassroots apocalyptic and millenarian movements across the lands of the king of France as a way of expressing the rising tide of anxiety. One of these movements was, arguably, the earliest grassroots religious movement of the Middle Ages. This was the so-called "Peace of God" initiative.

The Peace of God Movement sought to impose rules on warring nobles in order to protect noncombatants and to limit times of violence in feudal conflicts. Although it was a grassroots movement it also focused on stability as the world prepared for the second coming of Christ. Other movements that also took their cue from apocalyptic beliefs were less concerned about civilian casualties.

THE CRUSADES AS EXPRESSIONS OF APOCALYPTIC BELIEFS

In the year 1009, the Fatimid *caliph*, Abu Ali Mansur, also known as Al-Hakim bi-Amr Allah (The Ruler by the Order of God), destroyed the Church of the Holy Sepulchre in Jerusalem and forced Christians to convert to Islam (in his case, to the Shia Ismaili form). In France, where apocalyptic feelings had been running high for a generation, there was a wave of antisemitic violence as Jews were targeted. They were the "alien other" on the doorstep, substitutes for distant enemies. And, unlike those distant enemies, they were not armed.

In 1033, another wave of Peace of God mass assemblies occurred across France. These accompanied renewed attempted pilgrimages to Jerusalem. Many present at these Peace of God assemblies believed that they had made a covenant with God.[15] The stage was being set for the explosion of faith, violence, and millennial hopes that became intertwined in the crusading movement.

The astonishing success of the First Crusade—a Western response to a call for assistance from the hard-pressed Byzantine emperor against Islamic forces—made many of those involved feel that they were taking part in a divinely sanctioned activity that would accelerate the coming of Christ's kingdom on earth. This resonated with the enthusiasm that had been rising since the turn of the millennium in 1000. The capture of Jerusalem, in 1099, was accompanied by the slaughter of many Muslims and Jews living there. The traditional figure of 30,000 civilian casualties has been reduced to 3,000 in more recent studies and the point made that such killings of noncombatants was, sadly, a common feature of medieval warfare.[16] Nevertheless, the slaughter was appalling.

There were a number of features of the initial call to crusade that carried an apocalyptic subtext. The first was the idea of a march to Jerusalem, which called to mind prophetic verses concerning battles for the holy city and the idea of confronting the armies of antichrist (now identified as Muslims) in the Holy Land. The concept of such a colossal battle in the last days was found in Revelation as well as the Old Testament. It seemed, to many medieval Christians, that Gog and Magog (enemies of God in prophetic texts) had been loosed in the form of Islamic armies. What would follow would be a last stand of Christian armies at Jerusalem as they faced these forces of antichrist. Then Christ himself would appear in order to give the Christians victory, and his second coming would occur on the Mount of Olives.[17] It was a powerful message to those who heard it. The second feature was the millenarian excitement that had been building since the year 1000.

As with so many millenarian movements before and since, this was most vividly seen in the lower-class and popular expressions of

---

15. Landes, "Medieval and Reformation Millennialism," lines 100–103.
16. Dass, *Deeds of the Franks*, 123n41.
17. Rubenstein, *Armies of Heaven*, xii.

crusader enthusiasm. These often involved poorly organized groups of lesser knights and peasant volunteers and contrasted with the official (and usually better organized) groups that coalesced around powerful nobles and royalty. The most famous of these, the so-called People's Crusade, started in 1096 and was led by Peter the Hermit. It occurred in response to Pope Urban II's call for the First Crusade.

The extreme excitement, and the desire to be revenged on so-called enemies of Christ, led to pogroms against Jews and forced baptisms in western German cities such as Mainz, Speyer, Worms, and Cologne, as expressions of fanatical enthusiasm for becoming part of God's end-times judgment. Apocalyptic politics were, once again, assuming a character of extreme violence.

Another example of lower-class crusading enthusiasm can be seen in the events of 1212, in which a number of poorly organized attempts to reach the Holy Land and convert or conquer the Muslims are now remembered as the "Children's Crusade." Closer analysis suggests that there were, in fact, two broad movements, one in France and one in Germany, and that these involved lower-class followers of various ages.[18]

These examples of apocalyptic enthusiasm were radicalized, lower-class movements of a kind often associated with outbursts of activism linked to millennial beliefs. But, as in the past, these ideas were also accessed and manipulated by those higher up the social scale.

COMPETING APOCALYPTIC POLITICAL AMBITIONS

Supporters of Count Thierry of Alsace (died 1168), in his ambition to rule the city of Damascus, during the Second Crusade promulgated alleged prophecies that identified his family line as representing the final restraint on antichrist. This claim was applied by others to many different people and institutions. During the same crusade, a French preacher claimed that King Louis VII of France (died 1180) was the embodiment of God's chosen ruler in the last days.

Other leaders too were similarly acclaimed, or courted this role. During the First Crusade, Emicho of Flonheim, who led the pogroms against the Jews in the Rhineland, actually styled himself as the "Last World Emperor" and claimed that when he reached Constantinople,

---

18. Raedts, "Children's Crusade of 1213," 279–323.

Christ would crown him. When he finally reached Jerusalem in victory (which he never succeeded in doing), he would lay down this crown.

Others took a more socially radical approach and revealed just how revolutionary apocalyptic politics could be.

MILLENARIAN REVOLUTIONARY UPHEAVALS

The so-called "Spiritual Franciscans" or *Fraticelli* (Little Brethren) condemned the established church and world order as corrupt and worldly. Those who were part of this sinful structure would be damned. They were part of the wider Franciscan movement. In 1296, their beliefs were declared to be heretical by church authorities, but they did not go away. Throughout the fourteenth and fifteenth centuries the suppressed *Fraticelli* continued to appear in parts of Italy. Others, such as the "Apostolic Brethren," were rooted in the laity and set their faces against the Franciscan order (and monasticism generally) as being now too corrupt and worldly to be reformed. In 1300, the founder of the Apostolic Brethren, Segarelli, was executed. This set off a campaign of violent millenarian activism led by Fra Dolcino.[19] Dolcino led an insurgency in northwestern Italy against those maintaining Catholic orthodoxy, feudal overlords, and the wealthy. As a result, a mini-crusade was launched against them and he was captured and burned in 1307. In 1322, about thirty of Dolcino's followers were burned in Padua. Umberto Eco's novel *The Name of the Rose* (1980) is set in the aftermath of the crushing of Dolcino's movement and in the context of ongoing inquisitorial conflict with the *Fraticelli*. It is set in 1327.

Then, in 1320, an uprising of the so-called *Pastoureaux* (Shepherds) sacked the city of Paris as part of their demand that the king (Philip V) should go on crusade to the Holy Land. In ways reminiscent of the violence associated with the First Crusade, they launched pogroms against the Jews. In addition, they murdered clerics and academics. An earlier *Pastoureaux* uprising had occurred in 1251. There is evidence that they thought they could hasten the second coming by their actions.[20] Others were prompted to violent and murderous action by other factors.

In the years following the arrival of the Black Death in Europe, in the late 1340s, the Flagellant Movement arose in Central Europe and rapidly

---

19. Landes, "Patristic and Medieval Millennialism," lines 145–61.
20. Landes, "Patristic and Medieval Millennialism," lines 164–94.

spread from there. Engaging in acts of self-mortification, they believed that their pain would avert the wrath of God. They acted independent of the church structure and at times proclaimed messianic statements such as the movement lasting for thirty-three years (the age of Jesus at his crucifixion and resurrection), and only ending with the arrival of the millennium.[21] As in the earlier years of the crusades, panic at plague mortality led to mass murders of Jews. As the living embodiment of the "alien other," they were held responsible for outbreaks of disease. Thousands were slaughtered. In Germany and in the Low Countries, the Flagellant Movement played an enthusiastic part in committing these atrocities.[22]

The fourteenth century continued to be racked by apocalyptic and radicalized violence. In 1358, a lower-class revolt occurred in northern France. Called the *Jacquerie*, it involved horrifying levels of violence if the contemporary chroniclers are to be believed. While no manifesto accompanied these uprisings they had a millenarian character reminiscent of Fra Dolcino. The uprising was crushed, but unsettled times continued to lead to apocalyptic revolutionary actions.

In fifteenth-century Bohemia, the most radical wing of the Hussites, the Taborites, believed that their militant revolutionary activities would bring in the reign of Christ. They were eventually bloodily defeated, in 1434, by more moderate Hussites in alliance with Catholic forces. After 1452, they ceased to exist as a militant movement.

In the aftermath of the defeat of the Taborites—and clearly influenced by roaming bands of mercenaries who continued to quote some Taborite terminology, while actually terrorizing the Bohemian borderlands—a rogue Franciscan declared himself one called "the Anointed Savior" who would employ such mercenaries to destroy antichrist (the pope), the clergy, and all who opposed him. This was a heretical take on millenarianism. His spokesmen (Janko and Livin of Wirsberg) claimed that this "Anointed Savior," not Christ, was the Son of Man of Old Testament prophecy who would bring in the third and last age (the millennium kingdom) in 1467. However, in 1466, the church authorities crushed the movement.[23]

At other times of economic and political stress others also proclaimed the imminence of the second coming An example occurred in

---

21. Ziegler, *Black Death*, 93–94.
22. Tuchman, *Distant Mirror*, 115–16.
23. Cohn, *Pursuit of the Millennium*, 223–25.

1476, when the so-called "Drummer of Niklashausen" (near Würzburg, in Franconia, Germany), Hans Böhm, announced "messages" from the Virgin Mary. These included denunciations of the clergy and the arrival of the New Jerusalem focused on Niklashausen. Thousands of peasants flocked to hear him. To crush the movement, the authorities arrested him and he was tortured and then burned as a heretic.[24] Apocalyptic and radicalized politics had once again ended in violence.

---

24. Whittock, *When God Was King*, 124–25, 129.

CHAPTER 6

The Hope of a Persecuted Minority
Apocalyptic Beliefs within Medieval and Early Modern Judaism

THE DESTRUCTION OF the Jerusalem Temple in AD 70 created a situation in which "Jews were crushed physically and emotionally." This had added depths of grief because some of those involved in the uprising had "hoped the Messiah would arrive in time to save the Temple and the holy city."[1] It is not surprising that many of those who witnessed this catastrophe—and survived—continued to look for evidence that might indicate when the Messiah would appear and right what had gone so terribly wrong. Then the crushing of the revolt of Bar Kokhba—whom some declared to be the expected one—seemed to put an end to Jewish apocalyptic thinking.

It is often concluded that what replaced this was a more conservative and spiritualized approach to messianic hopes; focus on Torah knowledge and observance as the key characteristic of Jewish identity; and adherence to this as the main way by which persecution and assimilation should be resisted. It has been asserted that "The rise of rabbinic Judaism muted the millenarian impulse." In short, Judaism as a whole ceased to be an activist and politically radical apocalyptic religion.[2]

---

1. Popkin, "Introduction to the Millenarianism and Messianism Series," 1:viii.

2. Mor, *Second Jewish Revolt*, 463 examines this issue; as does Sheinfeld, "Decline of Second Temple Jewish Apocalypticism," 187–210.

There is a great deal of truth in this interpretation, since one can certainly see these profound developments shaping the character of post-Second-Temple Judaism. Yet, despite the trauma of defeat, it has been commented that "after a period of relative stability, some Jews were able to readopt, however timidly, apocalyptic forms of messianic hope."[3] Despite earlier disappointments, in the centuries that followed there could still be found members of the Jewish community who interpreted the antisemitic actions they often experienced as heralds of the revealing of the Messiah. Just as in the past, these believers identified aspects of their contemporary society as representing the fulfillment of the prophecies in Daniel. Analysis of these led to calculations concerning how far the present day had advanced between the end of the Roman Empire and the final day of God's judgment on the world.[4]

It is this reemergence of radical end-times beliefs within Judaism that we shall explore in this chapter. Over years of persecution, belief in the Messiah assisted in the keeping of Jewish faith. As early as the fifth century, a Jewish leader known as Moses of Crete claimed messianic status and declared that God would part the sea and then Moses of Crete would lead the Jews back to their homeland. The fifth-century Christian historian, Socrates of Constantinople, recorded a tradition that Moses fled when the sea failed to part. However, in the late-seventh-century work known as the *Chronicle of John of Nikiu*, it is stated that he drowned along with many of his disappointed followers.

MEDIEVAL JEWISH APOCALYPTIC BELIEFS

While Judaism after Bar Kokhba was clearly less focused on messianic activism, mass enthusiasm still could occur, even if not on the scale of the past. These events included the activities of the Jewish preacher Abu Isa al-Isfahani in the eighth century; David Alroy in the twelfth century; and leaders of messianic agitation in the Jewish communities of Western Europe in the eleventh and twelfth centuries.

Abu Isa al-Isfahani, often simply called Abu Isa, was a self-proclaimed Jewish prophet. He led a short-lived revolt in Persia in the eighth century.[5] Some sources give his first name as having been Obadiah. We do

---

3. Oliver, "Jewish Apocalyptic Expectations," 1:136.
4. Popkin, "Introduction to the Millenarianism and Messianism Series," 1:viii.
5. See: Lassner, "Abu Isa Esfahani."

not know as much about him as we would like, because the source material is fragmentary and lacks detail. However, from the evidence that has survived, it seems that he believed he was the last of five heralds, sent by God to announce the appearance of the Messiah. His followers claimed he was illiterate and that it was a miracle that allowed him to write down his prophecies. It seems that he did not claim messianic status for himself but that some of his followers proclaimed it. A distinctive feature of his preaching was the belief that both Jesus and Muhammad were true prophets. However, for Abu Isa their revelation was only to their own peoples. In addition, he prohibited divorce and increased the Jewish daily prayers from three to seven. This was based on Psalm 119:164, which reads: "Seven times a day I praise you for your righteous ordinances." He banned the consumption of meat and alcohol, in contrast with normal Jewish practices.

Some historians have suggested that Abu Isa represented a Jewish messianism that was influenced by the rise of Islam. Some in the contemporary Jewish community considered the arrival of the conquering Arab armies as signs of the impending end of the world. In terms of the ideology of his movement there are aspects that may have been derived from emerging Shia Islam. The claim that Abu Isa was an illiterate prophet, enabled to write by miraculous intervention, has been compared with Islamic beliefs concerning Muhammad and his receiving of the revelation of the Qur'an. Similarly, the idea of a succession of prophets bears comparison with Shia beliefs regarding Imams, linked to the anticipated coming of the *Mahdi*. The extent of the suggested influence of Shiism on him is disputed by different scholars who have studied his movement, with some arguing for ideas travelling both ways.[6] There is definitely a case for seeing his movement as related to messianic Shia sects which also emerged in the last years of the Umayyad caliphate.[7]

What is certainly clear is that Abu Isa represented a radicalized form of apocalyptic Judaism which had direct political implications, as he led a revolt against the Islamic authorities in Isfahan. Exactly when this occurred is open to question. According to a tradition preserved in Babylonian Jewish (*Karaite*) writings, the revolt occurred during the reign of the fifth Umayyad caliph Abd al-Malik ibn Marwan (685–705). In contrast, the seventeenth-century Persian poet Sahrestani thought that he lived

---

6. See: Wasserstrom, *Between Muslim and Jew*.
7. Lassner, "Abu Isa Esfahani," lines 16–17.

primarily in the time of caliph Al-Mansur (754–75), with his activities starting during the caliphate of Marwan II (744–50),[8] also known as Marwan ibn Muhammad. The lack of medieval references indicate that he was not considered a serious threat by those in power.

The later traditions claim that he gathered 10,000 followers who considered him the promised Messiah. The number is likely to be an exaggeration. What seems clear, though, is that he and his followers died in battle against the forces of the caliph, probably Al-Mansur. Some of his followers, who survived this defeat, thought he would return from the dead and usher in the apocalypse. A sect, the *Isawiyya*, which was focused on beliefs in him, seems to have survived into the tenth century.

Another and much more significant Jewish messianic figure was David Alroy, also known as Ibn al-Ruhi and David el-David. He was born in Amadiya, in Iraq, and was originally known as Menahem ben Solomon. The twelfth-century Jewish traveler and chronicler Benjamin of Tudela claimed his birth occurred sometime before 1160. He later adopted the name "David Alroy," which may have been derived from "the inspired one." The names "Alroy" and "Al-Ruhi" were probably corruptions of his family name in Arabic ("Al-Duji").

The movement associated with him probably began among the so-called "mountain Jews" of the northeastern Caucasus shortly before 1121. Sources are contradictory however, and some place the action in the second half of the twelfth century. It seems to have been prompted by the turbulence associated with the aftermath of the First Crusade (1096–99) and the ongoing conflict between Christian and Islamic forces that culminated in the Second Crusade (1147–49). This was a period when Jews were savagely persecuted by Crusader forces and many looked for relief to the coming Messiah. In addition, the wars had weakened the authority of Islamic rulers across a wide area and this had encouraged unrest and breakaway movements. The high level of war-related taxation further exacerbated this trend.

It was in this highly unsettled and traumatic context that David Alroy led a Jewish uprising against the Abbasid caliph in Baghdad, Al-Muqtafi (1136–60). Alroy summoned the persecuted Jewish community to follow him to Jerusalem. There he would be crowned king and would free the Jews from Islamic control and would restore their ancient capital city to them. This also envisaged freedom from Christian persecution.

---

8. Lassner, "Abu Isa Esfahani," lines 11–15.

Alroy sent out letters in which he declared his messianic mission to Mosul, Baghdad, and other settlements. His ambitions were encouraged by a contemporary rebellion by the Islamic sect of the *Yezidis*. They too sought independence from the rule of the caliph and the Seljuq sultan.

Alroy's authority was strengthened by reports that he had miraculous powers and had used these to free himself when captured by his Islamic enemy, the Seljuq sultan.

Some accounts say that he was eventually killed during an attack on the citadel of Amadiya, in Iraq (his birthplace). Other accounts describe his assassination on the orders of the Muslim governor of Amadiya. A number of his followers in Azerbaijan, who continued to believe in him after his death, became known as *Menahemites*. Alroy's death probably occurred long before the date (ca. 1160) recorded by Benjamin of Tudela. Much later, the nineteenth-century British prime minister Benjamin Disraeli wrote a novel, *The Wondrous Tale of Alroy*, in 1833, which was based on his legendary exploits. But, by that time, the tales had passed out of history and into fiction.

Other examples of Jewish apocalyptic beliefs emerged in Western Europe in the eleventh and twelfth centuries. This was a period, as we have seen, of heightened millenarian beliefs among Western Christians at the time of the early crusades. The same tendency was seen in Jewish communities, many of whom were experiencing ferocious persecution at this time. The Jewish apocalyptic text known as *Sefer Zerubbabel* contains symbolic imagery representing the forces that were opposed to Judaism and committed to its destruction or assimilation and reflects these concerns.[9] The text itself indicates that the looked-for Messiah would appear 990 years after the destruction of the Second Temple. This placed it ca. 1060. The references in the text to warfare centered on Jerusalem seems consistent with what occurred during the First Crusade at the end of the eleventh century. This has led to suggestions that the text, as it now exists, was composed as a direct result of the momentum leading to the First Crusade,[10] although tenth-century fragments suggest that the ideas found in it predated this period and its origins have been suggested as actually lying in the seventh-century context of Palestine.[11] The matter is made more complex because the longest of the surviving versions of

9. Latteri, "Dialogue on Disaster," 68–69.
10. Latteri, "Dialogue on Disaster," 72, 73.
11. Latteri, "Dialogue on Disaster," 70.

the text comes from a compilation manuscript that dates from the early fourteenth century. Consequently, there is a strong likelihood that, even if parts of the eventual text dated from before the crusading movement, its final form and content was heavily influenced by the crusades. This would have included a response to both the extreme Christian millenarians of that later time period and the atrocities committed against Jews at the time. The "Romans" and "Persians" who appear in *Sefer Zerubbabel* can be read as symbolizing Christians and Muslims, rather than the historic figures represented by these names.[12] In the early twelfth century, Rabbi Tobiah ben Eliezer (1050–1108), in a work titled *Lekach Tov*, referred to the existence of a popular Jewish belief, contemporary with the First Crusade, that the coming of the Messiah was imminent. It was this kind of outlook that we may see reflected in *Sefer Zerubbabel* and was clearly demonstrated in uprisings like that associated with David Alroy.

These ideas were not isolated occurrences. Messianic beliefs are also found in medieval Jewish philosopher Maimonides's *Thirteen Articles of Faith*. These ideas also influenced later apocalyptic visionaries and *kabbalistic* (Jewish esoteric) mystics. Among adherents to the kabbalistic approach were many who claimed a heightened ability to communicate with God and with angels. This included claims to be able to predict the future and also to perform miracles. Some Jewish kabbalistic thinkers, living in southern France and also in Spain, developed kabbalistic interpretations of biblical texts whereby they attempted to predict when the Messiah would appear. These often relied on "numerological" readings of Hebrew terms (where letters were accorded number values) in order to assist in these calculations. Some later kabbalistic scholars, such as Abraham Cohen de Herrera (1570–1635), paid less attention to these messianic calculations, but a great many other scholars did and this was often associated with their work.

The Jewish scholars who developed these ideas—though isolated from wider society by the antisemitic regulations that had developed over the medieval period—nevertheless engaged in exchanges of ideas with Christian writers who were equally fascinated with the apocalypse. Many of these Christians were keen to engage with the Old Testament in its original Hebrew as a way to better understand it and more accurately calculate the date of the second coming (despite New Testament prohibitions regarding this). Consequently, the late fifteenth century saw

---

12. Latteri, "Dialogue on Disaster," 73.

a significant exchange of ideas between Christians and Jews regarding prophetic interpretation. In Spain (prior to their expulsion in 1492), the writings of scholars such as the Portuguese Jewish philosopher, Bible commentator, statesman, and financier Don Isaac Abarbanel (1437–1508), who was a well-known theorist regarding Jewish messianic ideas, reveal an active interaction between Jewish and Christian beliefs. He was a prominent financial court adviser, firstly in Portugal and then in Spain. His *Ma'yanei ha-Yeshu'ah* (The Wellsprings of Salvation) was a commentary on the key Old Testament book of Daniel, while his *Yeshu'ot Meshiho* (The Salvation of His Anointed) and *Mashmi'a Yeshu'ah* (Announcing Salvation) interpreted rabbinic ideas about the Messiah and commented on messianic prophetic texts. He was highly critical of Christian interpretations of these texts.

EARLY MODERN "MESSIAHS"

If the late medieval period witnessed a resurgence of Jewish reflection on, and calculations concerning, the appearance of the Messiah, the turbulence of the late fifteenth and early sixteenth centuries further convinced many that the apocalypse was at hand. What occurred to the Jewish inhabitants of the Iberian Peninsula in that period was seared on Jewish consciousness: forced conversion, the end of Moorish rule, and then expulsion of the Jews from Spain and then Portugal. This was the end of a settlement there that stretched back centuries. Following the shock of their expulsion from Spain in 1492, many Jews were occupied more than ever with messianic hopes and eschatology.

In such an atmosphere, many turned to kabbalistic studies. At the same time—buoyed by their triumphs and the dramatic voyages of discovery—many Spanish Christians also considered themselves on the threshold of the millennium. Remarkably, Christopher Columbus, in a work entitled *Book of Prophecies,* told Queen Isabella of Spain that he would find enough gold in the Americas to rebuild the Jerusalem Temple.[13] To the vanquished and to the conqueror the signs of the times seemed clear.

Thinkers such as Don Isaac Abarbanel continued to explore messianic expectations in the context of these dramatic and distressing events. Recent studies have questioned the established view that his

13. Popkin, "Introduction to the Millenarianism and Messianism Series," 1:viii–ix.

postexpulsion thought was centered totally around messianic reflections and go on to suggest that Abarbanel's influence on sixteenth-century Jewish ideas regarding this was much less pervasive than has previously been assumed.[14] Nevertheless, we are still left with a clear impression that seeking news of the Messiah was a major topic within the displaced Jewish communities and among leading Jewish thinkers.

The intensity of messianic speculation after 1492 did not see the hopes realized. This was further disappointment to add to the trauma experienced by Jewish communities. Despite this, the messianic impact of the expulsions from Iberia did not wholly dissipate. In the latter half of the sixteenth century they again emerged in the kabbalistic work of Rabbi Isaac Luria. This, though, was not a radical call to action. Nevertheless, it was related to the highly activist apocalyptic movement that exploded in the 1660s in the movement centered on Sabbatai Zevi (1626–76).

Sabbatai Zevi (aka Shabbetai Tzevi) of Smyrna, in the seventeenth century, reminds us that Jewish apocalyptic hopes had not vanished. Sabbatai claimed to be the long-awaited one. From his claims arose the Sabbatean movement, which had a huge impact at the time. As with a significant section of his contemporary Jewish community, he was greatly influenced by mysticism and the kabbalah. Living in the context of heightened Christian millenarianism, he was also influenced by a Jewish text known as the *Zohar*. This text indicated that the year 1648 was the one when the messianic rescue of Israel would occur. The evidence suggests that a number of Jewish thinkers were "looking for some ray of hope after the expulsion of the Jews from Iberia,"[15] and they anticipated—with heightened expectation—the year 1648, in the hope that it would be "the moment of the arrival of the Messiah."[16]

It was in 1648 that Sabbatai announced to his followers in Smyrna that he was the expected one. To underscore this claim he began to speak out the *Tetragrammaton*. This was the unspeakable name of God, represented by the letters transliterated in the Latin alphabet as *YHWH*. Probably to be spoken as *Yahweh*, saying the holy name was prohibited to all except the Jewish high priest, in the Jerusalem Temple, on the Day of Atonement. It was sometimes represented by the letters *aHWY* or

---

14. Lawee, "Messianism of Isaac Abarbanel," 1:1–40.
15. Popkin, "Introduction to the Millenarianism and Messianism Series," 1:ix.
16. Popkin, "Introduction to the Millenarianism and Messianism Series," 1:x.

AHWY.[17] The form AHYH is also known.[18] With the destruction of the temple in AD 70, this practice of speaking "the name" stopped. Some later Jews (such as the Spanish thirteenth-century founder of the school of "Prophetic Kabbalah," Abraham ben Samuel Abulafia) believed that the hidden name of God would only be revealed to the Messiah.[19] This made the action of Sabbatai hugely significant—and highly controversial.

In about 1651 (some sources suggest 1654), the rabbis of Smyrna banished Sabbatai and his followers. There is uncertainty over where he immediately relocated to, but by 1658 he was in Constantinople. He then moved to Salonika; and then to Jerusalem in about 1663. Facing opposition there from the Jewish leadership, he relocated back to Smyrna where, in 1665, he once again declared himself to be the Messiah with the power to return the Jewish community to the Holy Land. There was great excitement, and he gained a large following. It has been asserted that in 1665–66, the widespread enthusiasm connected with him "swept up much of the Jewish world."[20] It was an extraordinary phenomenon.

Across Europe many Jews prepared for the return to their ancient homeland. Following widespread pogroms against Jewish communities in Eastern Europe, this desire for a secure home was very strong, and Sabbatai's claims spoke to this. Symbolically—but hugely controversially—he announced that the fast of the Tenth of *Tevet* (mourning the Babylonian siege of Jerusalem in the ancient past) would now be a time of feasting and celebration. It was the birthday of Sabbatai.

In 1666, he left again for Constantinople. Some of his followers claimed that he would assume the position of sultan. Instead, he was arrested—but messianic expectations increased rather than declined. Examples of excitement linked to Sabbatai are recorded from as far apart as Moravia and Morocco. Despite this, fractures were appearing in the movement. A rival prophet in Poland, Nehemiah ha-Kohen, declared himself to be the herald of the Messiah. He and Sabbatai did not agree. Moved by Ottoman authorities to Adrianople and threatened with execution (to prove his divinely ordained status) Sabbatai converted to Islam. He was followed in this by his wife Sarah and hundreds of his supporters. Those who converted became known as the *Dönmeh* (converts). They

17. Miller, *Name of God*, 20, 122.
18. Miller, *Name of God*, 20.
19. Miller, *Name of God*, 122.
20. Goldish, "Introduction," 1:xvii.

have been described as "crypto-Jews"[21] because, while outwardly living as Muslims, they secretly continued following Jewish practices—while still holding themselves separate and distinct from Judaism.[22]

The event was a disaster for his movement, which was then ridiculed by both Muslims and Christians. Sabbatai himself attempted to combine aspects of Judaism and Islam in his activities and attempted to revive his messianic claims in 1668, when he claimed to have been filled with the Holy Spirit at Passover, and among his followers it was said that he would convert Muslims to Judaism. To the sultan he declared the opposite. He was clearly running out of options and attempting to appeal to both groups. He was eventually exiled and died in 1676. His followers splintered, though some continued as Muslims while secretly practicing a form of messianic and mystical Judaism. Some descendants of these groups have survived in Turkey into the twenty-first century. But the high hopes of their time of greatest influence had been disappointed. Sabbatai was not the Messiah.

Sabbateanism did not stand alone. Rather, it took place at a time of wider change and turbulence, which means that analyzing its causes cannot be restricted to events within the Jewish community.[23] These reflected not only stresses and developments within Judaism but also reflected the way Jews related to wider European and Ottoman society.[24] Indeed, it was both a product of longstanding Jewish traditions and the particular pressures on the community, living as an often vulnerable minority.

What is also clear is that their gentile contemporaries paid close attention to these dramatic events. Protestant millenarians in England, New England, and the Netherlands were well aware of what was taking place in Turkey, and elsewhere in the Ottoman Empire. Viewing it from outside, they "tried to fit it into their own [apocalyptic] scenarios."[25] This was quite a challenge since they completely rejected any belief in a Messiah subsequent to Jesus. However, it gives an insight into the apocalyptic fervor of the seventeenth century and the way in which many Christian and Jewish millenarians were aware of each other's ideas and, at times,

---

21. Kohler and Gottheil, "Dönmeh," line 1.
22. Kohler and Gottheil, "Dönmeh," lines 10–12.
23. Barnai, "Some Social Aspects," 1:78–79.
24. Barnai, "Some Social Aspects," 1:77–90.
25. Popkin, "Introduction to the Millenarianism and Messianism Series," 1:xiii.

attempted to take the other into account while promulgating their own confessional approaches to the impending end-time events.²⁶

The interconnectedness of the millenarian world can be seen in the way that, in 1655, Rabbi Menasseh ben Israel of Amsterdam thought that the appearing of the Messiah was imminent because a Portuguese explorer reported finding members of an unknown tribe in the Andes. Thoughts quickly moved to the "lost tribes of Israel." Furthermore, ben Israel's study of Isaac la Peyrere's *Du Rappel des Juifs* (Reminder of the Jews)—published in 1643—led him to conclude that the king of France would soon lead the exiled Jews home to the Holy Land. Following this, the temple would be rebuilt and the king of France would rule as regent of the Messiah. This idea was promulgated by the French theologian and courtier Isaac la Peyrere (1596–1676). He was born in Bordeaux and raised a Calvinist; his family origin was among the converted Spanish Jews (or *Marranos*). It seemed that the "day of the Lord" was finally at hand.

In order to better facilitate this return to the Middle East, ben Israel contacted the government of Oliver Cromwell with a request to readmit Jews to England (they had been brutally expelled in 1291) as part of preparation for a messianic age that was very much on the mind of Cromwell too. We know this from accounts from England and from foreign diplomats who commented on the way the theme occupied the mind of the Lord Protector in London. For example, Swedish representatives—who wished to negotiate regarding the fur trade—found, instead, that "the only thing Cromwell would discuss was if there were any new reports about when the Messiah was coming."²⁷ On arriving in London, ben Israel even discovered that some in the city entertained the extraordinary belief that the son of Charles I (beheaded in January 1649) would soon rule the world as regent of Christ. Ben Israel was not convinced by this extraordinary claim and was more confident that such a role might be played either by the king of Sweden or the ruler of France.²⁸ Quite how such contradictory views of the Messiah—viewed differently as the second coming of Jesus, or the first coming of the Messiah in Jewish beliefs—could be reconciled is hard to imagine. But regardless, the looked-for millennium did not occur.

26. Popkin, "Christian Interest," 1:91–106.
27. Popkin, "Introduction to the Millenarianism and Messianism Series," 1:x.
28. Popkin, "Introduction to the Millenarianism and Messianism Series," 1:x.

The coming of the eighteenth century did not lead to the dissipation of Jewish hopes, despite the profound disappointments of the seventeenth century. In Poland, Jacob Frank, aka Jakub Lejbowicz (1726–91), claimed in 1755 that he was the reincarnation of Sabbatai Zevi and also of the Old Testament patriarch Jacob. His claim was encouraged by the fact that there were many Jewish Sabbatean secret societies (known as *Dönmeh*), in Eastern Poland. This was in areas that are now in Ukraine. In many ways it was an eighteenth-century Sabbatean revival.

Frank and his followers were soon involved in conflicts with local rabbis. Due to their rejection of the Talmud and their intimations that they were sympathetic to Christian Trinitarian beliefs, the Catholic Bishop of Kamieniec Podolski, in Poland, sided with Frank and his followers, and used this as a basis for attacks on orthodox Judaism and the destruction of huge numbers of copies of the Talmud. Despite this apparently positive attitude towards Christian doctrine, it was clear that Frank and his followers held beliefs that were as much at odds with Christianity as with Judaism. Frank was arrested in Warsaw in 1760, convicted of heresy, and imprisoned for thirteen years. Released in 1772, he lived in the Moravian town of Brno until 1786, protected by an armed retinue. There he was visited by both the future Russian tsar (Paul I) and the Austrian emperor (Joseph II).

In time, though, the Austrian authorities decided he could not be managed and he was forced to relocate to Offenbach am Main, in Hesse, Germany. Supported by the monetary contributions of his followers, he lived there in some comfort until his death in 1791. After this, his daughter took over leadership of the movement and a number of "Frankists" thought that Napoleon Bonaparte might be the awaited Messiah. The movement largely faded from view following the death of Frank's daughter in 1816.

There has been debate over the extent to which Frank's outlook was influenced by the beliefs of the *Dönmeh* and by Freemasonry later in his life, when he was living in Brno and Offenbach am Main.[29] What is clear is that the much-awaited millennium did not dawn. Of the earlier *Dönmeh* sect—called the *Ya'kubis*—it has been recorded that on every Sabbath a woman and her children were sent to the coast "to inquire whether the ship which is to bring Jacob is sighted."[30] But Jacob has not come.

---

29. Lenowitz, "Charlatan," 1:189–202.
30. Kohler and Gottheil, "Dönmeh," lines 58–59.

CHAPTER 7

Apocalypse Now!
The Impact of the Reformation

THE APOCALYPTICALLY ORIENTATED political effects of theological changes in the sixteenth and seventeenth centuries were dramatic. They ranged from justification for establishing virtual theocracies, such as that in Geneva under Calvin (as later in Massachusetts), to lower-class uprisings set on preparing the ground for the millennium, such as occurred during the German Peasants' War (1524–25) and which led to the deaths of approximately 100,000 people (the vast majority of them having been civilians) and the radical Anabaptist seizure of Münster, in Germany, in 1534–35.

During the seventeenth century, apocalyptic beliefs informed the political ideologies and demands of British groups as varied as the agrarian communist Diggers, the theocratic and militant Fifth Monarchy Men, and their North American Puritan equivalents after 1620. For many of these believers the second coming was imminent and they adopted an active—and, at times, highly muscular—approach towards preparing the way for it. At times they believed that they were implementing it in a way that merged human action with divine intervention. For them it was apocalyptic belief with attitude.

THE IMPACT OF THE REFORMATION ON POLITICAL ACTION

In 1521, Martin Luther made a decisive break from the authority of the pope. This followed the Diet of Worms, an assembly before the leaders of the Holy Roman Empire in which he laid out his criticisms of the Catholic Church. Luther himself had wanted no such break but had been hoping to reform the Catholic Church from within. It proved strongly resistant to reform. However, it has to be said that many of his contemporaries were in favor of a more radical break with the Catholic past and some of them were committed to challenging society as well as church. For the latter, things were about to get very radical indeed. Apocalyptic politics aimed to overturn the social order in many communities.

Across Germany in 1524 and 1525, peasants took their cue from a sense of change being possible and rose in revolt against their feudal masters. This was certainly not what Luther intended, but the unsettled nature of things encouraged them to act. Vast numbers died in the course of the German Peasants' War and its eventual defeat.

The violence prompted hugely differing reactions among early Protestant reformers. Martin Luther, for example, condemned the uprising and wrote a pamphlet entitled *Against the Murdering Plundering Hordes of Peasants*. In this pamphlet he advised lords to crush the peasants' revolt. In contrast, some other Christian leaders of a more revolutionary disposition applauded the uprising and later sought to emulate its attack on the wealth and power of the world. This soon developed into a sense of playing an active part in God's judgment on a sinful society, while offering the promise of an imminent New Jerusalem as part of a millennial new world order. This was where apocalyptic beliefs merged into violent radicalization. This was a much more radical definition of "reformation" than Luther had envisaged.

Later, radical revolutionaries, such as those at Münster in Westphalia in 1534–35, would see themselves as the heirs of this revolutionary tradition that had earlier been seen in the bloody violence of the German Peasants' War. For them the social upheaval was clearly interwoven into apocalyptic beliefs. Part of the broad Anabaptist movement, their activities would later thrill or horrify different Protestant groups—including the seventeenth-century British "godly"—depending on their outlook. The Reformation developed both a socially conservative and a revolutionary track. However, apocalyptic beliefs were integral to both, even if they were expressed in different forms. What can be described as a distinct Protestant apocalyptic character was emerging and would become a permanent part of a wide range of Protestant identities.

In 1541, any hope of reconciliation between Catholics and Protestants broke down. This followed the Diet of Regensburg and led to years of indecisive warfare between the Catholic Holy Roman Emperor and the various German princes who had adopted the Protestant faith. This finally led to the Treaty of Passau in 1552. The treaty recognized the continued existence of the Protestant German states and was followed by the Peace of Augsburg (1555), which ended this period of fighting. However, it was not the end of religious warfare.

THE NATURE OF PROTESTANT APOCALYPTIC BELIEFS

Millenarian beliefs were prevalent among sixteenth- and seventeenth-century Protestants. Many, perhaps most, identified the pope as the antichrist. Luther accused the pope of being this in the 1530 edition of the German Bible and continued to do so in later editions.[1] The identification was widespread. In Switzerland, John Calvin also asserted this in the 1559 edition of the *Institutes of the Christian Religion*. In the commentary accompanying the *Geneva Bible*, translated in 1560 by English Protestant exiles living in Geneva, the same identification occurred.[2] This outlook envisaged that once the pope had been defeated, the situation would be ready for the return of Christ; judgment would fall on those who had opposed the godly movements of the Protestants; and the heavenly kingdom would be established. Most of those who believed in the millennium in some form (neither Luther nor Calvin, it should be noted, envisaged a literal millennium) looked to God to bring it in, and armed millenarian revolts were certainly not envisaged or encouraged. It would be the preaching of the Protestant message that would lead to the defeat of antichrist.[3]

This was an outlook found across large areas of the emerging Protestant leadership; both those who were terming themselves "Lutheran" and those who preferred the term "Reformed." Prominent among the

---

1. Boyer, *When Time Shall Be No More*, 61.
2. Boyer, *When Time Shall Be No More*, 61.
3. Cohn, *Pursuit of the Millennium*, 243.

latter was Calvin who, though inclined towards a theocratic form of government and the rule of the saints in Geneva, was opposed to major changes in the economic status quo. This was a form of establishment Protestantism that was replacing establishment Catholicism. In other words, those who considered themselves "the godly" should take power, but there would not be an upending of the economic hierarchy. For Calvin, as for Luther, this was for a number of reasons. The first was that only God could establish the eschatological eternal kingdom. The second was that socially radical revolts got in the way of spreading the new Protestant message and prompted opposition from elites. Such political activism, it was feared, would discredit the Reformation.[4] But the key thing was that they simply did not believe in it as an outworking of the faith. The official concept was one that removed eschatological activism on the part of believers when it came to economics and social change. The elite Protestants were revolutionaries, but ones who set clear economic and social boundaries to the upheavals they set in motion.

However, this did not mean they lacked political goals. In Geneva, it was not until 1555 that Calvin and his supporters were finally able to gain control over the reformed church in the city. It was then that they used their power to implement changes. Anything not specifically mentioned in the Bible was forbidden in the church services; all ornaments and statues were removed from church buildings; the preachers wore simple robes instead of ornate Catholic-style vestments; all musical instruments were banned and congregational hymn singing was unaccompanied. This Reformed church structure came to be known as "Presbyterian" and was a tightly controlled and efficiently run system. In it church pastors and a council of lay elders constituted the government of the church. The pastors were chosen by other pastors and approved by the church members. A strict control was exercised over church members, their beliefs, and their behavior.[5]

The new church became increasingly influential in deciding the laws of Geneva, despite some opposition from the city's ruling council. As a result, between 1541 and 1546, fifty-eight people were executed for infringing laws promoted by the church; a further seventy-six were expelled from Geneva; taverns were shut; games of cards and dice forbidden. The controls went further. In 1547, certain types of fashionable

---

4. Cohn, *Pursuit of the Millennium*, 243.
5. Whittock, *When God Was King*, 13.

clothes were banned, and dancing was banned in 1550. Not surprisingly, all Catholic practices were banned.

In order to ensure compliance, homes in the city were inspected by church pastors in order to ensure godly conduct was maintained. Some said that they were so closely monitored in the city that it was like living in a community made from glass.[6] After 1555, the City Council conceded the power of excommunication to the church, which greatly increased its power. Numbers of excommunications escalated.

However, despite these godly ordinances, Calvin was only able to achieve this because key citizens were members of both the church and city governing bodies. Overall though, Geneva set a pattern for the trajectory that a godly community might follow in order to establish a semi-theocracy.[7] Those who did this firmly believed that they lived in the last days and were part of God's campaign against antichrist. It was institutional millenarianism, but one reluctant to speculate about dates.

It should also be noted that—though lacking official encouragement—millenarian beliefs circulated among some Catholic communities too. The expansion of Islamic Ottoman power in the fifteenth and sixteenth centuries seemed to threaten the very existence of Christian Europe as much as Protestants threatened the unity and orthodoxy of Catholic Christendom. The last days, it seemed, might indeed be at hand. Whereas Protestants accused the papacy of being antichrist, many Catholics (and some Protestants too) "saw the Turkish Empire as the last empire before the divine one."[8] These beliefs revealed themselves in the Iberian Peninsula in ways that contrast with ideas being discussed in northwestern Europe. In late-sixteenth-century Portugal, popular millenarianism looked for the reappearance of "Lost King Sebastian" as the herald of the appearance of Christ and the start of the millennium. Sebastian had been killed in 1578 in battle in Morocco against Islamic forces (where he was intervening in an Islamic civil war and fighting alongside Muslim allies). However, his body was not recovered. Hence he became known as *O Adormecido* (The Asleep) in Portuguese, and many looked for his "return" to restore Portuguese greatness. Then, in the same region in the seventeenth century, some asserted that the returning Jesus would come first to Portugal. There he would lead the *Marranos* (Jews who had

---

6. Whittock, *When God Was King*, 13.
7. Whittock, *When God Was King*, 14.
8. Popkin, "Introduction to the Millenarianism and Messianism Series," 1:ix.

converted, or had been forced to convert, to Christianity) and take them with him to the Holy Land. There they would rebuild the temple in Jerusalem and begin Christ's thousand-year reign on earth.[9]

However, the most radical and widespread millenarian beliefs—and those that had the most apocalyptic *political* impact—were to be found among Protestants.

RADICALIZED APOCALYPTIC POLITICS

In sharp contrast to Luther in Germany and Calvin and fellow Reformed leaders in Switzerland, there were other Protestants who adopted an altogether more muscular and radicalized approach towards bringing in the millennial kingdom of God. And their actions were designed to overturn the entire social order—including the economy and the class structure.

The most radical among those who espoused apocalyptic politics gravitated towards the Anabaptist wing of the Protestant Reformation. This term described those who rejected the validity of infant baptism in favor of adult believers' baptism. Many of these groups were the forerunners of Baptist churches that emerged in the seventeenth century, even if many of these later fellowships came directly out of infant-baptizing churches and did not have roots in the earlier Anabaptist movement.

The Anabaptists included both violent militant groups and pacifist fellowships. The one thing they had in common was a belief in the need for adult believers to make their own declaration of faith, independent of the power and sacraments of Catholic priests on one hand, and Lutheran and Reformed pastors on the other. It was a short step from this to challenging secular structures too. Consequently, they were regarded as highly dangerous and suffered as a consequence. In response, many began to adopt millenarian beliefs in the judgment of God that would vindicate the suffering poor and bring down the mighty. For some of the more radicalized this involved a redistribution of wealth and the holding of goods in common. They claimed scriptural validity for this from the practice of the very early church, as revealed in Acts 2:44–45.

This apocalyptic preaching was promoted in Germany by Thomas Müntzer and Niklas Storch, at the time of the German Peasants' War.[10] They attracted a large following among unemployed silver miners at

---

9. Popkin, "Introduction to the Millenarianism and Messianism Series," 1:x.
10. Cohn, *Pursuit of the Millennium*, 250–51.

Zwickau. This then spread to peasants and copper miners in Thuringia. From Mühlhausen, Müntzer issued a manifesto that called for uprisings and quoted eschatological passages from Ezekiel 34, Daniel 7, Matthew 24, and Revelation 6. For Müntzer and his allies, the apocalyptic confrontation was at hand. In May 1525, this uprising was bloodily suppressed by an army loyal to the German princes. Müntzer was captured and tortured. Finally he was beheaded.

Müntzer never actually described himself as an Anabaptist, although he was later venerated by the Anabaptist movement in the aftermath of the crushing of the German Peasants' War.[11] It is not surprising that, later in the seventeenth century, the term Anabaptist became "just a loose term of abuse like, 'Red.'"[12] What happened ten years later, in Westphalia, only served to increase the panic.

In 1534, John Mathias of Haarlem (in the Netherlands) and John Buckhold of Leiden (also in the Netherlands) led a group of radicalized Anabaptists who seized control of the German city of Münster. What occurred after this illustrated just how extreme the most radicalized form of apocalyptic politics could become. The entire social order of the city was overturned and a reign of terror began. There had been precedents for this in the *Bundschuh* (peasants' clog) uprisings that had escalated into the earlier German Peasants' War. Both the *Bundschuh* and what occurred in Münster represented lower-class revolt,[13] which proclaimed a God-sanctioned overturning of the entire social order.

The violence began to spiral out of control, as both Lutherans and Catholics were expelled from the city. Following this, the city was besieged by the Catholic bishop of Münster. It was then that Mathias declared that he was a prophet and began a reign of terror against all perceived enemies. The radicals seized all gold and silver and held it communally; all books were destroyed. In March 1534, Mathias was so convinced that he had been ordered by God to take a small force out of the city to break the siege that he led a force out of the city and was killed. He was replaced as leader by John Buckhold—later remembered as "Jan of Leiden"—who adopted the title "King of Justice, King of the New Jerusalem."[14] It was a heretical messianic self-promotion.

---

11. Cohn, *Pursuit of the Millennium*, 250–51.
12. Hill and Dell, *Good Old Cause*, 160.
13. Whittock, *When God Was King*, 15.
14. Whittock, *When God Was King*, 15.

Buckhold then proclaimed a policy of polygamy and took fifteen wives. After this, any women who refused to be given in arranged marriages to one of Buckhold's supporters were executed on his orders. Women who argued with their husbands were also executed.[15]

In August 1534, he declared that he, not Christ, was "Messiah of the last days" and would rule the world as a descendant of the Old Testament King David. It was an attempt to seize the idea of messianic Davidic kingship that dated from the years after the revolt of the Maccabees. Buckhold's coinage proclaimed that "The Word has become Flesh and dwells in us." It was clear that this text referred to him.[16] The city starved, but he lived in luxury, claiming that the cobblestones of the town would turn into loaves of bread in order to feed the starving people.[17]

Finally, in 1535, the chaos ended as those besieging the place finally gained entry to the town, slaughtered the Anabaptists and captured "King John," who was tortured to death with red-hot irons.[18]

Despite the crushing of the revolt, others took inspiration from it. In 1567, a cobbler named Jan Willemsen set up yet another New Jerusalem, and this one was also in Westphalia. He also declared that he was the Messiah. In time, he and his supporters were captured and executed.[19]

Such views continued to circulate among the more extreme Anabaptist groups, and conflicts such as the Thirty Years War and the British Civil Wars only added to this sense of being in the middle of apocalyptic events. Consequently, radical millenarian beliefs were very much in the Protestant godly mainstream and were not just held by fringe groups. As political order broke down in the British Isles in the 1640s, a heady cocktail of ideas was being mixed.

RADICAL APOCALYPTIC POLITICS IN BRITAIN

In the 1640s and 1650s, the British Isles were convulsed by civil wars, during which apocalyptic politics were energized by the literal reading of prophecy. This was encouraged by the Reformation changes that had overturned the medieval Catholic view of them as allegorical. Large

---

15. Whittock, *Reformation*, 35.
16. Whittock, *When God Was King*, 16.
17. Whittock, *Reformation*, 35.
18. Whittock, *Reformation*, 35.
19. Whittock, *When God Was King*, 16.

APOCALYPSE NOW!

numbers of people became radicalized as they saw themselves as the ones through whom these prophecies were being fulfilled.

One group, known as the Diggers, called for the total reordering of the system of land ownership in a country where, in 1650, about 83 percent of the English population lived in the countryside.[20] Given that wealth was still measured primarily in terms of land and agricultural products, the idea of the communalization of agriculture was shocking. It was as radical as Communist ideology in the twentieth century. Their manifesto—*The True Levellers Standard Advanced*—claimed that all the well-known Old Testament prophecies about the "restoration of Israel" (referring to justice and freedom from want) involved what these radicals called "digging" (communal agricultural work and ownership).

Another group, called the Fifth Monarchists, took their distinctive name from the content of Daniel 7, with its vision of four kingdoms (or monarchies) that would be succeeded by the rule of one "like a son of man" who would appear with the clouds of heaven and would be established as ruler of an eternal kingdom by God (the "Ancient One" or "Ancient of Days" in the prophecy). This was the "Fifth Monarchy" and was interpreted as referring to the millennial kingdom of Christ. Christ, they believed, would reign on earth with his saints for 1,000 years before the final judgment and the creation of a new heaven and a new earth.

The Fifth Monarchists took planning for the impending theocratic government seriously. Some of them argued for an assembly elected by the "gathered churches" (the fellowships of which they approved). On the other hand, some wanted Oliver Cromwell to personally select a modern Sanhedrin (the ancient Jewish ruling council). Others wanted representatives chosen by the officers of the godly parliamentary army. However, by the end of 1653, they were of one mind that Cromwell's protectorate was not the rule endorsed by God and referred to in the prophecies. Any last lingering support for Cromwell evaporated.

Two plots against Cromwell failed: first in 1657, and then in 1659. In January 1661, a couple of leading Fifth Monarchists, Thomas Venner and Vavasor Powell, led an abortive uprising in London against the newly restored Charles II. Their evocative battle cry was: "King Jesus and the heads upon the gates."[21] The revolt was finally put down with the deaths of some twenty-two of the rebels and another twenty were executed. In the

---

20. Chalklin, *Rise of the English Town*, 5.
21. Greaves, *Glimpses of Glory*, 138.

face of such resolute government action and the failure of their prophetic hopes to materialize (the apparently numerically significant year of 1666, the mark of the beast in Revelation, did not have prophetic significance) the Fifth Monarchy movement rapidly faded away.

To return to Cromwell. He was no Fifth Monarchist, but he too believed that a monumental movement of God—that was of end-times significance—was occurring. He was convinced that a theocratic form of government should be established in order to facilitate the further fulfillment of prophecy. Consequently, in 1653, he called together a new parliament now remembered as the "Barebone's Parliament," the "Nominated Parliament," or the "Parliament of Saints." The unusual first name is taken from the striking surname of one of its members: Praise-God Barebone, who represented the City of London. It was made up of those whose names were nominated by the so-called "independent" churches (basically the Puritan congregations Cromwell approved of). Cromwell declared to its members, "You are as like the forming of God as ever people were . . . You are at the edge of promises and prophecies."[22] They were heady words. It looked as if the apocalyptic mood of the times had finally combined with the radicalism that it and the civil wars had generated to create an assembly that would prepare the world for the second coming of Christ. Cromwell was less specific about this than some of its members. But if he was not exactly "on the same page," he was certainly reading the same general "book."

The Barebone's Parliament finally met from July to December 1653, but the aims of the millenarian radicals in it alarmed those who were of a more conservative disposition. It also alarmed Cromwell. Like Calvin in Geneva, he wanted to prepare for the millennium without overly disturbing the economic and class order of his day. Within six months, the conservatives organized a vote for the dissolution of the assembly and engineered it to occur while the millenarians were absent at a prayer meeting. The apocalyptic "rule of the saints" was eventually replaced by Cromwell becoming Lord Protector. Radicalism was becoming replaced by something that was institutional. The second coming did not occur. Cromwell died in 1658. The Stuart monarchy was restored in 1660. The era of apocalyptic politics in Britain was over.

22. Fraser, *Cromwell*, 424.

THE APOCALYPSE IN NORTH AMERICA

The same apocalyptic mood that shook Britain in the 1640s and 1650s also permeated the Puritan settlements of New England. However, there it did not suffer the same degree of decline as the century wore on.

Despite the fame of the Mayflower Pilgrims of 1620, most of the godly who emigrated to North America travelled there between 1630 and 1640. This was triggered by the personal rule of Charles I and mounting pressure on Puritans. This was the same process that led to civil wars in their homeland. Those who emigrated spoke of their new home as a "New England Canaan." It was part of their reimagining themselves in the role of God's chosen people, embarking on the conquest of a new promised land.[23] In this construct, the indigenous peoples could easily be simply presented as idolaters, slated for extermination. They also considered themselves living in the last days and this they took as sanction for their warfare against those they considered opponents of God. It was the well-known trope of colonial violence, but energized by apocalyptic ideology.

In 1636, war broke out between the New England settlers and the Native American Pequots. In it, the settlers exterminated the natives in a way that shocked their own native allies who were used to wars that minimized fatalities. Then further hostilities broke out in 1675 (King Philip's War). In it, former Puritan native allies, such as the Narragansetts in collaboration with other Algonquian tribes, collaborated to oppose the English. It was perhaps the bloodiest "Indian War" in the history of the North American continent. Native relations with the colonists never recovered.

In the long term, the apocalyptic outlook became a vital ingredient in the development of US nativism and "American exceptionalism." Those who laid its foundations were arguably more socially homogeneous and religiously active than any comparable colonial group in North America.[24] This gave them a distinct ideological character. The historian Michael Zuckerman called their tightly knit communities "a totalitarianism of true believers."[25] The infamous Salem witch trials of 1692–93 illustrated the dangers inherent in such a community of the

---

23. See: Bercovitch, *American Jeremiad*, and Bercovitch, *Puritan Origins*. Also, Kaplan, *Our American Israel*, 5.

24. See: Fischer, *Made in America*, ch. 4, "Groups."

25. Fischer, "Pilgrims, Puritans," line 29.

godly—where high levels of mutual policing, combined with hunting out imagined "others" and a sense of the imminent end times—while normal standards of legality were suspended. At the same time, women's inferior place was emphasized, as female names like Be-Fruitful, Comfort, Fear, Patience, Prudence, and Silence made clear.[26]

The godly semi-theocracy was effectively at an end by the 1690s, as British royal authority was reasserted over the New England communities, but its political and cultural legacy was enduring. When the British Parliament passed the Boston Port Act in 1774 (a response to the Boston Tea Party) to force the town to compensate the royal treasury and the East India Company for losses incurred, several local ministers announced a fast day. Tellingly, they also preached that the British crown was a tool of "Satan" that had unleashed King George, "the great Whore of Babylon," to ride her "great red dragon" upon America.[27] Eschatology went hand-in-hand with American patriotism. It has been argued that, among its more extreme exponents in the eighteenth century, there were those who expected "a star-spangled Millennium."[28] In 1776, Timothy Dwight looked forward to two centuries of US progress, which would climax in the year 2000 with the second coming of Christ.[29] In the nineteenth century, the westward advance of the frontier, which became known as "Manifest Destiny," owed much to both the individualistic personal self-confidence, and the sense of providentially approved community purpose, that was inherited from the earlier national myth. "It satisfyingly justified the precocious confidence of a newly minted and assertive state."[30] Once again, apocalyptic politics and culture had become institutionalized and normalized.

This outlook would affect US cultural development again and again. Key features of the ideology of the twenty-first-century evangelical right—and its eschatological outlook—can be traced back to these formative years of the mid-seventeenth century.[31] Apocalyptic politics can have a long reach.

---

26. UShistory.org, "3d. Puritan Life," lines 34–36.
27. Elliott, "Legacy of Puritanism," lines 246–47.
28. Boyer, *When Time Shall Be No More*, 73.
29. Boyer, *When Time Shall Be No More*, 73.
30. Roberts and Whittock, *Trump and the Puritans*, 76.
31. See: Roberts and Whittock, *Trump and the Puritans*.

CHAPTER 8

Islamic Apocalyptic Response to Colonialism in Sudan

WHEN THE *MAHDI* movement exploded in Sudan in the 1880s (and defeated and killed the British General Gordon at Khartoum) it was a vivid reminder that apocalyptic preoccupations continued to influence Islamic as well as Christian and Jewish thinking from the medieval into the modern period of history.

The experiences of Western imperial expansion prompted a revisiting of this central Islamic belief and saw its reinterpretation in radical military and political forms at times (the *Mahdi* movement in the Sudan being an extreme example).

Such radicalized politics were both a well-rooted aspect of traditional Islamic beliefs and also a response to Western imperialism and the apparent humiliation of Islamic communities that accompanied Western colonial expansion.

APOCALYPSE AND JIHAD

We have seen how Islamic eschatology is a major feature of Muslim belief, both in the Qur'an and in the hadith traditions. Islamic scholars have long debated the actual nature of *jihad* (often translated into English as "holy war"). It is clear that the term covers a number of activities. These primarily consist of: the Muslim believer's personal internal struggle to live in a way consistent with Islamic beliefs; the struggle to construct a society that is in line with Islam; holy war, using physical force, to defend Islam; and holy war, using physical force, to conquer territory and establish and/or extend Islamic rule.

Islamic traditions frequently refer to "internal *jihad*" as the one taught by Muhammad as being the "greater *jihad*." This is a matter debated by different Islamic and non-Islamic scholars depending on their assessment of the source of this tradition. The idea that, in its highest form, it means personal (nonviolent) commitment to living an Islamic life explains why *Jihad*, along with *Mujahid* (effectively "doer of *jihad*"), appear as Islamic personal names. The latter, for example, has appeared as a personal name from the early Islamic period to the present day.[1] Modern Muslims with these names should not be considered as violent holy warriors but, instead, as one engaged in a personal struggle for holiness as understood within Islam.

However, even for those who consider this understanding of the term to be its most important aspect, the notion of it as also encompassing military action in the service of Islam seems clearly rooted in Muslim writings and history. Such an understanding of *jihad* as "holy war" need not have an apocalyptic tone. We have seen the use of the Arabic singular form, *mujahid*, as a personal name in everyday use. However, and more pertinent to this study, it could be (and has been) deployed in order to encourage and justify armed resistance to non-Islamic forces as diverse as the medieval resistance to Western crusaders and the modern resistance of the Afghan *mujahideen/mujahidin* to the Soviets and their Afghan allies in the late twentieth century, and the military and political forces of the US and its allies from 2001 to 2021. The same outlook has also characterized the modern, militarized Islamic activity, by other so-called "jihadists," in places as diverse as Chechnya, Myanmar (Burma), and the Philippines. Often these have been reactions against forces regarded as antagonistic to Islam: foreign imperialists, non-Muslim governments at home, aspects of modernity viewed as corrupt and un-Islamic. The fact that the term *mujahideen* means "strugglers or strivers, doers of *jihad*" reveals how closely connected the term *jihad* and military struggle can become. In this sense the term *mujahideen* has been translated as "those engaged in *jihad*."[2]

---

1. Editors of Encyclopaedia Britannica, "Mujahideen, Islam," lines 3–4.
2. Editors of Encyclopaedia Britannica, "Mujahideen, Islam," line 1.

While the term *jihad* need not necessarily carry apocalyptic meaning, it certainly can do so. This is not surprising, given the fact that (as we saw in chapter 4) Islamic eschatology envisages titanic struggles occurring as the prelude to the "end of days" and the culmination of the current world and cosmic order. Consequently, apocalyptic and radical politics and military action can become intertwined with Islamic attitudes towards *jihad,* and this has, at times, led to extremely radicalized action by those who regard themselves as not only furthering the current purpose of Islam, but also playing a role within the drawing of world history to its close.

We shall later explore how, when ISIS/ISIL/*Daesh* established their short-lived and bloody "caliphate" in Syria/Iraq—at its height stretching from Aleppo in Syria to Diyala in Iraq (2014–18)[3]—they did so believing in the imminent day of judgment and the end of the current world order. In this emphasis they differed from other Islamist and *jihadist* movements, including *al-Qaeda*.

However, they were by no means the first to see their political program as being part of apocalyptic events. Others in modern times have approached events in a comparable way. While there are a number of striking examples, certain ones stand out as particularly dramatic in their apocalyptic activities. The one we will focus on here took place in Sudan. Then, by way of contrast, we will briefly see how a more compliant form of end-times beliefs could also arise as a response to colonialism.

APOCALYPTIC POLITICS IN THE SUDAN

The so-called *mahdist* State in Sudan, which is also sometimes known as the Sudanese *mahdiyya*, was a polity arising from a combined religious and political movement that was started in 1881 by Muhammad Ahmad bin Abdullah (later known as Muhammad al-*Mahdi*).

It was originally conceived as a Sudanese movement acting against the khedivate of Egypt, which had ruled Sudan since 1821. Muhammad Ahmad declared a *jihad* against the Egyptian-run administration based in Khartoum. This was a government dominated by Egyptians and Turks. That he declared a *jihadist* uprising against fellow Muslims indicates how complex such activities can be. In his eyes they were compromised in their Islamic credentials and were virtually *kafir* (infidels). Muhammad

3. Glenn, "Timeline."

Ahmad considered the Egyptians as wealthy and worldly (and, by definition, un-Islamic), whereas the poverty of Sudan was acclaimed as exemplifying its spiritual purity. Many accepted his claim to be the promised *Mahdi*. This added a volatile eschatological character to his revolt and movement.

Initially, the government in Khartoum played down the threat posed by the *Mahdi*'s uprising. However, two expeditions sent to capture him were defeated in the course of one year. It was clear that he was not going away. In the wake of these failed attempts to suppress him, his power increased. The message of revolt spread across Sudan, with his growing movement becoming known as the *Ansar* (helpers). Thus a deliberate parallel was drawn between his movement and the original *Ansar*, who were the inhabitants of Medina who had, in Islamic tradition, taken Muhammad and his followers (the *Muhajirun*) into their homes when they had relocated from Mecca during the *Hijra*.

The Sudanese *Ansar* are often described as a *Sufi* religious movement, a term used to describe a form of "Islamic mysticism."[4] Early Sufiism had developed as a reaction against the perceived worldliness of the early Umayyad Caliphate (661–750) and, while usually drawn from Sunni Muslims (as in the Sudan), some Sufi practices also developed within Shia Islam during the late medieval period. The key points are that the movement was (and is) characterized by asceticism and Sufi groups coalesce around a "grand master," often referred to as a *wali* (master/custodian) in Arabic. Such a person was, and is, regarded as standing in the direct line of successive teachers of true Islam that stretches back to Muhammad. The term "friend of Allah" was sometimes used to describe such a person. Muhammad Ahmad *al-Mahdi* came to be described as such a person.

Since Egypt was increasingly dominated by British imperial interventions, this drew the British into events within Sudan. During the same period as the rise of *al-Mahdi*, what was termed the *Urabi* Revolution broke out in Egypt. In response to this nationalist uprising, the British eventually occupied Egypt in 1882. Following this, they appointed Charles Gordon as the governor-general of the Sudan in 1884. So-called "Chinese" Gordon was a British army officer who had gained fame leading Chinese troops during the massive and bloody civil war known as the

---

4. Milani, "Cultural Products of Global Sufism," 659–80.

Taiping Rebellion (1850–64), an apocalyptic revolt that we shall examine in a later chapter.

Prior to his appointment in 1884, he had served the khedive of Egypt in the region from 1873–80 (this had occurred with British government approval). In his role he had put down revolts against Egyptian rule and worked to suppress the local slave trade. He had then returned to Europe in 1880.

Now he returned to the Sudan with instructions to evacuate loyal soldiers and civilians and to leave with them. However, in the event, he defied his orders and stayed. After about a year in Khartoum, with the city under siege—and following several battles with the *Mahdi*'s forces—the *mahdists* succeeded in capturing Khartoum. Gordon was killed on the steps of his residence in January 1885. His disobedience had antagonized the imperial government of Prime Minister Gladstone in London, who had no wish to be drawn further into the tangled politics of Sudan. As a result—though Gordon was popular with the British public—the government delayed sending a relief force. As a result, it arrived just two days after the city had fallen and Gordon's death. It was a great humiliation of imperial power. And it had occurred at the hands of an apocalyptic Islamic leader and his followers.

An Apocalyptic Regime

Muhammad Ahmad (later acclaimed as *Al-Mahdi*) was the son of a Dongola boat-builder on the Nile in northern Sudan. He became a disciple of Muhammad ash Sharif, who was the head of the *Sammaniyah* Sufi order. Eventually emerging as a *sheikh* of this Sufi group, Muhammad Ahmad then spent several years in seclusion. He soon gained a reputation as both a mystic and teacher.

He claimed he received direct revelations from Allah and that he was *Al-Mahdi al-Muntazar* (the rightly guided expected-one). His mission was to prepare the way for the second coming of prophet *Isa* (Jesus) and to prepare the faithful for their promised salvation. This was end-times ideology and was the foundation of his self-belief and the radical nature of his movement. It was clear that, while his movement might be starting with challenging Ottoman-Egyptian and then British forces, it was envisaged that it would end with supernatural intervention that would vindicate the *Mahdi* and bring the world order to a close.

In this process, Muhammad Ahmad first reacted against what he saw as the corruption of the Muslim Ottoman-Egyptians and then the intervention of the Christian British imperialists. Opposing both forms of externally driven power seemed to signal the start of an eschatological conflict in which the poverty and the puritanical ideological simplicity of his Sudanese followers was considered to be evidence of their pre-ordained role in bringing end-times events to pass. In this sense, his reaction to two different forms of colonial intervention in Sudan was imbued with eschatological meaning. It was a nineteenth-century claim to be realizing and implementing an ancient Islamic article of faith: that in a time of turmoil the *Mahdi* would be revealed.

The movement that grew out of this conviction reminds us that such apocalyptic outlooks—though usually the preoccupation of a minority within Islam, as in other world religions—has the capability of injecting extraordinary energy into a political movement. As has been noted by a number of modern scholars,

> Islam probably began as an apocalyptic movement, and it has continued to have a strong apocalyptic and messianic character throughout its history, a character that has manifested itself in literature as well as in periodic social explosion.[5]

What occurred in Sudan also reminds us that, while today apocalypticism is an outlook often associated with Shiism, it also occurs within the majority Sunni community too. The Muslims in Sudan were Sunni. What occurred there is also a reminder that, while "scholars of the Islamic world are confined mostly to the simple narration of signs and features of the apocalypse without trying to apply it to a specific time,"[6] this is not always the approach "on the street." While this may generally represent a marginal trend, when it surpasses a critical mass in a particular time and society those subscribing to it "tend to transform the passivity of the worshiper into active identification of the signs of the *Mahdi*'s return."[7] It is that which occurred within Muhammad Ahmad's movement.

Later in this book we will see that it has also energized communities as different as the Sunni ISIS caliphate and (via a reaction against traditional eschatological passivity) the Shiite outlook of radicals in Iran.

5. Cook, *Contemporary Muslim Apocalyptic Literature*, 1.
6. Khalaji, *Agenda Iran*, 4.
7. Khalaji, *Agenda Iran*, 5.

More on that in due course, but first we need to address the apocalyptic politics of Sudan in the early 1880s.

Muhammad Ahmad preached a puritanical doctrine that demanded a return to what he considered to be the early principles of Islam as he understood them from the Qur'an and the hadith. Men should give up alcohol and tobacco, and women should be strictly secluded.[8] To Muhammad Ahmad, holy warfare against those classed as "unbelievers" was mandatory. In fact, he considered it as essential as the *Hajj* (pilgrimage to Mecca). His prominence in the movement was made clear in the statement adopted by his followers: "Muhammad Ahmad is the *Mahdi* of God and the representative of His Prophet." In another change to Muslim practice, *zakat* (almsgiving) became a tax paid to the state that he was establishing.[9]

Muhammad Ahmad was keen to differentiate his movement from other Sufi groups. It was this that led to him forbidding the use of the Arabic word *darwish*, plural *darawish* (known in English as *dervish* to describe ascetic *Sufis*) to identify them. Instead—and in an act that directly drew a comparison between his movement and the founder of Islam—it was replaced with the term *Ansar*. Despite this, the group description of *dervish* continued to be used by the imperial forces into the 1890s, often in a dismissive way.

The *mahdist* rebels overthrew the Ottoman-Egyptian administration in a war that lasted from 1883 to 1885 and set up what they considered a truly Islamic government, with its capital at Omdurman. It ruled with a form of *sharia* law, as revised by the *Mahdi*.

Muhammad Ahmad appointed *caliphs* or *khalifa* to administer the state under him. These were: Abdallahi (or Abdullah) ibn Muhammad, Ali wad Hilu, and Muhammad Sharif (his cousin and son-in-law). This was in a deliberate imitation of Muhammad who, in the seventh century, was followed by the four caliphs: Abu Bakr, Umar, Uthman, and Ali. In Sunni Islam these are referred to as "*Rashidun* (Rightly Guided) Caliphs." The pattern was broken in Muhammad Ahmad's version because one of his followers—Muhammad ibn Ali as-Senussi—who was to have taken the place of Uthman in this structure, refused the honor offered him. This behavior reflects the extreme spiritual confidence of Muhammad Ahmad in his divinely foretold eschatological role of being *Al-Mahdi*.

8. Fadlalla, *Short History of Sudan*, 27.
9. Fadlalla, *Short History of Sudan*, 29.

This situation lasted from 1885 until Anglo-Egyptian forces defeated the movement in 1898.

Although the end of days was expected, what occurred was the devastation of the economy of the Sudan. The dislocation caused by warfare was accompanied by famine and disease which halved the population. At the same time, all who did not accept Muhammad Ahmad as *Al-Mahdi* were designated as *kafir* (infidels). They were killed and their women and property seized as booty. The apocalyptic state, as so often the case throughout history, was becoming a killing field within its own borders. This was before it became engulfed in conflict with external enemies.

The End of an End-Times State

Muhammad Ahmad *al-Mahdi* did not long outlive General Gordon. He too died in 1885. The end of days had not occurred. However, as so often is the case in such radical movements, this did not cause a collapse of the ideology. Instead, what had begun as an eschatological program developed into a radicalized ongoing community. Eschatology gave way to seminormalized administration.

His successor was the *caliph* named Abdallahi ibn Muhammad. As the new ruler he took action to consolidate the Islamic state. He did this by establishing administrative and judicial systems based on the interpretation of Islamic law developed under Muhammad Ahmad *al-Mahdi*. Abdallahi ibn Muhammad had been born around 1846 and had been educated as a preacher and holy man. He had become a follower of Muhammad Ahmad in about 1880 and had been named as one of the caliphs in 1881.[10] On becoming leader of the movement he took the new title of *Khalifa al-Mahdi*. This combined his existing title with that which he clearly felt he had inherited in 1885.

What has been termed the *mahdist* state (1885–98) was run as a *jihad* state. The courts had earlier equally enforced *sharia* law and the recorded decisions of the *Mahdi*. Following the death of Muhammad Ahmad *al-Mahdi*, his successor—*Khalifa al-Mahdi* Abdallahi ibn Muhammad—developed this into a more traditional structure based on *sharia*. This *jihad* state attempted to expand its influence and conducted a campaign against Ethiopia in 1889 and killed its ruler, King John, which

---

10. Lipschutz and Rasmussen, *Dictionary of African Historical Biography*, 1.

caused chaos in his kingdom.[11] Assisted by this, the Italians then conquered parts of that country in 1890.[12]

The *mahdist* state did not survive long. After the loss of Dongola to the British in September 1896, and further defeats at the hands of Kitchener's army in 1897, the *Khalifa al-Mahdi* Abdallahi's army experienced another defeat at the Battle of Atbara River in April 1898. From there his forces fell back to his new capital located at Omdurman. They were finally defeated at the Battle of Omdurman in September 1898. There, his army of 52,000 men was destroyed and the apocalyptic *jihad* state came to an end. The *Khalifa al-Mahdi* fled south, going into hiding, accompanied by a small number of followers. However, he was finally caught and killed by an Egyptian column, commanded by Sir Reginald Wingate, at Umm Diwaikarat in Kordofan in November 1899.[13] The British reconquest of the Sudan in 1898 officially stated it would be jointly run between Britain and Egypt. In practice it became a British colony.

Despite the condescension found in many imperial accounts, the ferocity of the *mahdist* warriors—in their distinctive patched uniforms—during these battles won the respect of the British. The poem "Fuzzy-Wuzzy" by the English author and poet Rudyard Kipling was published in 1892 as part of a collection titled *Barrack Room Ballads*. Although it is couched in the racist language and attitudes of the imperial infantryman, it nevertheless conveys the grudging respect felt by British soldiers for the bravery of the Hadendoa warriors who believed in the cause of the *Mahdi* and who fought the British army in the Sudan with extraordinary ferocity.

> So 'ere's to you, Fuzzy-Wuzzy, at your 'ome in the Soudan;
> You're a pore benighted 'eathen but a first-class fightin' man;
> An' 'ere's to you, Fuzzy-Wuzzy, with your 'ayrick 'ead of 'air -
> You big black boundin' beggar - for you broke a British square![14]

The "square" in question refers to the British infantry formations used to repel attacks with a block of outward facing soldiers bristling with bayonets and pouring volleys of rifle fire. The rolling, accented speech and slang was written to reflect that which was used by working-class British soldiers of the time.

11. Searcy, *Formation of the Sudanese Mahdist State*, 137.
12. Searcy, *Formation of the Sudanese Mahdist State*, 137.
13. Fadlalla, *Short History of Sudan*, 30–31.
14. Kipling, "Fuzzy-Wuzzy," lines 45–48.

Despite these defeats, scattered remnants of the *mahdist* state survived in the Darfur region until as late as 1909. Furthermore, the *Mahdi*'s eldest surviving son—Abd al-Rahman *al-Mahdi*—became the religious and political leader of the surviving *Ansar* for much of the colonial period in Anglo-Egyptian Sudan (1898–1955). Many of his followers identified Abd al-Rahman with prophet *Isa* (Jesus), which indicated the continuation of eschatological expectations focused on him, as on his father. There is evidence that this identification included a belief among them that he would drive the colonists out of Sudan. The colonial authorities found evidence that Abd al-Rahman communicated with other anticolonial leaders in Nigeria and Cameroon, and that in these communications he predicted that the *mahdists* would eventually expel the white colonial Christians.[15] Despite this, the British colonial administrators seem to have generally considered him to be a moderate leader of the *Ansar*. This role continued for a few years after Sudanese independence in January 1956.[16]

Abd al-Rahman finally died (aged seventy-four) in 1959. His son, Sadiq *al-Mahdi*, replaced him as the spiritual leader (an *imam*) of the *Ansar*, until his death in 1961. He was succeeded in this role by his brother, Imam al-Hadi *al-Mahdi*.[17] But by this time, what had once been an Islamic apocalyptic state had become a sect within Islam.

THE AHMADIYYA MOVEMENT

The Islamic groups in Sudan who resisted British colonialism were not alone in equating the idea of holy war *jihad* with resistance to imperialism. The term *mujahideen* (those engaged in *jihad*) was first coined in the eighteenth century in India where it described Islamic revivalism that sought to confront what was considered decadence in aspects of contemporary Islamic society, and also to resist incursions by non-Muslims. In this way, the expansion of the Maratha, Jat, and Sikh armies into Muslim areas was resisted by those who regarded themselves as holy warriors.

Later proponents of this belief saw British rule as equally threatening to the maintenance of Islamic society, since they thought that only

---

15. Warburg, *Islam, Sectarianism, and Politics*, 89, 125–27.
16. Stiansen and Kevane, "Introduction," 23–27.
17. Warburg, *Islam, Sectarianism, and Politics*, 171.

Islamic rule could ensure its survival and development.[18] This in itself did not inevitably imply apocalyptic ideology.

However, there were those within the Islamic community of British India who certainly did hold beliefs with end-times implications. However, this did not always lead to militant opposition to British rule.

The *Ahmadiyya* movement was just such an Islamic messianic movement with millenarian elements. It was founded by Mirza Ghulam Ahmad (died 1908), who claimed to be the *Mahdi*, during the late nineteenth century. The movement had its origins in northern India, where Mirza Ghulam Ahmad was born in 1835, and was, and is, generally regarded as heretical by mainstream Muslims. This is because the claims of Mirza Ghulam Ahmad led to the development of a movement that does not believe that Muhammad was the final prophet sent to guide mankind. Mirza Ghulam Ahmad considered himself chosen by Allah as a renewer of Islam.

In 1880, he announced that he was the *Mahdi*. He further claimed that he was the incarnation of prophet *Isa* (Jesus), and also of the Hindu deity Krishna, and that he was also a reappearance (*buruz*) of Muhammad. This was a heretical claim that set him on a collision course with orthodox Islam, Christianity, and Hinduism. His followers claimed that he was not himself a "lawgiver." Instead, his role was to support and declare those preached by Muhammad. The *Ahmadiyya* movement claims that Jesus did not die on the cross (a belief also held by many orthodox Muslims) and, consequently, did not experience resurrection. Instead, they claim that he travelled to India, where he died at the age of 120.

In sharp contrast with events in Sudan, the *Ahmadiyya* movement did not advocate militant opposition to colonial rule. For the *Ahmadiyya* movement, *jihad* was a peaceful activity. Furthermore, its founder believed that *jihad* should not be declared against the British because he considered them promoters of liberty of religion and, therefore, not enemies of Islam.[19]

However, as with so many messianic movements, it faced the challenge of its leader not guiding the world into a new order. In short, the end times did not occur. In 1914, the movement split. Some recognized a new leader—Ghulam Ahmad—as a "prophet" (*nabi*), while others only

---

18. Editors of Encyclopaedia Britannica, "Mujahideen, Islam," lines 5–16.
19. Basit, "Loyalty to the British Raj," lines 30–36.

accorded him the title of a "reformer" (*mujaddid*). Once more, an apocalyptic sect faced the challenge of the end times not being revealed.

This absence of the apocalypse is reflected in what might be described as the development of very down-to-earth versions of eschatological expectation. Maulana Muhammad Ali (died 1951) wrote Qur'anic commentaries that claimed that the expected opening of the graves is represented by the mining of minerals; the afterlife is seen as an example of the unceasing progress also experienced on earth; resurrection is when new realities are discovered in the here-and-now; and heaven will be experienced on earth as well as after death.[20]

In 1947, the *Ahmadiyya* community moved its headquarters from Qadian in India to Rabwah in Pakistan. In 1974, a constitutional amendment in Pakistan declared the *Ahmadiyya* to be non-Muslims. In the 1980s, they were banned from using the word "mosque" to describe their meeting places. They were also banned from spreading their faith. In response, the movement relocated to the UK. Persecution of the *Ahmadiyya* community has occurred in a number of Muslim countries.

The movement illustrates that apocalyptic ideology does not always lead to violent action.

---

20. Robinson Waldman, "Eschatology," lines 265–74.

CHAPTER 9

African Syncretistic Anticolonial Apocalypse

A MIXTURE OF THE APOCALYPTIC beliefs of Christianity, Islam, and indigenous African religions has characterized a number of syncretistic African millenarian movements. The formation of the earliest ones was stimulated by Western exploitation, which prompted these apocalyptic movements to focus on resisting aspects of Western colonial power. However, this was resistance that drew heavily on indigenous beliefs and culture, while often also revealing the influence of non-African millenarian religious beliefs that had spread across the continent.

Postcolonial Africa has also seen such movements, some with huge impact. In these later movements the syncretistic apocalyptic trends became further complicated by the pressing issues of political reorganization, turbulence, and national consolidation in the newly independent (and at times politically unstable) new states.

Within Africa, these millenarian and apocalyptic movements have a history that is at least two centuries old and, in its complex multireligious origins, bears resemblance to aspects of some Chinese and Native American apocalyptic movements.

THE XHOSA CATTLE-KILLING MOVEMENT, 1856–57

An apocalyptic movement that affected the Xhosa people of southern Africa occurred in the 1850s. In April 1856, fifteen-year-old

Nongqawuse—accompanied by a friend named Nombanda—was sent to scare birds from her uncle's crops in the fields at the mouth of the Gxarha River. This was in the still-independent land of the Xhosa people, but bordering British colonial territory in the Eastern Cape of South Africa. This is significant, as tensions were rising between the indigenous people and the British colonists. As so often in the period of imperial expansion, this was because Europeans were encroaching on land belonging to indigenous peoples. Nongqawuse was an orphan and had been raised by her uncle, who was named Mhlakaza. He himself was the son of a councilor of the Xhosa king, Sarili kaHintsa. This meant that Nongqawuse was in proximity to political power within her community.

On returning from the bird-scaring, Nongqawuse told her uncle that she had been met by the spirits of two of her ancestors while out in the fields. What she said next was even more astonishing. She claimed that these two spirits had told her that the Xhosa people should destroy all their crops and slaughter all their cattle. Since this would mean the destruction of both wealth and food this was an extraordinary instruction. In addition, new houses and enclosures should be constructed, and the people should abandon witchcraft, along with adultery and incest. In return for this, the spirits assured her, the ancestral dead would rise from their graves, and all Europeans would be swept away into the sea.

It was a radical message that can be found expounded among many indigenous peoples who were experiencing—or feared—the destruction of their society at the hands of European newcomers. It also had a common millenarian future promise that, following the removal of Europeans, the granaries would again be full and new cattle (with greater beauty and health than those slaughtered) would be given to them. It is noteworthy that Xhosa cattle were suffering from diseases that may have been brought into the region by European cattle. Consequently, the message promised deliverance from both Europeans and their diseases.

Nongqawuse claimed that if the Xhosa followed these instructions then the promised transformation would occur by 18 February 1857. Accompanying this, the sun would turn blood red.

What followed was a frenzy of cattle-killing that gripped the entire Xhosa nation. When the prophesied transformation did not occur as expected, more prophetic claims were made that it would take place within eight days. This accelerated the destruction of livestock. These renewed claims had attracted the attention of Sarili kaHintsa, the Xhosa king, who appeared to validate the prophecies of Nongqawuse. It has been estimated that over 400,000 cattle were destroyed.¹ The result was a catastrophe. By 1858, over 40,000 people were dead as a consequence of the famine that followed the destruction.² The Europeans did not vanish. The cattle and crops were not restored. The disappointed followers of Nongqawuse blamed this on those who had not followed her instructions, whom they termed *amagogotya* (mean ones). Nongqawuse was eventually handed over to the British and died in the Alexandria district of the Eastern Cape in 1898. The failure of this desperate, anticolonial apocalypse was no isolated incident.

THE MAJI MAJI REBELLION, 1905-07

The Maji Maji Rebellion was an armed rebellion against colonial rule in German East Africa, Tanganyika (now Tanzania), between 1905 and 1907. As in the Xhosa cattle-killing, this again involved beliefs in indigenous spiritualism and animism, although in this case mixed with what one might term "folk Islam." A man with the status of a spirit medium, named Kinjikitile Ngwale, claimed he was possessed by a snake spirit that was called Hongo. Kinjikitile then took the name Bokero. He declared a war against German colonists and claimed that the "war medicine" that he gave his followers would turn German bullets into water. In fact, the "war medicine" consisted of water (known as *maji* in the Kiswahili language) that had been mixed with castor oil and millet seeds.³

In the resulting uprising, European trading outposts were attacked and cotton crops (imposed as a crop by the Germans) were destroyed. As a result, Kinjikitile was arrested by the German authorities and hanged. But this was not the end of the revolt as within about a month—in August 1905—Ngindo tribespeople attacked a safari party and killed the missionaries taking part in it. The dead included the Roman Catholic bishop of Dar es Salaam.⁴ The revolt spread and German garrisons were attacked throughout the colony. One group of rebels, known as the Qadiriyya Brotherhood declared a *jihad* against the German colonists and this brought many Muslims into the revolt.

1. Hackett, "Millennial and Apocalyptic Movements in Africa," 388.
2. Hackett, "Millennial and Apocalyptic Movements in Africa," 388.
3. Pakenham, *Scramble for Africa*, 616–21.
4. Pakenham, *Scramble for Africa*, 616–21.

The Germans responded with extreme force; something frequently seen in such colonial reactions. Large numbers of German reinforcements were sent to put down the revolt. The Germans were armed with machine guns, and it soon became apparent that the "war medicine" was of no avail against modern weapons. Villages and crops were destroyed and, when open warfare was replaced by guerrilla attacks, it was accompanied by terrible famine that was partly a deliberate policy by the Germans to break resistance. By August 1907, the rebellion was over. It has been estimated that it took the lives of fifteen Germans, 389 native soldiers fighting for the colonial authority, and tens of thousands—possibly hundreds of thousands—of Africans (both rebels and civilians affected by the war).[5] While some estimates for Maji Maji fighters killed stand at about 75,000,[6] other estimates suggest that as many as 200,000 to 300,000 Africans died in total.[7] The apocalypse might not have occurred—but the cost was apocalyptic in its scale.

THE SATIRU REBELLION, NIGERIA, 1906

Even as the people of German East Africa were rising in revolt, another millenarian movement occurred in British-administered Nigeria. Here, as in German East Africa, Islamic reaction to Christian colonial rule was also apparent.

Unrest started in February 1904, in the village of Satiru, which was situated fourteen miles southwest of Sokoto, in the extreme northwest of Nigeria. It was then that the village chieftain declared that he was the awaited *Mahdi*, and his son was prophet *Isa* (Jesus). This was a direct claim to end-times status. In response the sultan of Sokoto arrested the chief and he died in prison. However, the matter was not over, because when his son succeeded him as chief he continued to claim prophetic status.

Things went quiet until the start of 1906, when a preacher named Dan Makafo arrived in Satiru in the company of a large group of followers. He had fled from the French colony of Niger after a failed uprising there. He was attracted to Satiru because he had heard of the claims of its (new) chief. This reignited the millennial phenomenon that had lain

---

5. Hull, "Military Culture," 161; Hull, *Absolute Destruction*, 157.
6. Beverton, "Maji Maji Uprising," lines 35–36.
7. "Maji Maji Rebellion," line 118; See: Iliffe, *Modern History of Tanganyika*.

dormant since 1904. The restating of the claim to be *Isa* forced locals to make a choice. The inhabitants of the nearby village of Tsomo refused to recognize this claim. So-called *Isa* and his followers attacked the "unbelieving village" and killed about fourteen of its inhabitants. He then declared a *jihad* against the British authorities.

When colonial forces arrived, they faced some 2,000 men in arms. In the resulting conflict, two civilian officials and a military officer were killed, along with twenty-nine of their soldiers. Their Maxim gun (an early machine gun) was captured by the *jihadists*. It was a humiliating defeat.

However, in the conflict, the man claiming to be *Isa* was mortally wounded and leadership passed to Dan Makafo. The *jihad* then rapidly unraveled. The sultan of Sokoto, along with local emirs, remained loyal to the British. The reorganized British responded with a strong military force equipped with two Maxims and a field gun. The *jihadists* suffered huge numbers of casualties; those fleeing were shot, and Makafo was captured. Those who had escaped into the bush were hunted down.

It has been estimated that more than 2,000 *jihadists* were killed and over 3,000 women and children were captured. The village of Satiru was burned and totally destroyed. By March 1906, the *jihad* was over. Following the uprising, Dan Makafo and five other leaders were tried in the Sultan's court and executed.[8] This meant that the British could maintain a distance from the retribution that was meted out.

THE CHILEMBWE UPRISING, 1915

Occurring in 1915, in Nyasaland (modern Malawi), this movement was led by the Baptist minister John Chilembwe, and included members with millenarian beliefs. He preached black advancement through hard work and education and was influenced by the ideas of the black American educator Booker T. Washington. He also encouraged his followers to adopt European-style dress.

However, during the First World War there was huge recruitment of Africans to support the British forces in East Africa. Large numbers died of disease. Chilembwe opposed the recruitment. At the same time, millenarians in the region were preaching that the war would lead to

---

8. Dewhirst, "Satiru Uprising."

Armageddon and the end of colonial rule.[9] In January 1915, he and his followers rose up against the colonists.

The colonial forces rapidly mobilized. Facing defeat at the hands of the British, Chilembwe and a number of his followers tried to escape into Portuguese East Africa (modern Mozambique). However, many were captured. Following this, forty rebels were executed and 300 imprisoned. Chilembwe himself was shot dead by a police patrol near the border.

THE IMPACT OF MUMBOISM, 1913–21

Mumboism, which is also referred to as "the Mumbo cult," was founded by Onyango Dunde in 1913. Its epicenter was in the Nyanza region of Kenya, near Lake Victoria. As with many other African uprisings, it was committed to the destruction of European colonial rule.

Onyango Dunde preached that he had been swallowed by a serpent in Lake Victoria. When the serpent spat him out it gave him a prophetic message:

> I am the god Mumbo whose two homes are in the sun and in the lake. I have chosen you to be my mouthpiece. Go and tell all the Africans . . . that from henceforth I am their God. Those whom I choose personally and those who acknowledge me, will live forever in plenty . . . the Christian religion is rotten . . . All Europeans are your enemies, but the time is shortly coming when they will all disappear from the country.[10]

The millenarian nature of the movement was clear in the golden age that Onyango Dunde promised would be ushered in. He gathered many followers to his movement. His promise of a golden age, similar to that preached by Nongqawuse at the time of the Xhosa cattle-killings, may have been influenced by Christian apocalyptic teachings. He claimed that the drinking water would turn to blood, only the *mumboites* would have drinking water, all white people would vanish, and only Africans would remain. An alternative claim was that the Germans would come and mutilate those "in clothes," by which was meant Europeans and Africans who had adopted Western fashion.[11] In short: "The projected utopia would be a time of role reversal, healing, and plenty that could only be

---

9. Strachan, *First World War in Africa*, 132.
10. Pickens, *African Christian God-Talk*, 133–34.
11. Hackett, "Millennial and Apocalyptic Movements in Africa," 389–90.

effected by traditional sacrifices and rituals."[12] Some of his followers reportedly purchased lamps, in preparation for the darkness that would accompany the end of the world.[13] This again suggests borrowing from Christian apocalyptic traditions.

The movement was rooted in earlier revolts that had occurred in 1905, 1908, and 1914, and its appeal lasted for decades, flaring up again and again at times of economic distress.[14] This was despite the exiling of its leader, in 1921, to the island of Lamu in the Indian Ocean.[15] The movement was finally proscribed during the later Mau-Mau emergency in 1954.[16]

A similar millenarian movement to *Mumboism* developed in the interwar wars (1918–39) among the Kamba people living around Machakos, also in Kenya, which was focused on Ndonye wa Kauti, who was believed to be a prophet.[17] The British similarly deported him to Lamu Island, off the Kenyan coast.

THE SOUTH AFRICAN "ISRAELITES," 1907–21

Enoch Mgijima was a Wesleyan Methodist in South Africa. In 1907, he declared that he had seen visions in which an angel told him to instruct people in the Old Testament worship of God in order to escape the judgment when the world ended. This came at a time of deteriorating economic conditions for a black population that was already oppressed by white rule. He claimed that the appearance of Halley's Comet in 1910 vindicated his prophetic claims.

In 1912, Mgijima—who was a lay preacher and evangelist—broke away from the Wesleyan Methodist Church. He joined the "Church of God and the Saints of Christ," which was a small church based in the US. Prior to this, he had become influenced by the African American William Crowdy, who claimed that black people were descended from the "lost tribes of Israel."[18]

12. Hackett, "Millennial and Apocalyptic Movements in Africa," 390.
13. Hackett, "Millennial and Apocalyptic Movements in Africa," 390.
14. Maxon, *Conflict and Accommodation in Western Kenya*, 74–75.
15. Pickens, *African Christian God-Talk*, 133–34.
16. Hackett, "Millennial and Apocalyptic Movements in Africa," 390.
17. Maxon, *Conflict and Accommodation in Western Kenya*, 74–75.
18. Grossman and Raboteau, "Black Migration," 313.

Mgijima predicted that the world would end before Christmas Day 1912. As a result of this claim, his followers stopped farming and suffered impoverishment as a result. Despite the failure of this prediction, and the resulting social costs, the movement did not collapse.

Mgijima's apocalyptic preaching became increasingly violent as he predicted end-times wars between blacks and whites. As a result, in 1914, he was excommunicated from the "Church of God and the Saints of Christ." From this time onwards, he and his followers described themselves as the "Israelites," keeping the Jewish Sabbath and celebrating Passover.

In 1919, after Mgijima failed to get permission to host the Passover at the location he had previously used, he was given permission to host it at Bulhoek in the Eastern Cape. After the festival, a number of his followers remained there and began building an illegal settlement. By 1921, there were about 3,000 "Israelites" living there. Facing opposition from the authorities they armed themselves with traditional spears and *knobkerries*.

In May 1921, the police arrived to disperse the camp. In the ensuing battle almost 200 people died. It became known as the "Bulhoek Massacre." Mgijima and his brother were arrested and sentenced to six years' hard labor.[19]

Current followers of the teachings of Mgijima still take part in an annual pilgrimage on 24 May to the mass grave where the "Israelites" were buried in 1921.

POSTCOLONIAL APOCALYPTIC MOVEMENTS: THE "HOLY SPIRIT MOVEMENT," 1986–87

This movement emerged in Uganda between 1986 and 1987. It arose out of a combination of traditional African beliefs in spirit mediums, particularly found in this area of Uganda, with aspects of Christian beliefs (particularly regarding personal morality). Within the regional Catholic Church, belief in so-called spirit divination meant that many people were prepared to accept the claims of the founder of this movement. In a context of social and political disintegration—when many people had lost trust in the Ugandan state—those who claimed to be spirit mediums appeared to offer ways in which events could be both understood

---

19. Hackett, "Millennial and Apocalyptic Movements in Africa," 388–89.

and influenced. This was especially the case in a society where suffering and death were often considered to be caused by witchcraft and spiritual activities.[20]

This involvement (of those claiming to be spirit mediums) in guerrilla movements had earlier been seen in Zimbabwe. Here the postcolonial government, in its attempts to build local power-bases, had worked to co-opt them. However, greater international interest was focused on that which occurred within the Acholi-speaking region of northern Uganda in the late 1980s.[21]

In contrast to Zimbabwe, where the spirit mediums claimed to be possessed by ancestral spirits, those in northern Uganda claimed to be possessed by strangers. What occurred in Uganda represented a "version of tradition" that was assisted by the adoption of "imported Christian imagery," while using aspects of Christian beliefs that, it has been suggested, facilitated "the possibility of resolving contradictions" in some aspects of traditional beliefs regarding spirit mediums.[22]

In 1987, Alice Lakwena led her so-called "Holy Spirit army" in an attempt to overthrow the National Resistance Movement (NRM) government of Yoweri Museveni and its military wing, the National Resistance Army (NRA):

> There will probably never be agreement as to what led to what, but a common view is that rogue NRA units took to arresting and even killing ex-military men from the region, and persecuting old regime supporters. The north rose in arms, first through the Uganda People's Democratic Movement/Army [UPDA]—which eventually cut a peace deal with Kampala in 1988. Then, most famously, there arose the millennial Holy Spirit movement, led by a former prostitute turned spirit medium, Alice Auma.[23]

The government forces were disconcerted by "an adversary who didn't fear death or take cover in the face of heavy fire."[24] These particular "Combatants walked into battle in cross-shaped formations while

---

20. See: Allen, "Understanding Alice," 370–99.
21. Allen, "Understanding Alice," 370.
22. Allen, "Understanding Alice," 370.
23. "Alice Lakwena," lines 1–10.
24. "Alice Lakwena," line 28.

swaying, shaking and singing hymns."[25] This had occurred due to the preaching of Alice Auma.

Alice Auma claimed to be channeling messages from the spirit of an Italian First World War veteran who was buried near Murchison Falls. She named him as Lakwena. As a result of this claim, she called herself Alice Lakwena. Alice claimed that she underwent a forty-day immersion in the Nile before giving advice to the UPDA. Gaining support from this group assisted her to launch her "Holy Spirit" movement.

She preached what she termed "Holy Spirit Safety Precautions" for her followers in order to achieve victory, which allegedly included: singing Christian hymns when going into battle; rubbing themselves with shea butter oil as protection against bullets; throwing stones that would transform into grenades; avoidance of contact with nonmembers of the movement; avoiding killing bees and snakes, the allies of the "Holy Spirit Movement"; and following the Ten Commandments. It was a combination of indigenous religious beliefs, magic, and aspects of Christian belief.

In November and December 1986, her forces achieved two surprising victories over NRA forces. This encouraged belief in her "spirit power" among the Acholi population. When her followers were killed, she asserted that this was because they lacked purity or strict adherence to her instructions. She also launched attacks on UPDA groups who did not accept her authority.

Despite these initial successes, 1987 brought defeat for the Holy Spirit Movement. After these defeats, she was forced to withdraw and reorganize. She also carried out "purification" activities in an effort to reverse these setbacks. In September, she once more marched on Kampala, gathering support along the way. The extent of belief in her was seen in the fact that these supporters included Professor Isaac Newton Ojok, who had been Minister of Education under President Obote. However, in November, her forces were defeated; suffering huge losses as they advanced, convinced in a spiritual protection that, in the event, failed to protect them from machine guns. Alice Lakwena fled into exile in Kenya, where she died in a refugee camp in 2007.

---

25. "Spirits in Uganda," line 51.

POSTCOLONIAL APOCALYPTIC MOVEMENTS: THE "LORD'S RESISTANCE ARMY" 1987–2022

After the defeat of the Holy Spirit Movement, surviving members splintered to form other rebel groups. A number of these copied its religious message of belief in the impending millennial rule of Christ.

The most infamous of these was "The Lord's Resistance Army" (LRA). With its massive impact on civilians in eastern Africa, this movement has caused the deaths of thousands. Estimates of civilian victims stand at more than 100,000.[26]

Joseph Kony, who some believe to be Alice Lakwena's cousin, formed this group in 1987. He claimed to receive messages from God and declared that the LRA was fighting in the name of God with the aim of overthrowing the Ugandan government and replacing it with a government that has the Ten Commandments as its constitution.

However, horrific violence was chosen as the strategy deployed to make Uganda ungovernable, disrupt civilian life, spread terror, and undermine trust in the government. At its height, LRA ranks were filled by some 25,000 child-soldiers who had been kidnapped and then forced to commit horrific acts of extreme violence, including abduction, mutilation, rape, and torture.[27]

> This group has a philosophy that blends elements of Christianity, Islam and traditional Acholi beliefs into a murderous world view that has terrorized Kony's own Acholi people and set back development in the North [of Uganda] by years if not decades.[28]

When the Acholi people failed to offer the LRA the support demanded, it responded with massacres, abductions, and atrocities. The (LRA) has terrorized large areas of central Africa since the late 1980s.

The LRA was eventually expelled from Uganda by the end of 2006. Following this, it became a problem in nearby countries. It has continued to terrorize and to raise revenue by elephant poaching and by looting diamonds and gold from miners operating in eastern Central African Republic.[29] In recent years it has been worn down in conflicts with regional armies, assisted by US Special Forces, an African Union counter-LRA

26. Neiman, "Enduring Harm," line 29.
27. "Spirits in Uganda," lines 58–59.
28. "Alice Lakwena's Holy Spirit Movement," lines 35–36.
29. United Nations Security Council, "Lord's Resistance Army," line 29.

task force, UN-supported sanctions, and actions by the International Criminal Court (ICC).

Today, the group numbers in the low hundreds, and is dispersed across areas of the Democratic Republic of Congo, Central African Republic, South Sudan, and Sudan. Yet, despite the reduction in its size, in 2020–21 the group still carried out forty-two attacks, leaving thirty-one dead and 192 abducted.[30] This occurred mostly in the remote border area of Democratic Republic of Congo-Central African Republic-South Sudan. "This represents a 48 percent decline in attacks compared to the previous year."[31]

The ongoing impact of the LRA has been greatly reduced in the last decade. Nevertheless, the appalling scale of death and suffering caused by its activities makes it one of the bloodiest political apocalyptic movements. Its impact continues to be felt in many African communities.

---

30. "Uganda's Brutal Lord's Resistance Army," lines 46–47.
31. "Uganda's Brutal Lord's Resistance Army," line 48.

CHAPTER 10

New World—New Apocalypse?

As in Africa, several apocalyptic political movements arose in North, Central, and South America as a reaction against colonialism. Some—but by no means all—combined indigenous religious beliefs with ingredients borrowed from Christianity. Consequently, these examples are reminiscent of those syncretistic African apocalyptic movements already discussed.

It is not possible to cover all such revolts, but the following give some idea of the kind of millenarian resistance that has been documented.

MEXICO: THE TEPEHUÁN REVOLT, 1616

An uprising known as the Tepehuán Revolt broke out in Mexico in 1616. This was when the Tepehuán people attempted to break free from Spanish colonial rule. This revolt was finally crushed by 1620, after a very large loss of life on both sides in the conflict. The revolt was an attempt to expel Spanish colonists and priests and return to traditional ways. The Tepehuán people lived on the eastern slopes of the Sierra Madre Occidental uplands. This was primarily in the future state of Durango.

The arrival of Europeans had brought devastating diseases to the area. This may have reduced the population of the Tepehuán and neighboring tribes by as much as 80 percent. The population before Spanish colonization may have been as high as 100,000. By the time of the revolt, it had collapsed to somewhere in the region of 20,000.[1]

In addition, Jesuit insistence that the Tepehuán give up warfare marginalized warriors in the tribal society and their traditional way of achieving status. The resulting revolt was, arguably, partly these warriors' response to this marginalization. It was also a result of a clash of cultures in which the Tepehuán felt that their distinctive character and way of life was vanishing.

Spanish settlers first reached Tepehuán country in the 1570s. They came there to mine silver and raise cattle. Jesuits began Christian missionary work there in 1596. They established missions at Santiago Papasquiaro, Santa Catarina de Tepehuánes, and El Zape. At first the Tepehuán seemed relatively friendly towards the missionaries. However, they refused to live near the Jesuit missions and eschewed working in the Spanish silver mines and on the Spanish estates (*haciendas*). Being warlike, they often mounted raids against indigenous peoples who were friendly with the Spanish. Despite this, by 1615, a Jesuit assessed that the Tepehuán "showed great progress and were in the things of our holy faith *muy ladino*" (much like the Spanish).[2]

This apparent accommodation with the Christian Spanish was illusory. In 1616, a messianic leader named Quautlatas began to preach among the Tepehuán communities. He had been baptized as a Christian but now mounted a campaign against the Catholics. He carried a broken cross and preached that the ancestral gods were angry because the Tepehuán had abandoned their old beliefs. In order to assuage this anger, they needed to kill or expel all the Spaniards from their lands—especially the missionaries. He mixed Christian and indigenous beliefs in a syncretism reminiscent of some African anticolonial movements. He declared that he was a "bishop" and promised that all those killed by the Spanish would rise again after seven days. There was something in this reminiscent of the hope later expressed by the North American "Ghost Dance Movement." With the Spanish dead, he claimed that the old ancestral gods would bless the land with good crops and fat cattle.[3] The message of Quautlatas was like many millenarian movements that have appeared in societies experiencing extreme cultural (and socioeconomic) stress.

1. Reff, "'Predicament of Culture,'" 70.
2. See: Gradie, *Tepehuan Revolt of 1616*, 148.
3. Gradie, *Tepehuan Revolt of 1616*, 149.

Not surprisingly, Quautlatas was identified with the antichrist by the Jesuits, who believed that the revolt was the work of the devil. They considered the Spanish blameless for all that ensued.[4]

The revolt resulted in the deaths of more than 200 Spanish colonists, many slaves and servants, and ten missionaries, eight of whom were Jesuits. Churches and missions were burned and silver mines wrecked. The number of the Tepehuán who died was estimated by one Spanish source at 4,000. Quautlatas was also killed during the Spanish campaigns against his movement.[5] By the time the Spanish authorities quelled the revolt, the region had been devastated. The event resulted in a reaffirmation of Jesuit missionary activity in Mexico; but it also altered Spanish colonial methods in "New Spain,"[6] where military imposition of Spanish Catholic culture increased. This ended the previous policy of "peace-by-purchase pacification." The new "mission-presidio" approach saw missionaries and the military working in closer alliance.

Despite this, the Spanish continued to face opposition to their cultural influence. Hostility arose again when they tried to establish a mission station among the Tepehuán in 1707. Christianization of the Tepehuán did not accelerate until after 1745.

NEW MEXICO: THE PUEBLO REVOLT, 1680

This was a revolt of Pueblo people in what is now New Mexico. It occurred in alliance with the Apaches and was successful in overthrowing Spanish rule in New Mexico for twelve years. The Pueblo were not a warlike people, but they had experienced much hardship following Spanish colonization of the region after 1598. Missionaries enforced conversion to Catholic Christianity, destroying tribal ceremonial pits (*kivas*), sacred masks, and other religious objects. In addition, the Pueblo found themselves subject to trial in Spanish courts, where brutal punishments included whipping, hanging, removal of hands or feet, and enslavement.

After 1645, there were several revolts against Spanish rule. After each of these, Spanish punitive actions targeted religious leaders ("medicine men") who were considered central to Pueblo cultural resistance. One of these "medicine men" targeted for repression was named Popé of

4. Reff, "'Predicament of Culture,'" 66–67, 81.
5. Gradie, *Tepehuan Revolt of 1616*, 1.
6. See: Gradie, *Tepehuan Revolt of 1616*.

the San Juan pueblo. Following imprisonment, he declared that he was commanded by the tribal ancestor spirits (the *kachinas*) to drive out the Spanish and restore the old religion.

The Pueblo were banned from riding horses, so those carrying messages concerning the planned revolt travelled on foot. They carried knotted string. The communities to whom they gave these were told to untie one knot every day and rise against the Spanish when the last knot was untied. It was a simple but effective way to ensure that the rising occurred in unison.

On 21 August 1680, the revolt exploded into action. The Spanish were forced to evacuate the region, leaving 401 dead, including twenty-one priests. After Pueblo warriors laid siege to Santa Fe, the Spanish survivors were forced to flee to El Paso. All Europeans encountered were killed: men, women, and children. European culture was treated as a contagion that needed to be totally removed. It was indicative of the bitterness caused by Spanish brutality and oppression. The Pueblo celebrated their victory over the colonists by "washing off" Christian baptism, annulling all Christian marriages, and destroying all churches.

Even after Spain reasserted control over New Mexico twelve years later, the Pueblo peoples were not fully subjugated. Having faced such massive opposition, the Spanish were forced to recognize some Pueblo land rights and accord the communities some autonomy. In addition, tribal members were allowed to lodge legal complaints when they suffered mistreatment at the hands of colonial officials.[7] It was far short of independence but nevertheless revealed the way the revolt had shocked the Spanish colonial authorities.

The continued memory of the revolt and its significance can be seen in the graffito that was written on the wall of the New Mexico History Museum in Albuquerque in 2020. It read: "1680 Land Back!"[8]

UNITED STATES: TENSKWATAWA, THE "SHAWNEE PROPHET" 1809–26

In North America, indigenous people similarly attempted to defend their culture in the face of European settlement. While most of this took the

---

7. Romero, "Why New Mexico's 1680 Pueblo Revolt," lines 55–59.
8. Romero, "Why New Mexico's 1680 Pueblo Revolt," line 5.

form of straightforward (though unsuccessful) warfare, other responses took on an apocalyptic character, with strong millenarian characteristics.

One of these was led by Tenskwatawa the "Shawnee Prophet," who called for a return to ancestral ways and the defeat of European colonial power in ways reminiscent of the "Ghost Dance" of the later nineteenth century.

Tenskwatawa (also known as "The Prophet") was born in 1775. Originally named Lalawethika (the Rattle), he faced marginalization within his tribe due to his physical limitations, lack of military prowess, and disablement (he was blind in one eye). This dramatically changed in 1805. In that year, according to tradition, while lighting his pipe, he entered into a deep trance. So severe was the event that his family prepared his body for burial. However, Lalawethika was not dead. He regained consciousness and claimed that a Shawnee deity—called the Master of Life—had visited him while he was in the trance.

Lalawethika told his listeners that the Master of Life instructed him that the native people of the Ohio region should abandon all the ways of life of the Europeans—their customs and their goods. Of these, he was told, dependence on guns, iron cooking pots, glass beads, and alcohol were the worst things. Once these were abandoned, the Master of Life would drive out all the Europeans. It was, once more, the millenarian hope of a community facing a threat to its very existence. In addition, all tribes should give up intertribal warfare. It was at this time that Lalawethika changed his name to Tenskwatawa, meaning "open door" in Shawnee.[9]

The religious movement saw the development of an alliance between Tenskwatawa and his warrior brother, named Tecumseh, who was trying to form a united front of Native American nations west of the Appalachian Mountains. The combined movement soon attracted considerable support among several different tribes (including the Seneca, Wyandot, and Ottawa) living in the state of Ohio and the Indiana Territory. His fame increased in 1806 when he predicted an eclipse of the sun.

In 1808, Tecumseh and Tenskwatawa moved their combined followers to Prophet's Town, which was located near the Tippecanoe River in the Indiana Territory. This was followed by Tenskwatawa declaring his opposition to the Treaty of Fort Wayne (1809), in which some Native American chiefs ceded 3 million acres to the United States.

---

9. "Tenskwatawa," lines 10–18.

In 1811, the US army moved against him. Tecumseh was away and Tenskwatawa led their forces against the army at what became known as the Battle of Tippecanoe. Tenskwatawa claimed that bullets would not harm his warriors. Despite heavy losses inflicted on the assembled army, Tenskwatawa's forces also experienced high casualties and were forced to withdraw. The army burnt Prophet's Town and his followers began to lose faith in his power.

During the War of 1812, Tecumseh and Tenskwatawa allied themselves with the British against the US forces. During the war, Tecumseh was killed at the Battle of the Thames in 1813. Tenskwatawa was unable to maintain resistance without his brother. In 1826, after a brief time in Canada, he moved with most of the Ohio and Indiana Shawnee to a reservation in modern-day Kansas. The relentless pressure of European settlement had broken his resistance movement. He died in 1837.

UNITED STATES: THE GHOST DANCE, 1889–91

The destruction of Plains Native American culture in the 1870s and 1880s as a culmination of the "Plains Indian Wars" led to one of the most tragic and poignant apocalyptic movements, arising from the despair and desperation of Native American communities.

From 1889 to 1891, the "Ghost Dance" (*Nanissáanah*) movement rapidly spread among Native American communities recently forced onto reservations. This new religious movement tapped into several different Native American belief systems. It was based on the teachings of the Northern-Paiute spiritual leader Wovoka. Reports that reached the Lakota, living on the Standing Rock reservation, situated on the border between North and South Dakota, described him as the Messiah, Christ returned to earth as a Native American.[10]

His teachings claimed that the proper practice of the "Ghost Dance" he taught would bring back the Native American dead; reunite the living Native American communities with the spirits of their ancestors; cause the spirits to fight on their behalf; sweep away the white settlers; bring back the (almost extinct) buffalo herds; return the wild horses; and usher in an era of peace, prosperity, and unity for Native American peoples. There were aspects of it that seemed to mirror the Christian concept of the rapture, with the claim that those who danced the Ghost Dance

---

10. Brown, *Bury My Heart at Wounded Knee*, 342.

would be lifted into the air while below them the making of a new earth would remove all "white people."[11]

Sweeping through much of the western United States, it galvanized huge numbers of Plains Native American communities and rapidly affected areas as far apart as California and Oklahoma. Among the Lakota (Sioux) people it took on strident millenarian features, such as wearing "ghost shirts," thought capable of repelling bullets.[12] These events alarmed US government "Indian agents" and the military. Some US experts at the time compared the millenarian preoccupation of the Lakota with that of Christian Seventh-Day Adventists (who had a strong apocalyptic character). But the Seventh-Day Adventists were white; the Ghost Dancers were not.

In December 1890, Indian Police (in US government service) shot and killed the famous chief Sitting Bull (who had led the tribes at the destruction of Custer in 1876 at the Battle of Little Bighorn). Then, at Wounded Knee Creek, South Dakota, the US army killed at least 153 Minneconjou and Hunkpapa from the Lakota people in a massacre. One estimate of the dead stood as high as 300. Twenty-five soldiers died, most hit by friendly fire from other soldiers.[13] Those responsible were from the 7th Cavalry. They had taken revenge for the events of the Battle of Little Bighorn. Twenty US soldiers received Medals of Honor for their actions in this massacre.

The events of the Ghost Dance period were the final acts in the suppression of "Plains Indian" culture. Their apocalyptic hopes had been dashed.

BOLIVIA: THE GUARANI/ CHIRIGUANOS WAR, 1892

The Battle of Kuruyuki in 1892 saw an attempt by the eastern Bolivian Guarani (then called "Chiriguanos") to resist the spread of Christianity and Bolivian settlers. It was part of a long-term pattern of resistance that saw this tribal group fight against (in succession) the Inca Empire, the Spanish Empire, and the Bolivian state. In a similar fashion, the Guaycuruan-speaking Toba attempted to regain control of the Gran Chaco in Argentina in 1904. Both failed.

11. Brown, *Bury My Heart at Wounded Knee*, 342.
12. Brown, *Bury My Heart at Wounded Knee*, 343.
13. Brown, *Bury My Heart at Wounded Knee*, 351.

The nineteenth-century conflict was a response to encroachment on their lands by Spanish-speaking ranchers and *creole* (mixed-race) settlers and was also resistance to the spread of Christianity.[14] Led by a man named Chapiaguasu, who was considered a prophet and healer, it was a millenarian movement comparable with the Ghost Dance in the US and anticolonial movements in Africa and China.[15] It aimed to expel all missionaries and nonindigenous settlers and envisaged the restoration of a traditional society. As with many similar apocalyptic movements it promoted the promise of a new "Golden Age." Chapiaguasu called himself *Apiaguaiki Tumpa* (the Eunuch of God). Although he was familiar with Christianity from time at the Franciscan mission of Santa Rosa, near Cuevo, his messianic message was deeply rooted in tribal society and spirituality. However, as with many such movements, it was arguably also partly influenced by the Christian millenarian tradition.

The immediate trigger of the uprising was the rape and murder of a Chiriguano girl by the mayor of Cuevo. In response, *Apiaguaiki* led his followers in an uprising. Early ambushes of Bolivian army patrols and attacks on local ranches were successful, but the success did not last. On 21 January 1892, *Apiaguaiki* led an attack on the mission at Santa Rosa, where Spanish-speaking settlers and a large number of Chiriguanos (who did not side with *Apiaguaiki*) were sheltering. The attack failed. Following this, a combined force of Bolivian soldiers, *creole* volunteers, and Christian Chiriguanos counterattacked. On 28 January, *Apiaguaiki* and his followers were heavily defeated at the Battle of Kuruyuki. In the aftermath of the defeat, the Bolivian army slaughtered huge numbers of those Chiriguanos who surrendered. They also sold women and children into slavery. It has been estimated that 6,000 died at the hands of the army and its allies.[16] *Apiaguaiki* escaped after the battle but was betrayed, then tortured, and executed.

BRAZIL: THE CONTESTADO REBELLION, 1912–16

In this rebellion, somewhere in the region of 25,000 millenarians fought against about two-thirds of the Brazilian army (7,000 men) in a conflict set in a contested border region located between the two Brazilian states

---

14. Langer, *Expecting Pears from an Elm Tree*, 11–18.
15. Adas, *Prophets of Rebellion*, xix.
16. Combés, "Las batallas de Kuruyuki," 224.

of Paraná and Santa Catarina.[17] The area was contested by both these states and also by Argentina (hence the name *Contestado*).

Railway construction and the arrival of large numbers of European immigrants in the area had destabilized the existing social and economic system, which was based on cattle ranching. As local landowners sold off land to incomers, the *agregados* (ranch hands and sharecroppers) who worked the land were dispossessed.

Resistance to these developments was led by a "prophet" named José Maria. Many believed that he was a previously "martyred prophet" come back to life.[18] Named Atanás Marcaf, he took the alias of João, or José Maria. The uprising was one of three mass messianic movements that shook undeveloped "back-lands" areas of Brazil from 1889 to 1930.[19] José Maria proposed the creation of "holy cities" that would be inhabited by believers; and he called for the return of the Brazilian monarchy (the country had been a republic since 1889).

The Brazilian army mounted a scorched-earth campaign against rebel areas, which starved them into submission. José Maria was killed/disappeared in 1912; but his followers hoped for his resurrection for some time after this and the uprising lasted from 1912–16.

JAMAICA: RASTAFARIANISM IN THE 1930s

The impact of colonization in the Americas not only provoked apocalyptic reactions from indigenous peoples; comparable responses also occurred among those who were brought to the Americas as enslaved people as part of the colonization process.

Although it is now better known as a black cultural movement, Rastafarianism originated in Jamaica in the 1930s with clear millenarian characteristics. Drawing on Jewish and Christian beliefs, the movement described people of African descent, both in the Americas and around the world, as being "out of Africa" and, so, "exiles in Babylon." Tested by *Jah* (God) through the imposition of slavery, the original movement awaited a literal deliverance from captivity and a return to "Zion" (Africa, particularly Ethiopia).

---

17. Diacon, "Contestado Rebellion," lines 1–3.
18. Siegel, "Contestado Rebellion, 1912–16," 202.
19. Siegel, "Contestado Rebellion, 1912–16," 202.

Many believers originally saw the Ethiopian emperor, Haile Selassie I's coronation in 1930 as the second coming of Christ, which would redeem black people. The emperor's name before his coronation was *Ras Tafari Makonnen*. Many cultural factors flowed into the emergence of Rastafarianism, perhaps most significantly the nineteenth-century pan-African movement and the teachings of the Jamaican-born Marcus Garvey (died 1940). He reportedly told his followers to "Look to Africa where a black king shall be crowned, he shall be the Redeemer."[20] The movement later became known globally through the music of Rastafarian Bob Marley (died 1981).

By the time of the death of Haile Selassie in 1975, the movement had grown in cultural complexity and diversity (it had always been a highly decentralized movement, with no central creed) and had grown beyond its original roots in a movement where many looked to a millennial literal return to Africa through the actions of a god-emperor. While one cannot generalize about the complexity of modern Rastafarianism, it seems clear that today the original idea of "Babylon" has "developed to represent all oppressive organizations and countries in the world."[21] And repatriation to "Zion" is now more likely to be regarded as "voluntary migration to Africa, returning to Africa culturally and symbolically, or rejecting Western values and preserving African roots and black pride."[22]

US ETHNIC APOCALYPTIC MOVEMENTS TODAY

Today, apocalyptic ethnic politics remains a feature of the US political landscape. Within areas of the black community these include ones that are comparable with the historic movements explored in this chapter.

Some take the form of semireligious cults, often focused on surviving a future cataclysm or cosmic event. An example would be the black supremacist and UFO cult of the "Nuwaubian Nation." While some factions of this group still exist, most followers abandoned it after the imprisonment of its founder, Dwight York, in 2004.

Other groups have a more explicit political and revolutionary agenda. For example, the "Nation of Islam"—infamous for its antisemitism, homophobia, belief in innate black superiority over whites, and

---

20. History.com Editors, "Rastafarianism," lines 19–21.
21. "Rastafarian beliefs," lines 94–95.
22. Murrell, "Introduction," 6.

the separation of black people from other ethnic groups—is rooted in a "hybrid creed with its own myths and doctrines,"[23] preaching a coming apocalyptic overthrow of the white "devil" and the appearance of God on earth.[24] The latter claim was originally linked to belief in the divinity, or *Mahdi* status (sources vary), of Wallace Fard Muhammad (died/disappeared 1934), the founder of the original Nation of Islam. In many ways one can recognize distinct—if mirror—characteristics of those found among modern white supremacist groups in the US. The "Nation of Islam" should be differentiated from mainstream Islam. However, a number of other radical groups have also engaged with what can be termed "Black Muslim Radical Theology," and a number of these contain apocalyptic and millenarian tendencies.

Some groups, instead of connecting with a form of Islam, have adapted other religious traditions. An example of this is the "Black Hebrew Israelites" movement, which draws on Christian and Jewish beliefs while reinterpreting them in a way that is radically different to either of these two religions. The group claims that African Americans are descended from the ancient Israelites. The movement is complex and some groups within it exhibit extreme antisemitic, antiwhite, and black supremacist beliefs.[25] The group should not be confused with Judaism, despite its name.

Quite what form such ethnically separatist and politically radical groups in the US will take in the future is currently hard to predict. But what is clear is that several of them are rooted in a violent reaction against dominant white culture that has been (in various forms) part of the American apocalyptic phenomenon since the sixteenth century.

---

23. "Nation of Islam," lines 53–54.
24. "Nation of Islam," lines 57–58.
25. "Black Hebrew Israelites," lines 9–10, 15–18.

CHAPTER 11

Apocalypse in the Philippines

IN THE PHILIPPINES, as in other areas of the world, politically radical anticolonial movements developed millenarian trends when they faced destruction at the hands of colonial forces. The movement of *Cofradía de San José* and that of *Santa Iglesia* both combined Catholic outlooks with indigenous nationalism. The followers of both movements believed that their leaders' millenarian prophecies were realizable; this adapted and refocused traditional Christian apocalyptic beliefs. Consequently, they joined the uprisings in the hope that these apocalyptic expectations would be realized.

While these movements were anticolonial protests designed to liberate themselves from colonial exploitation, those taking part did not think of their liberation in modern political revolutionary terms. Instead, they viewed their context within a Catholic frame of meaning—seeking their liberation by the power of God—and this was expressed through apocalyptic terms and outlooks as a result of this.

THE COFRADÍA DE SAN JOSÉ, 1832–41

The *Cofradía de San José* first appeared in 1832 in the province of Tayabas (now Quezon), and its activities soon spread to the adjacent provinces of Laguna and Batangas and broke out into a full millenarian uprising in 1841.

The movement was prompted by the refusal of Catholic religious orders to admit native Filipinos (*indios*) as members. In response, a devout Catholic of peasant stock named Apolinario de la Cruz—better known as Hermano Pule—decided to form a religious order that would only admit native people. He called the order the *Cofradía de San José* (Confraternity of St. Joseph). At its height it had somewhere in the region of 4,500 to 5,000 members, living in the provinces of Tayabas, Batangas, and Laguna.[1] Apolinario became known to his followers as Hermano Pule (Brother Pule). The movement banned Spanish colonists and *mestizos* (mixed-race locals) from joining unless given specific permission by Pule.

The movement combined Roman Catholic beliefs and practices with some that were native pre-Christian, such as the wearing of *anting-anting* (talismans).[2] In this it drew on a mixed heritage that was distinctive to the Philippines. The Catholic conversion process there had occurred in a complex way, which saw some areas rapidly Christianized, while in other areas (particularly mountainous regions) the process was more spasmodic and lacked depth. As a result, Catholicism in the Philippines "incorporated elements of animism, that is, belief in spirits called *anito*, and other elements of indigenous culture."[3] This meant it exhibited distinct differences when compared with Catholicism as practiced in Spain and Latin America (particularly Mexico), which had been the base of a number of those later involved in work in the Philippines. This characteristic made Catholicism in the Philippines distinct;[4] and something of this trend can be traced in the nature of the *Cofradía de San José*.

Attempts to have the movement recognized by the Catholic Church in the Philippines failed and, from 1840, the colonial authorities began to mobilize against the group. As well as accusing the group of heresy, there was a fear that the size of the movement might pose an armed threat to colonial government. In October 1840, 243 *cofradía* members were arrested. Further attempts to persuade ecclesiastical authorities that the group was not heretical failed.

The governor-general, Marcelino de Oraá Lecumberri, declared the movement subversive and ordered the arrest of its members. This forced

1. Palafox, "193rd Birth Anniversary," lines, 44–45.
2. Guerrero, "Colorum Uprisings," 65–78.
3. Setsuho, "Popular Catholicism," 109.
4. See: Schumacher, "Syncretism in Philippine Catholicism," 261–69.

Pule into hiding. Fearing further persecution, he rallied those members who had avoided capture, and about 4,000 of them gathered at Barrio Isabang, which was situated on the slopes of Mount Banahaw. There they were joined by Aetas (a still-pagan indigenous people) living in the Sierra Madre Mountains. They made common cause against the Spanish colonial authorities.

It was in this atmosphere of mounting threat of military intervention that the millenarian nature of the movement emerged. Prior to this, some acceptance by colonial church authorities might have ensured that the group generally operated within official church boundaries and would have prevented its development into an armed force. Whether this could have occurred, given its mixed religious ideology and origins outside of official ecclesiastical structures, is perhaps unlikely. What is certain is that the racist exclusivity of the religious orders—and a refusal to dialogue with the group—accelerated its movement towards radicalization.

Official armed forces attacked the *cofradía* camp but were initially defeated. It was at this point that the *cofradía* members there crowned Pule as "King of the Tagalogs" (an indigenous people). Pule and the other *cofradía* leaders promised that God would intervene to grant them victory: they would be protected from enemy bullets; angels would appear and assist them in battle; and the ground would open and swallow the enemy soldiers.[5] However, in the ensuing battle the *cofradia* were heavily defeated, losing perhaps as many as 500 members, compared with government casualties that numbered just eleven wounded.[6] A movement that had finally developed a millenarian character in response to colonial persecution had collapsed in its final apocalyptic struggle.

Pule was eventually captured, tortured, and executed in 1841. His quartered body parts were put on public display by the Spanish colonial authorities. About 200 others who had joined in the resistance were also executed at the same time.

Members of the *Cofradía de San José* who survived the crushing of the revolt continued as a religious movement and became known as *colorums*. This was derived from the phrase "*saecula saeculorum*" (to the ages of ages), used to end prayers during the Catholic Mass. But the politically revolutionary millenarian character of the group had been extinguished.

---

5. Ileto, *Pasyon and Revolution*, 59.
6. Duka, *Struggle for Freedom*, 106–7.

THE *SANTA IGLESIA* MOVEMENT, 1900

The *Santa Iglesia* movement was popular in the central Luzon provinces of Pampanga, Bulacan, and Nueva Ecija. Founded by Felipe Salvador, the movement known as the *Santa Iglesia* (Holy Church) was a messianic society that aimed to defeat the colonial government of the United States in the Philippines. The US had gained control of the Philippines following their victory in the Spanish-American War of 1898. Prior to this, the revolutionary society known as the *Katipunan*—which sought independence from Spain—had begun the Philippine Revolution in 1896. Independence from Spain was declared in 1898, and the First Philippine Republic was established in 1899. However, Spain had ceded the islands to the US (along with Puerto Rico and Guam) following defeat in the Spanish-American War. The Americans did not recognize the Philippine Republic and, in the resulting Philippine-American War, somewhere between 250,000 to 1 million civilians died. Most of these deaths were due to famine and disease.[7]

Salvador founded the *Santa Iglesia* in 1900, after the defeat of the Filipino forces of General Emilio Aguinaldo by the Americans. He had earlier joined the *Katipunan* who were fighting the Americans (having exchanged one colonial occupier—Spain—for another—the US). Sheltering in the mountains, he used these as a base for resisting US control.

The *Santa Iglesia* fused religious and nationalist ideology. Its underpinning beliefs were strongly anticolonial and anti-Catholic. Salvador took the title "pontiff" (pope), grew his hair long, wore clothing reminiscent of biblical figures, and was revered by his followers as a prophet. He carried a large crucifix. As he preached, twelve of his followers would face him; another twelve would face the assembled people. As with many such movements experiencing severe cultural stress, it was accelerating into millenarian extremism. Salvador prophesied the coming of a second "great flood" (as in the days of Noah in the Old Testament) that would drown all nonbelievers. Other accounts refer to a prophecy of a "rain of fire." Following this, gold and jewels would rain down on his followers. As they prepared to fight the US military, he also promised that God would turn their knives into rifles. All they needed to do was fight bravely and stay loyal to the movement. Once victory was achieved, land would be redistributed to the poor. The impoverished and the landless flocked to his apocalyptic cause.

7. Tucker, *Encyclopedia*, 478.

The *Santa Iglesia* stood within a very particular religiopolitical revolutionary tradition in the Philippines in which "prophets, saints and *babaylan* [Filipino shamans, often women] saw the war years as part of the great cataclysm that would signal the end of the world."[8] As with the earlier *Cofradía de San José*, it combined millenarian Christian beliefs and folk themes with nationalist hostility towards the Spanish and then the Americans. It was an explosive mixture of features.[9] In this combination of driving factors, it shared a character with other East Asian millenarian movements, such as the Boxers in China and the Tonghak movement in Korea.[10]

Salvador was captured in 1901, but escaped in 1902. He was now something of a folk hero to poor people. However, facing military defeats at the hands of the Americans and their allies, the movement began to collapse, and he went on the run. He was finally captured by US forces in 1910, sentenced to death, and hanged in 1912. After his death, a cult focused on him—called *Apo Ipe*—emerged and was noted as still being in existence as late as the 1920s. After him, other millenarian leaders continued to gain followers by claiming they had eaten with him or talked with him. This messianic status continued for a surprisingly long time after his death.

THE TWO MOVEMENTS COMPARED

Modern experts have compared these two dramatic movements that occurred in a comparable period within the same country. A persuasive analysis has listed several points of direct comparability.[11]

Firstly, it is asserted that the two movements did not embrace apocalyptic millenarianism from the beginning. They did not begin as radical end-times movements. Both began as spiritual initiatives, designed to meet the needs of those believers who were being excluded from the ecclesiastical structures of colonial society. It was the persecuting responses of the colonial authorities that ratcheted up the crisis and created a situation within which radicalization would occur. The two movements became increasingly millenarian in direct proportion to the antagonism

---

8. Churchill, "History of the Philippine Revolution," lines 44–45.
9. See: Setsuho, "Uprisings of Hesukristos in the Philippines," 143–74.
10. Phillips, *War, Religion and Empire*, 215.
11. See: Setsuho, "Millenarian Uprisings," 3–36.

they faced from the authorities. In short, repression triggered apocalyptic responses.

Secondly, the two movements were able to rapidly morph into millenarian mode because there was a pre-existing form of marginalized and lower-class Catholic faith in the Philippines that had been primed by the restricting and racist attitudes prevalent among colonial authorities and the leadership of the Catholic Church. This was vividly seen in the responses to the pre-existing *Pasyón* (Passion) tradition in the Philippines. The *Pasyón* was—and is still—a Philippine epic that narrates the passion, death, and resurrection of Jesus Christ. It is organized in stanzas of five lines (of eight syllables each), in which the standard elements of indigenous epic poetry are interwoven with this dramatic faith theme. In the Philippines, the uninterrupted chanting or *pabasa* (reading) of the narrative from start to finish is a popular Catholic devotion that occurs during Lent; it is particularly enacted during Holy Week (the week leading up to Easter). The *Pasyón* narrative was an adaptation of pre-Hispanic Filipino cultural activities geared to the chanting of epic poems as a part of oral traditions. The best-known form of the *Pasyón* narrative was first written by Gaspar Aquino de Belén and was known as *Ang Mahal na Pasión ni Jesu Christong Panginoon Natin na Tola* (The Sacred Passion of Jesus Christ, Our Lord, Which Is a Poem). It was first written in this form in 1703 and approved in 1704 for use in Catholic events. By the nineteenth century, and the time of the emergence of the *Cofradía de San José* and the *Santa Iglesia*, it was both well known and deeply engrained in popular culture and experience.

Celebrating the *Pasyón* acquainted people with the New Testament apocalyptic vision connected to Christ's suffering and victory and helped them to look forward to his coming again in glory. Those who took part in these enactments injected popular and lower-class enthusiasm and excitement into these narratives in ways that were not controlled by the church hierarchy. In this, lower-class leaders could identify with millenarian themes and come to represent them in the local environment. This meant that when later leaders articulated such beliefs in times of turbulence, many people were prepared to positively respond due to their existing engagement with such themes. To them it seemed that such millenarian prophecies and expectations were realizable in the here and now. Such attitudes made people more likely to join in with the uprisings.

Thirdly, the *Pasyón* experience also influenced the formation of the character of the leadership of both movements. A common belief developed through the *Pasyón* that *Hesukristo* (Jesus Christ) was particularly the savior of the poor, dispossessed, and downtrodden. As a result, the leaders of both movements likened themselves and their mission to the well-known image of *Hesukristo*. In so doing, their claims resonated with popular religious beliefs and gained the respect and support of many ordinary people.

Finally, both movements were supported by marginalized people who could readily connect their suffering and problems with the economic and political activities of the ruling classes. As a result, these millenarian movements were rooted in national spirituality but also in anticolonial ideology. Liberation from exploitation and oppression in the here and now could, therefore, swiftly be linked to liberation in an eternal sense and the hope of end-times justification. As a result, both movements can be clearly differentiated from many modern anticolonial movements that take their frames of reference from secular political ideologies (such as Marxism and/or socialism). In contrast, those who supported the *Cofradía de San José* and the *Santa Iglesia* framed their actions within the mindset of Catholic (especially apocalyptic) theology and saw their liberation as depending on the direct intervention of God. As a result, these movements were forms of "realized eschatology," which sought to both enact the values of the age to come and, by their direct involvement, to hasten its occurrence. The colonial authorities actively and energetically oppressed both movements precisely because they recognized their ideology as an existential threat to the economic and social status quo.

Consequently, while the two movements did not start as proponents of anticolonial apocalyptic politics, they rapidly developed this character, and this accelerated their radicalized agenda and impact.

THE RIZALISTA CULTS

The *Cofradía de San José* and the *Santa Iglesia* are not the only examples of apocalyptic and millenarian movements in the Philippines. A number of others have also existed and continue to do so. These are often described as "Rizalista cults."[12]

José Rizal was a martyr who died during the struggle against Spanish rule that occurred in the years immediately before the Spanish-American

---

12. See: Scott, *Decoding Subaltern Politics*, 56–57.

War. The "Rizalista cults" were, and are, syncretistic, as we have seen in a number of anticolonial millenarian movements. As such, they combined Catholic religious beliefs with pre-Spanish Malay and Filipino features in order to give hope to the poor and the oppressed.

The Rizalista cults believe in the divinity of José Rizal, a national hero who was martyred by the Spanish in 1896. The son of a wealthy landowner, Rizal was educated in Manila and later at the University of Madrid, in Spain. Originally a medical student, he soon became committed to reforming the nature of Spanish rule in the Philippines. However, he did not actually espouse Philippine national independence. He lived and wrote in Europe between 1882 and 1892 but returned to the Philippines in 1892. On arrival, he founded a nonviolent reformist society called the *Liga Filipina* (League of the Philippines) in Manila. In response, the colonial authorities deported him to Dapitan, in northwest Mindanao. There he remained in exile for the next four years.

In 1896, the *Katipunan*—the nationalist secret society we came across earlier—revolted against Spain. Despite having had no connections with that organization and its uprising, Rizal was arrested and then tried for sedition by the colonial authorities. Found "guilty," he was publicly executed by firing squad. This took place in Manila. It was an act of colonial oppressive violence and it backfired spectacularly. His martyrdom convinced many ordinary Filipinos that there was no viable alternative to full independence from Spain. While awaiting execution, Rizal wrote *Último adiós* (Last Farewell), which is regarded as a masterpiece of nineteenth-century Spanish verse. In a way that would have astonished the colonial authorities, their brutal killing of this nonviolent thinker accelerated support for him—and in the most extraordinary ways.

Many lower-class Filipinos began to proclaim his divinity or to assert that he was the second (and specifically Filipino) Christ. Some identified him as representing a divinity drawn from the pre-Spanish Malay religion of the Philippines. These cults continue to proclaim a variety of beliefs about him, such as that he continues to live, or will return in order to free believers from poverty and oppression. Many exhibit ideologies proclaiming "classic themes of liberation and symbolic reversal."[13]

These Rizalista cults include the *Iglesia Sagrada ni Lahi* (Holy Church of the Race); the *Iglesia Watawat ng Lahi* (Banner of the Race Church); *Bathalismo* (named from Bathala Maykapal, a Tagolog pagan

---

13. Scott, *Decoding Subaltern Politics*, 57.

deity in the Philippines); *Adarnistas* (named after "Mother Adarna," its founder); *Iglesia Sagrada Filipina* (Sacred Philippine Church); and *Samahan ng Tatlong Persona Solo Dios* (Organization of the Three Persons One God). A number have adopted a synthesis of Roman Catholic rituals, holy images, and church organization, with pre-Christian Filipino religious beliefs and features. The *Iglesia Sagrada ni Lahi* has its own "bible," supposedly kept secret until Rizal appears as God on earth.

Today about 300,000 people in rural areas are still members of these various cults.[14] A number of these groups stress a feminized hierarchy in the "church." This acknowledges the principal role that women have long had as *babaylan*, or spiritual and community leaders in the Philippines. By including Rizal in their theological framework, they reference the proindependence ideology of their followers.

The Rizalista groups provide an insight into the continued role of apocalyptic and millenarian cults within the Philippines. Although in these latter cases many no longer have a radical political role, this has not always been the case. The belief in an upturning of the social order has meant that "the sect passed, by turns, from quietism into rebellion [in the past]."[15] How this will develop in the future is hard to predict, but what is clear is that these sects are rooted in a distinctly Filipino version of a syncretistic apocalypse.

---

14. Editors of Encyclopaedia Britannica, "Rizalist Cult," lines 11–12.
15. Scott, *Decoding Subaltern Politics*, 57.

CHAPTER 12

Apocalyptic Slaughter in China

THE FOCUS ON apocalyptic beliefs and politics has remained enthusiastically supported by many groups within the Christian church over 2,000 years. However, as we have seen, at other times it has morphed into cults that have broken away from mainline Christianity in highly radicalized forms and that have led to warfare and deaths comparable with the sixteenth-century German Peasants' Wars and the radical Anabaptists.

The most dramatic and lethal of these involved Chinese members of the Taiping Rebellion (1850–64). As with aspects of the Lord's Resistance Army (recently explored), a syncretistic movement (combining indigenous beliefs with some of those introduced by Christianity) drove forward the most radical political expression of Chinese apocalyptic political ideology: the Taiping Rebellion.

As we shall see, the lives lost as a result of this millenarian uprising constituted the heaviest death toll associated with any millenarian movement. The suffering and mortality were huge. In this drawn-out series of bloody wars (often unheard of in the West) somewhere in the region of 30 million Chinese people died.[1]

---

1. White, "How Many Died?," line 1.

THE ORIGINS OF THE TAIPING REBELLION

Led by Hong Xiuquan, the self-proclaimed brother of Jesus Christ, the Taiping movement proclaimed the overturning of the contemporary Chinese moral and social order. Setting up the "Taiping Heavenly Kingdom" in Tianjing (present-day Nanjing)—in opposition to the ruling Manchu-led Qing dynasty—the rebels eventually controlled much of southern China, ruling a population of about 20 to 30 million people.[2]

The Qing dynasty (also called the Manchu dynasty), the target of the rebellion, was the last of the imperial dynasties of China and lasted from 1644 to 1912 (there was a brief restoration of the dynasty in 1917). The Qing dynasty was not formed by Han Chinese—who make up the majority of the Chinese population—but by Manchu rulers. Living in what are now the northeastern Chinese provinces of Jilin and Heilongjiang, the "Manchu" (from which Manchuria takes its name) were made up of different groups of Tungusic-language speakers, who were united under one dynasty in 1616. In 1636, this was designated as the *Qing* (pure) dynasty. In 1644, the Manchus capitalized on disunity within the Ming state to commence the conquest of the Chinese lands ruled by the Ming.

Under this new—Qing—dynasty, the territory ruled by the Chinese Empire tripled in size compared to the preceding Ming dynasty (1368–1644). Accompanying this territorial expansion, the population under the Qing grew from about 150 million to 450 million people.[3] Many of the non-Chinese minorities living within the empire were subjected to Sinicization, with the goal of creating greater cultural and linguistic unity. At the same time, a more integrated national Chinese economy developed that drew more of the population into the expanded system. As the Manchus extended their rule over this vast empire, they spread Chinese culture over territories as far from the original Han-Chinese heartlands as Central Asia, Tibet, and Siberia. In addition, the Manchus also annexed Chinese cultural traditions. They did this as a way by which they could demonstrate their legitimacy as "Confucian-style rulers."[4]

It was this dynasty that was targeted by the Taiping Rebellion. The area that was the original center of the Taiping unrest covered the provinces of Guangdong and Guangxi. This was the homeland of the Taiping people and, in the run-up to the rebellion, it had experienced

---

2. Ai, "Envision of the Land," 99.
3. Editors of Encyclopaedia Britannica, "Qing Dynasty," lines 8–9.
4. Hearn, "Qing Dynasty." lines 4–7.

considerable social unrest. By the time of the rebellion, the great days of the Qing were in the past and the dynasty was facing increasing disruption and turbulence. A series of great famines, natural disasters, economic problems, and escalating defeats at the hands of colonial foreign powers in the nineteenth century fed into what has become known as China's "century of humiliation."[5] Deep resentment at this foreign interference still informs large parts of twenty-first-century Chinese national identity and attitudes towards outside "interference" in Chinese affairs. It was during this "century of humiliation" that the Taiping Rebellion added a new and unique form of mayhem to the cocktail of crises facing China.

The immediate background was the first Opium War with Britain (1839–42), a humiliating defeat at the hands of an external power that led to a huge decline in Qing Government prestige. As this occurred, Qing officials found it increasingly difficult to resolve societal conflicts and feuding between different cultural and social groups. The most significant cultural conflict relevant to the eventual revolt was that between native inhabitants and *Hakka* (guest settlers) who had migrated into western Guangdong and Guangxi. It is significant that the core followers of the movement that eventually emerged were found among the miners, the charcoal workers, and the poor peasants in central Guangxi. Most of these were *Hakka* and felt highly vulnerable. This made them particularly open to an ideology that promised radical change and an improvement in their social and economic positions.

The focal figure in the rebellion was named Hong Xiuquan (1814–64) He was a man who had failed to enter the imperial civil service through its demanding and extensive series of examinations. As well as experiencing severe personal disappointment, he was clearly influenced by Christian teachings, particularly those with a millenarian character.

While suffering from fever in 1837, he claimed to have had a series of visions. In these "visions" he allegedly travelled to a heavenly land, which was situated to the east. There it was revealed to him that demons were destroying humankind. He was given a sacred sword, and with the help of a heavenly brother, he battled against the demons and the king of hell. After this spiritual battle, Hong remained in heaven, took a wife, and had a child with her. After this, Hong returned to earth, with the title: "Heavenly King, Lord of the Kingly Way."[6]

---

5. Chesneaux, *Peasant Revolts in China*, 23–24.
6. History.com Editors, "Taiping Rebellion," lines 18–24.

Following these experiences, by 1843 he came to believe that he was a Son of God, the younger brother of Jesus Christ. This was based on his reading of Christian missionary literature. As a result of this, he reinterpreted the fevered vision as indicating that the father in his dream was Father God of Christianity, the older brother of the dream was Jesus, and the king of hell was the serpent in the garden of eden (in Genesis).[7] This then made Hong the younger brother of Jesus and placed on earth with a divine calling.

With this messianic status, he claimed that he had been sent to reform China. Once again, as in so many apocalyptic movements, a self-confident messianic figure had arisen at a time of cultural turbulence and conflict.

Feng Yunshan, an associate of Hong, assisted in the organization of a new religious group based on Hong's claims. It was known as the *Bai Shangdi Hui* (God Worshippers' Society). The group rapidly gained followers among the poorest peasants living in Guangxi province. This accompanied new millenarian spiritual claims by others who were accepted into the growing religious movement. In 1848, this included a charcoal burner by the name of Yang Xiuqing who claimed to be a spiritual channel for God, and a peasant named Xiao Chaogui who said he was a channel for Jesus. Ecstatic followers claimed to be transported to heaven. Others recounted claims of angelic beings who saved local villages from crises. A movement that accelerated the desperate hopes of downtrodden people was beginning to gain real traction.

In January 1851, Hong proclaimed the beginning of a new dynasty: the *Taiping Tianguo* (Heavenly Kingdom of Great Peace). It was then that Hong openly took the title of *Tianwang* (Heavenly King). The movement was now entering a new phrase of apocalyptic claims and territorial expansion.

THE COURSE OF THE REBELLION

In September 1851, the expanding Taiping movement relocated to the city of Yong'an (modern-day Mengshan, in Guangxi province). There they were besieged by the imperial army until April 1852. At that point they broke the government siege and, following this breakout, expanded their influence across Hunan.

7. History.com Editors, "Taiping Rebellion," lines 44–48.

As this revolutionary, largely peasant army took new territory, it pulled in support from other armed groups, including members of Chinese secret societies and outlaws. Taking Wuhan, the capital of Hubei province, they went on to push north through the Yangtze River Valley. Reaching the eastern city of Nanjing, they captured it in March 1853, renaming it *Tianjing* (Heavenly Capital). It then became their territorial base. From there they mounted a northern expedition that aimed to seize the Qing capital, located at Beijing. Although this venture failed, another push—into the upper Yangtze valley—was highly successful and defeated several of the Qing imperial armies sent against it. Despite this, the northern expansion had ultimately failed by the spring of 1855 and the provinces in the Yangtze River Valley became the main theatre of conflict with Qing forces.

At the same time, by 1856 the internal cohesion of the movement had begun to unravel. Yang Xiuqing, one of the ministers of the apocalyptic state, attempted to encroach on the powers of the *Tianwang* (Heavenly King). In the resulting violence, Yang Xiuqing and thousands of his followers were killed. This destruction was ordered by the *Tianwang*. Fearing a similar fate, another Taiping general, Shi Dakai, defected and took many soldiers with him.

These internal divisions were accompanied by military reversals. In 1860, an offensive by the Taipings, directed towards Shanghai, was stopped by the "Ever-Victorious Army," which was Western-trained and commanded by an American named Frederick Townsend Ward. Later, command would pass to the British military officer Charles ("Chinese") Gordon, who would later die in the Sudan facing the *Mahdi*. Within this army, large numbers of Chinese mercenary troops in the pay of the imperial government were assisted by being equipped with Western weapons. The Taiping were gradually forced back. In October 1861, Anqing, the capital of Anhui, was taken by the Hunan Army in the service of the Qing. It was clear that the *Taiping Tianguo* (Heavenly Kingdom of Great Peace) was now doomed.

This failure was exacerbated by the lack of support for the movement from landowners and gentry, who opposed both the radical anti-Confucianism of the Taipings and their social and economic policies. Under the leadership of Zeng Guofan, a Qing official, the opposition to the *Taiping Tianguo* coalesced, and in July 1864, Nanjing was captured for the Qing. The fall of Nanjing was, in effect, the end of one of the greatest civil wars that had ever occurred in world history. It was the end of the apocalyptic revolution.

Hong—the erstwhile *Tianwang* (Heavenly King)—committed suicide in June 1864. Prior to this, he had installed his fifteen-year-old son as the next *Tianwang*. However, the Taiping could not recover. While scattered acts of Taiping resistance continued in other parts of the country until 1868, the *Taiping Tianguo* was over.

THE IDEOLOGY AND NATURE OF THE *TAIPING TIANGUO* (HEAVENLY KINGDOM OF GREAT PEACE)

What emerged as the Taiping religion was a strange mixture of distorted Christian beliefs (influenced by Protestant missionary theology), Chinese religious traditions, hatred of the Manchu, and opposition to Chinese cultural traditions that underpinned the Qing regime. Despite the movement's perceived opposition to traditional Confucianism, there was much about it that drew on this tradition and on earlier religious rebellions in China. There was little in the movement that referenced New Testament concepts of forgiveness and compassion, but much that referenced Old Testament beliefs regarding theocratic government, worship, and obedience.

In the early years, this syncretistic belief radicalized the followers of the movement to a striking degree. The whole population was expected to give all their belongings to what was termed a "general treasury," which would be shared out by the new government. This clearly attracted the poor and dispossessed, although it was not widely practiced outside the early core of *Hakka* followers.

The ideology of the rebellion was rooted in the shared ownership of land and property that appealed to large numbers of impoverished peasants, town-workers, and miners. Redistribution of land was planned but only partly carried out. This lack of radical redistribution was partly caused by the fact that many of the new administrative posts in the villages were filled by former landlords or by those who had acted as clerks of the local government under the Qing. As a result, the old order proved remarkably resilient. In addition, the short-lived nature of the *Taiping Tianguo* meant that it is not possible to see how it would have developed in the long run.

Taiping propaganda against the Manchu rulers of China being foreigners also encouraged support for the movement. This propaganda helped create a force of perhaps a million fighters who were disciplined and fanatical in their commitment. These were organized into separate men's and women's fighting divisions. The depth of this commitment was revealed when about 100,000 Taiping followers opted for death over surrender when Nanjing eventually fell.[8]

Social policies included the banning of adultery, gambling, prostitution, opium smoking, foot-binding, and slavery. In addition, the use of tobacco and alcohol was banned. The Chinese language was simplified. Gender equality was declared. Strict discipline was applied in the army, both in camp and when on the march. A new puritanical and disciplined order was envisaged. Some within the leadership—influenced by Western ideas—proposed industrial expansion and the creation of a democratic system.

The rebellion failed for a number of reasons arising both from its ideology and its form of governance. Arguably, the main cause of the failure of the movement was rooted in internal divisions among the leadership in Nanjing. We have seen how this internecine violence started as early as 1856 with the actions of Yang Xiuqing.

Alongside this, many of those in leadership soon began to exhibit behavior far removed from the puritanical aims of the movement. It was a falling away from radicalism that is common to the leadership of many millenarian movements. In addition, it proved hard to recruit new leaders to oversee rural reforms, and this led to the continued influence of old elites, which meant that the program of radical land reform soon ran into the sand. This disillusioned many poor peasants who had pinned their hopes on this.

On the other side of the coin, though, it was also religious fanaticism that posed a threat to the movement. What motivated armies was not always the best mindset for managing complex military, social, economic, and administrative affairs.

As part of this radicalism, negative attitudes toward traditional culture alienated many of the gentry and peasantry in a deeply traditional society. Too radical? Not radical enough? The Taiping faced the age-old revolutionary dilemma—and failed to solve it.

---

8. Grant, "Third Battle of Nanjing," lines 29–30.

THE DEATH TOLL

The death toll of this series of wars was enormous. As well as being caused by the fighting and disruption centered on the main regions involved, the chaos spread out into wider areas of China. For example, the first half of the nineteenth century had already witnessed the destructive activities of marauding gangs called *Nian* in the regions of northern Anhui, southern Shandong, and southern Henan. As the Taiping Rebellion was getting under way this increased as the numbers of the *Nian* swelled with starving peasants who had faced flooding of the *Huang He* (Yellow River) in 1851 and 1855. The Qing government was unable to provide assistance due to being distracted by both the Taiping Rebellion and by Western aggression.[9] At the same time (1856–59), these *Nian* groups were both encouraged by the early successes of the Taiping against government forces, and also presented themselves as allies of those rural communities who feared the upheaval brought by the approach of Taiping armies. Many significant clan leaders threw in their lot with the *Nian*. Plundering of other areas by these *Nian* forces only added to societal misery and turbulence. The region was finally pacified when imperial forces established lines of fortifications along the *Huang He* and the Grand Canal after 1866, which contained the revolt. By 1868, the *Nian*-related uprisings had been suppressed.

At the same time that warfare was centered on the areas ruled by the Taiping leadership and under the control of the *Nian*, violence erupted in other areas too. This was accelerated by the reduced power of the Qing government. For example, longstanding rivalry between Chinese and Muslim miners in central Yunnan led to a severe outbreak of intercommunal violence in 1855. This resulted in the slaughter of many Muslims in and around the provincial capital, Kunming. This added to the escalating death toll of this violent decade. As well as being caused by religious and ethnic tensions and the weakness of imperial administration, there is evidence that imperial officials supported non-Muslim Chinese communities, which led to Muslims rebelling against both their non-Muslim Chinese neighbors and the imperial government generally. The 1855 conflict triggered a wider uprising of Islamic communities in Yunnan that lasted until 1873, long after the collapse of the Taiping Rebellion.

All of this exacerbated the problems caused by the Taiping Rebellion itself and added to the huge number of casualties. The Taiping

---

9. Shichor, "Crackdowns," 98.

armies, those who opposed them, and those other groups who had risen up in arms, carried out acts of terrible brutality. Mass conscription[10] was accompanied by the devastation of the land and populations in "enemy" areas. Tens of thousands were deliberately slaughtered. In Nanjing, the Taiping are estimated to have butchered about 40,000 Manchu civilians.[11] In Ts'ang-chou the Taiping slaughtered some 10,000 Manchus.[12] The Qing forces retaliated in similar fashion. As Guangxi was the epicenter of the rebellion, vast numbers of rebels who spoke its dialect were killed.[13] Mass killings of *Hakkas* in the province of Guangdong reputedly reached a million people dead.[14]

This was accompanied by famine and disease, which attended such widespread disruption of farming and trade, and the movement of war-related refugees. Indeed, it has been concluded that

> A few thousand died in battle, but the ultimate toll was in the tens of millions, because agriculture and commerce were disrupted; the vast majority of deaths were from starvation or from local breakdowns of law and order systems.[15]

However, it should be added that breakdowns in law and order included the deliberate killing of civilians. And the atrocities committed against civilians by armed forces were many and appalling. We should not assume that the vast numbers dead were solely collateral damage attending societal breakdown. This undoubtedly was a major factor; but the fact remains that vast numbers of unarmed civilians of all ages were deliberately put to death.

Overall, it has been estimated that somewhere between 20 and 30 million people died due to this rebellion and related upheavals.[16] Some figures have ranged as high as 50 million deaths.[17] What is striking is that civilian deaths far outnumbered military casualties.[18] The lower Yangtze provinces, for example, lost huge numbers of their population, although

---

10. Spence, *God's Chinese Son*, 172–91.
11. White, *Atrocities*, 289.
12. Clodfelter, *Warfare and Armed Conflicts*, 256.
13. Ho, *Studies on the Population of China*, 237.
14. Kiang, *Hakka Odyssey*, 120.
15. Anderson, *East Asian World-System*, 219
16. Meyer-Fong, *What Remains*, 1–2.
17. Shichor, "Crackdowns," 98.
18. Nishikawa, *Human Security in Southeast Asia*, 2.

immigrants from less-damaged areas moved in to take over abandoned land. The area that experienced the Muslim rebellions also suffered massive devastation and depopulation. It has been estimated that as late as the start of the twentieth century many affected areas had not yet recovered from the severe damage caused to industry and farming.

The long-term impact of this devastation was to further undermine the effectiveness and capability of the imperial Chinese government. Although the Qing had won, the dynasty was so weakened by the rebellion that it was never again able to establish an effective hold over the country that was officially under its rule. Weaknesses in the regime had already been ruthlessly exploited by Western colonial powers in the first half of the nineteenth century; but this process was accelerated by the chaos facing the imperial government due to the Taiping Rebellion and related civil unrest within China from 1850 onwards.

The Qing regime had only succeeded in suppressing the revolts by relying on local armies, provided and funded by the regional gentry, and whose aim was to defeat popular uprisings that threatened their social and economic position. As a direct consequence, the central government survived because it relied on a process of continued militarized decentralization that further weakened its effective control over the country. Manchu rule, in effect, was only sustainable because of actions that enhanced the power of those Chinese warlords who had put down the various rebellions in the name of the Manchu rulers.

Later events—such as the Sino-Japanese War of 1894–95 and the wars with Japan that devastated China in the twentieth century—were hugely influenced by outside forces making the most of the opportunities occasioned by the further weakening of imperial power that had been accelerated by the nineteenth-century internal upheavals. Japan was now added to the Western colonial powers who had already been aggressively exploiting China for their own ends. The continuation of the "century of humiliation" was further accelerated by the failed apocalyptic rebellion of the Taiping.

Curiously, both the later Chinese Communist Party and the Chinese Nationalists (who lost in the civil war they fought with the communists) have traced some of their origins to the Taipings. What is indisputable is that the Taipings made a huge contribution to the way China developed after 1864.

ECHOES OF MILLENARIANISM AFTER THE TAIPING

The Taiping Rebellion was not the only Chinese apocalyptic movement. The "Righteous Harmony Society" during the "Boxer Rebellion" (1899–1901) was a Chinese movement reacting against Western colonialism.[19] Like the Taiping, it also had apocalyptic characteristics. Its supporters—known as "Boxers" to the English—blamed problems facing China on foreign influence and on China's Christian converts who the Boxers claimed had supposedly alienated the traditional Chinese gods.

The Boxers destroyed foreign property and murdered Christian missionaries and Chinese Christians. In June 1900, the Boxers, convinced that they were invulnerable to foreign weapons, moved on Beijing. Their slogan was: "Support the Qing government and exterminate the foreigners."

Foreign diplomats, Christian missionaries, foreign soldiers, and some Chinese Christians took refuge in the diplomatic Legation Quarter in Beijing. There they were besieged for fifty-five days by the Chinese Imperial Army and the Boxers. An eight-nation invasion of China broke the siege, defeated the Boxers, and forced major concessions from the Qing government. Another Chinese apocalyptic movement—this time in support of the Qing dynasty—had ended in defeat and the further weakening of the Chinese state.

---

19. See: Purcell, *Boxer Uprising*.

CHAPTER 13

When the Millennium Goes Rogue
The Thousand-Year Nazi Third Reich

THE NAZIS TRUMPETED 1933 as the start of a "Thousand-Year Reich." This was no mere coincidence of numbers in its echoing of the thousand-year millennium concept. For while the Nazi Party was not a Christian organization in any way, shape, or form (indeed, for all its frequent mentions of God, it was explicitly anti-Christian for anyone who cared to look in detail), it drew heavily on a cultural hinterland of Christian millenarian traditions combined with the Norse and later Wagnerian concept of the "Twilight of the gods" (*Götterdämmerung*).

This chapter explores how this manipulation of apocalyptic themes and tropes—torn out of their cultural contexts and largely secularized—led to the semireligious cult of both the messianic leader (Hitler) and the nature of the "millennial reich" itself. This revealed itself in Nazi racial elitism, iconography, and pageantry.

The appalling genocide of the Holocaust, committed against the Jewish population within territories controlled by the Germans or by compliant collaborationist regimes, was termed the "Final Solution" (*Endlösung*) precisely because the Nazis saw it (and their constructed fantasy of so-called "Jewish-Bolshevism") as a struggle between what they termed "good" and "evil." It was, in effect, political eschatology.[1] This was, for the Nazi regime, an end-times "struggle" (*kampf*)—a favorite Nazi term—which would settle the fate of humanity for all future time.

1. See: Redles, "National Socialist Millennialism," 545.

It was the most prominent among a series of racially inspired genocides by which the Nazis sought to remove all those whom they proclaimed had no place within their "New Order" (*Neuordnung*). This latter term was an implicit secular echo of eschatological language of transformation through conflict and purging. It is significant that Hitler specifically used this term, at Berlin *Sportpalast*, in the year that Germany began its titanic struggle with the USSR and escalated its murderous persecution of the Jews to outright genocide: "I am convinced that 1941 will be the crucial year of a great New Order in Europe."[2]

Then, as the Third Reich imploded in 1945, the doom-laden determination to see a world go down in flames once more revealed the secularized apocalyptic obsession of the Nazi leadership and its exultation of death and judgment falling on a "failing" German people who (in the eyes of the leadership) had not lived up to their responsibilities as a new "chosen people." This also reached back to the ancient, pagan Norse idea of the catastrophic day of *Ragnarok*. But this Nazi version was not a mythological construct. Instead, in 1945, it was a catastrophe enacted on the streets of German cities.

THE BACKSTORY OF THE GERMAN *VÖLKISCH* MILLENARIAN APOCALYPSE

The roots of Nazi ideology were firmly embedded in nineteenth-century nationalism and racism. In its origins, the Nazi Party was originally one of many tiny *völkisch* (ethnic/racist) parties in Bavaria. The common feature of such groups was their racist belief in the purity of German blood and German culture. Beyond that core ideology, their beliefs were a mixture of extreme nationalism, antisemitism, and militarism, blended with a radical and semisocialist resentment of capitalism, large department stores, and unearned profits. As such they were difficult to place on any political spectrum, since they represented the anxieties, fears, and resentments of those who felt themselves squeezed from both "above" and "below." "Below them were the unionized workers with their internationalist allegiances to class rather than race; above them were the more comfortably off and the rich, whose nationalism was basically conservative."[3]

---

2. "Hitler Quotes," Line 78.
3. Whittock, *Brief History of the Third Reich*, 4.

While expressing their allegiance to Christian values (Catholic in southern Germany, Protestant in the north) in the face of atheistic communism, they actually represented a secularized semireligious exaltation of the *völk* (race). This was rooted in nineteenth-century biological/racial nationalism, a form of "bastardized Darwinism." This held that the "Aryan race" (white and Germanic) was the superior race. As such, the Aryans had both the right and the obligation (as defenders of civilization and culture) to rule over all other races. "The Jews, in complete contrast, were seen as a kind of 'anti-race,' dangerous inhuman beings in seemingly human form."[4] In the Nazi racial view there was a hierarchy of races, and while Jews were depicted as occupying the key malevolent place at the very bottom of it, the view also subjugated all other ethnic and racial groups to the Aryan. To the Nazis, races were in a constant state of conflict for dominance. It has been described as "Social Darwinism."

The Nazi ideology was rooted in a wide range of earlier philosophical, biological, anthropological, and nationalist writings by people as diverse as: Friedrich Nietzsche (died 1900), Herbert Spencer (died 1903), Arthur de Gobineau (died 1882), Wilhelm Marr (died 1904), and the music and culture espoused by Richard Wagner (died 1883). However, it was also undeniably rooted in a long tradition of Christian antisemitism. However, unlike this belief, which was rooted in ideas about faith and culture, the *völkisch* antisemitism developed by the Nazis claimed to be biological and scientific. Nevertheless, the shared heritage of intolerance allowed them to present themselves as modern representatives of a traditional Christian position.

What is also clear is that the *völkisch* concept of conflict between what was perceived as "good" versus "evil" also drew on adapted and hijacked themes and tropes that were well known in the European Christian millenarian and apocalyptic tradition. The Nazis presented history as characterized by this struggle and culminating in what was, in effect, a secularized version of Armageddon that would see a titanic struggle settling the future destiny of humanity. In many ways it was the imagery and themes of the book of Revelation reimagined as a secular *völkisch* war (fought both culturally and actually). The victory of the *völk* would lead to a golden age of earthly harmony, following the destruction of racial enemies. That this was termed a "Thousand-Year Reich" was a clear echo of the millenarian language of Christianity. The number was

---

4. Silberklang, "Roots of Nazi Ideology," lines 3–9.

no coincidence. On the other hand, the Nazis clearly felt little sympathy with Christianity (despite their manipulation of Christian imagery and themes), and this is seen in their enthusiasm for reimagined Germanic pagan customs and ceremonies.

THE FIRST WORLD WAR AS THE BEGINNING OF A TIME OF "STRUGGLE"

Most millenarian movements have a trigger moment that they view as setting the "end-times clock" running. The conflagration—and for Germany, the eventual humiliation—of the First World War played a major part in the Nazi millenarian outlook.[5]

As Germany faced defeat in November 1918, it was disintegrating: sailors mutinied in the ports of Wilhelmshaven, Kiel, and Hamburg; workers and ex-soldiers set up revolutionary *soviets* (revolutionary councils, named after those recently established in communist Russia) in Berlin and other cities; the German Emperor—Kaiser Wilhelm II—fled to Holland. In 1919, the new democratic Weimar government agreed to the Treaty of Versailles that formally ended the war. The victorious Allies imposed a very harsh set of demands on Germany to weaken it so that it would never again threaten the peace of Europe.

This fueled the foundation myth of the Nazis and other German nationalists. Unable to accept that the German army had been defeated, they preferred to believe it had been betrayed by socialist politicians, communists, and Jews (despite the small size of the German Jewish population and its high level of integration into German society). In addition, the harsh treatment of Germany by the Treaty of Versailles made it easier to direct anger at Germany's enemies abroad than admit that German military ambitions had brought many of these problems on itself.

The situation was made worse in 1923 when the French occupied the German Ruhr coalfields, leading to hyperinflation. Money rapidly lost its value. By November 1923, it cost 200,000,000,000 marks to buy just one US dollar.[6]

In many ways, 1918–19 started the "end-times clock" ticking for German nationalists, which would lead to a future conflict designed to

---

5. Redles, "National Socialist Millennialism," 530–31.
6. Whittock, *Brief History of the Third Reich*, 9.

reverse the situation. Symbolically, Hitler titled the account of his political awakening and these turbulent years as: *Mein Kampf* (My Struggle).

HITLER AS "MESSIAH" FOR A RACIST MILLENNIUM

A self-conscious "messiah cult" developed around the person of Adolf Hitler.[7] It was one that he consciously fostered[8] and that was willingly taken up by followers who had lost whatever faith they once had (if any) in democratic norms and processes. This cult of the *Führer* (Leader) defied rational analysis and encouraged blind faith in one "sent by God" to rescue Germany from its plight. The terms "God" and "the Almighty" were used to express the idea that Hitler represented a providentially ordained path for the German people. The terms were empty of any theological content and could mean anything or nothing to those who used them.

The vacuous nature of Nazi religious belief was clearly demonstrated in the fact that the most dedicated Nazis hankered for a return to a semipagan set of vague rituals and beliefs picked out of the Germanic pagan past. They filled Nazi religiosity with whatever ideas and images suited their new "pick-n-mix," semipagan faith. Those Catholic and Protestant Germans who hailed Hitler as God's representative demonstrated a cognitive dissonance of extraordinary proportions. The SS, for example, provided a black-uniformed "nationalist religious order," and regarded themselves as Nazi crusaders and members of a military order of Nordic men that was engaged in holy war against enemies of Nazism.[9] Semipagan marriage rites were favored by the SS along with celebrations of the solstices. A cult grew up around those who had died in Hitler's failed coup in Munich in 1923. The Nazi rallies—with their use of light, flags, and sound—were events that were designed to encourage a religious fervor towards Hitler and the Nazi movement. German farmers attended the "Reich Harvest Thanksgiving Festival" (*Das Reichserntedankfest*) between 1933 and 1937 on the Bückeberg, a prominent hill near the town of Hamelin. Based on the Nazi concept of "Blood and Soil" (which Nazis

---

7. Redles, "National Socialist Millennialism," 529.
8. Redles, "National Socialist Millennialism," 534–37.
9. Stein, *Waffen SS*, 122–23.

believed underpinned German racial existence), in 1937 the festival was attended by approximately 1.2 million people.[10]

Revealingly, it was the Nazis who coined the term "neopaganism," although Himmler (head of the SS) was always more of an enthusiast than Hitler.[11] The former did not believe in much when it came to religion, and the latter basically believed in nothing much beyond himself.[12] In the period between 1933 (Hitler's accession) and 1945 (the end of the Third Reich) this neopaganism had a following within the party, but it did not receive official encouragement from the state.[13] That would have been going too far in a traditionally Christian nation. However, it seems that it would have been more actively pursued in the event of a German victory and in the aftermath of a failure to successfully dominate the German churches. Hitler believed that Nazism and organized religion could not coexist in the long term.[14] Science, he believed, would eventually destroy what he termed "superstition."[15] In short, those members of the Christian churches who in 1933 had hoped for some kind of working relationship with the Third Reich had been in a state of denial regarding the nature of the new regime.

THE FINAL TITANIC STRUGGLE: THE NAZI VIEW OF WAR AND GENOCIDE

A world war was not the original aim of Hitler in 1939. Since the mid-1930s he had broken international agreements and then aggressively acted towards neighboring states without facing the consequences. When he led Germany to war against Poland, in September 1939, he clearly thought he could do the same. Then the additional victories of 1940 in Western Europe reinforced this confidence. It was not to last. Britain and its empire would not come to terms. Then, in 1941, Germany and its allies invaded the USSR and, in December, Hitler declared war on the US. A "world war" was now being fought, and the struggle was becoming an existential conflict for survival. As this occurred, the Nazis came to view

---

10. Benz, *Concise History*, 82.
11. Morris, *Religion and Anthropology*, 293.
12. See: Overy, *Dictators*, 281
13. Stackelberg, *Routledge Companion to Nazi Germany*, 137.
14. See: Overy, *Dictators*, 287.
15. Evans, *Third Reich at War*, 547.

it through an eschatological lens. For them it was the equivalent of the "great tribulation" referred to in the New Testament and in two millennia of Christian thought. As war escalated, it was accompanied by racially motivated genocide(s).

The Nazis were always committed to racially motivated persecution of those they considered inferior in the Nazi "New Order." However, it was the escalating nature of the war, and especially the war with the USSR on the Eastern Front, that saw savage persecution develop into explicit genocide.

In *Mein Kampf* (written in 1923), Hitler's earlier attacks on Jewish capitalists became overshadowed by his new focus on what he called "Jewish Bolshevism."[16] According to this construct, the Jews dominated the world through their control of the two (actually contradictory) forces of Bolshevism (Russian communism) and world capitalism. The fact that these two groups were completely opposed to each other posed no difficulty to Hitler and the Nazis. As far as they were concerned the Jews were behind both, and both were the enemies of German nationalism. It was the equivalent of traditional antisemitism—that saw the "hand of the Jew" behind every calamity—and twenty-first-century "deep state" conspiracy theories that attempt to link a wide range of opponents through a fantastical, imaginary, worldwide group of enemies.

These Nazi theorists (as modern believers in QAnon) lived in a strange mental landscape that suited their personal needs and phobias but bore no resemblance to the landscape of the real world. As a consequence, for Hitler, the struggle was one to the death between Germany and these two linked systems.[17] When, in 1941, Germany invaded the USSR, it was the climax of this crusade against "Jewish-Bolshevism."[18] The "Nazi great tribulation" was leading to their own version of Armageddon.

Long before 1941, it was clear that Europe's Jews were to be targeted for brutal treatment in this struggle.[19] SS atrocities against Jews occurred in the first weeks of the Polish campaign in September 1939. However, the long-term Nazi intention at this point in the war was not clear. In September 1939, Heydrich (a senior SS officer) made a speech to SS *Einsatzgruppen* (special action groups) explaining that the "final

16. Michaelis, "'Jewish Bolshevism,'" 112.

17. Kershaw, *Hitler, 1889–1936*, 244–46; Redles, "National Socialist Millennialism," 542.

18. Redles, "National Socialist Millennialism," 543.

19. Redles, "National Socialist Millennialism," 543.

goal" (*Endziel*) was a territorial solution whereby all Jews (including Jews from Germany) would be sent to eastern reservations. At this point in the war the destination probably envisaged was the Lublin area, in the eastern part of German-occupied Poland.[20] One of the earliest uses of the term "Final Solution" (*Endlösung*) appeared in December 1939, in a document produced by the Jewish Affairs specialists of the SS security service (the SD) in Berlin. But, at this time, it still implied a form of brutal reservation.[21] This policy was accompanied by driving Jews into ghettoes, where huge numbers died from disease and brutality. But this was not yet outright genocide.

This changed in 1941. As the Germans prepared for war against the USSR—and then as they put this plan into operation—there was widespread talk at the highest levels of nothing less than serial genocides.[22] In May 1941, a meeting of German state secretaries calculated mass starvation of the civilian population in the USSR. Later that year (in November 1941), Reichsmarschall Göring told the Italian foreign minister that, within a year, 20 to 30 million people would starve to death in the USSR. At the same time the SS chief Himmler oversaw the production of a resettlement plan that envisaged the deportation of 31 million people to Siberia, consisting of all Jews, 80 to 85 percent of Poles, 75 percent of Belorussians, and 64 percent of western Ukrainians.[23] Hitler (according to notes made by the German general Halder, after a meeting in March 1941) specifically stated: "This is a war of extermination."[24] The "Nazi great tribulation" was becoming a "racial Armageddon."[25]

From the early stages of the invasion of the USSR, SS *Einsatzgruppen*, SD security police units, and Order Police battalions (units drawn from the German police force and employed in the occupied territories) began a process of killing people described as "Jewish-Bolshevik enemies" and encouraging pogroms by the local populations. After 15 October 1941, the deportations eastwards of German Jews and those in German-occupied Czech lands (soon to be extended to all Jews in Europe) extended the scope of Nazi killing. A number of historians have suggested that the

20. Friedländer, *Years of Extermination*, 30 and 187; Gellately, *Lenin, Stalin and Hitler*, 370.
21. Kershaw, *Hitler, the Germans, and the Final Solution*, 19.
22. Gellately, *Lenin, Stalin and Hitler*, 425.
23. Gellately, *Lenin, Stalin and Hitler*, 423–25.
24. Gellately, *Lenin, Stalin and Hitler*, 422.
25. Redles, "National Socialist Millennialism," 545.

expansion of the killing accompanied the Soviet counteroffensive before Moscow and Hitler's declaration of war on the US in December 1941 that turned the conflict into a world war.[26] This seems convincing as it escalated the war into an existential struggle.

On 11 December 1941, Germany declared war on the US. The very next day Hitler met with Nazi *gauleiters* (regional Nazi Party leaders), and Goebbels' diary records the message he gave:

> He prophesied to the Jews that if they once more brought about another world war, they would experience their extermination. That is no mere talk. The World War is here, the extermination of the Jews must be the necessary consequence.[27]

On 18 December, Himmler, after a meeting with Hitler, noted in his desk calendar: "Jewish question: to be exterminated as partisans."[28]

In March 1942, it has been estimated that 75 to 80 percent of the victims of the "Final Solution" (Holocaust) were still alive. However, by the end of March 1943, only about 20 to 25 percent of those who were to be murdered were still living. The bulk of the killing, in 1942–43, took place at three extermination centers: Belzec, Treblinka, and Sobibor. These were the "Operation Reinhard Camps" and were named after senior SS officer Heydrich, who had been assassinated in June 1942. The genocidal killings also took place at centers that functioned as both concentration camps and extermination sites. These were Chelmno, Majdanek, and, most infamously, at Auschwitz-Birkenau. In total the "Operation Reinhard Camps" murdered 1.7 million people in their period of operation (between March 1942 and December 1943). At Auschwitz alone, over 1 million Jewish people and 250,000 non-Jews were murdered between 1941 and 1945.[29] Auschwitz was the site of the greatest number of deaths in one place in the Nazi extermination campaign. This was genocide unparalleled in history.

While the victims were overwhelmingly Jewish, this apocalyptic slaughter also included huge numbers of Slavs, Roma, and Sinti. Others who died included the mentally and physically disabled, homosexuals,

---

26. Gerlach, "Wannsee Conference," 106–61.
27. Gellately, *Lenin, Stalin and Hitler*, 458.
28. Gellately, *Lenin, Stalin and Hitler*, 458.
29. Whittock, *Brief History of the Third Reich*, 248–49; Hilberg, *Destruction of the European Jews*, 3:894.

and political opponents. The Nazi New Order created a sea of blood and suffering.

"ARMAGEDDON" 1945

The war against the USSR and the US and their allies was unwinnable. As Germany spiraled into defeat in 1945, the destructive nature of Nazism turned inward as well as outward. Hitler's outlook on life had always been expressed in the term: *flucht nach vorn* (in essence meaning: "when in a tight spot, attack"). As a political gambler, his instinct was always to go for broke. In the past it had wrong-footed opponents and amazed allies; after 1941 it was escalating crisis into disaster. As the Third Reich imploded after 1943, the *Führer* reverted more and more to type: wild gambles, refusals to give ground, preposterous versions of reality, and a refusal to hear any criticisms of his actions. Field Marshal Paul von Kleist judged Hitler's mentality, by this stage in the war, as being "more of a problem for a psychiatrist than for a general."[30] The personality and strategies that had once propelled him to power were now accelerating Germany into the abyss of cataclysmic defeat.

The "Nazi messiah" was incapable of self-criticism. His apocalyptic ideology was creating an Armageddon that was now engulfing Germany, as it had already engulfed Europe, and those who had failed him in his millenarian mission were now judged unworthy of survival. Hitler ordered the destruction of Germany as his forces retreated (an order often ignored by those who now looked to the possibility of a future after the Nazis). He cared nothing for the people that he had once hailed as the Aryan supermen and superwomen.

He was not alone in this callous abandonment of his own people. Goebbels expressed similar sentiments to one of his subordinates:

> "I never compelled anybody to work for me, just as we didn't compel the German people. They themselves gave us the job to do. Why did you work with me? Now, you'll have your little throat cut." Striding towards the door, he turned round once more and shouted: "but the earth will shake when we leave the scene..."[31]

---

30. Roberts, *Storm of War*, 531.
31. Noakes and Pridham, *Nazism 1919–1945*, 28–29.

At about 3:30 pm on 30 April 1945, Hitler committed suicide in his underground bunker below the Reich Chancellery. Above him, Berlin was a blazing ruin. His brutal vision of life had finally ended in a defeat that was reminiscent of Wagner's *Götterdämmerung* (the mythical war of the Norse gods that in ancient Germanic legend was thought to bring about the end of the world), also known as the Norse Day of *Ragnarok*. The Nazi millennium had failed and had been engulfed in apocalyptic violence.

The Third Reich was to have lasted 1,000 years; in reality, it lasted less than thirteen. But in that time it had caused the deaths of about 40 million people, led to the genocide against the Jews, destroyed vast areas of Europe, and had enslaved millions.

CHAPTER 14

Contested "Zionisms"

"Zionism" is a term that describes a Jewish nationalist movement that has as its objective the creation and the support of a Jewish homeland (a Jewish nation-state) in Palestine. As a result of the crushing of Jewish resistance to Rome in the first and second centuries AD, Jewish people had been dispersed across large areas of the eastern parts of the Roman Empire. This forcefully added to a diaspora that had already seen significant Jewish communities being established in Egypt, Asia Minor, and further afield in the centuries before the cataclysmic events of the early Christian era, which had seen Jewish aspirations for political independence crushed by Rome. The geographical focus in Zionism is on a return to the ancient homeland of the Jewish people and faith. In Hebrew this place is called *Eretz Yisra'el* (the Land of Israel).

Modern "Zionism," as we will see, originated in eastern and central Europe in the latter part of the nineteenth century. However, the movement was the latest manifestation of a deep connection of Jewish people with a particular area of the Middle East and the city of Jerusalem. One of the hills of this ancient city was known as Zion, hence the term "Zionism." For centuries, at Passover Jewish people have declared the hope: "Next year in Jerusalem."

However, the story—already traumatic and complex—is made more complicated still by the relationship of Christianity with Judaism; by contested focus on the Holy Land between Christianity, Judaism, and Islam; and by the deep interconnection between Jewish and Christian end-times beliefs and the role of the Jewish people within this. While aspects of this are shared by Islam, the belief in a providentially approved "return of Israel to the land" is a Judeo-Christian one.

As a result, the competing claims to the "holy land," the shared prophetic Scriptures, and the interaction of national identity with end-times hopes and aspirations means that this focus on the geography of "the land" and its role within providential history is much contested. As a result—while "Zionism" primarily refers to Jewish aspirations—Christians too have, in effect, laid claims to it. There are "contested Zionisms," and while some describe secular political programs, others describe apocalyptic visions and claims that are themselves subject to, at times violent, competition. And this is before one adds the Islamic dimension, since Islam too lays claim to Jerusalem as a holy city and a key place within end-times concepts and expectations.

THE CHRISTIAN DIMENSION

Within Christian beliefs, ideas regarding the place of the Jews in salvation (and cosmic) history have, at times, been highly significant. For while traditional Christianity from the later Roman Empire to the Reformation (and into modern times for a number of Christians) saw the church as inheriting the spiritual and temporal role of the "chosen people" of God (known as replacement theology or supercessionism), a revitalizing of interest in prophecy following the Reformation challenged key aspects of this outlook.[1]

Some Puritans (as we saw in chapter 7) saw themselves as being a "New Israel" and American colonies were even described as an "American Israel." It was as if all the expectations within Old and New Testament prophecy, which were anchored (figuratively or literally) in and around Jerusalem, had been reimagined and relocated to the North American continent.[2] This had a profound effect on emerging American self-image. It later had a huge impact on Mormonism in the nineteenth century, when it was claimed that Israelite tribes had migrated to North America.

Other Puritans, though, regarded a literal return of the Jews to the Middle East as necessary before the second coming of Jesus. This would accompany their conversion to Christianity. It is here that what is termed

---

1. Whittock, *End Times, Again?*, 112, 121.

2. See: Bercovitch, *American Jeremiad*; Bercovitch, *Puritan Origins*. Also see: Kaplan, *Our American Israel*, 5.

"Christian Zionism" became closely related to what would later emerge as "Jewish Zionism." The two shared a similar geographical preoccupation with the future of the "holy land." But there were, and are, major areas of difference between the two as well. A connected—but competing—set of "Zionisms" was being put in place. Within the Christian version a new and more positive attitude towards the Jews began to compete with the centuries-old antisemitic view of them as "Christ-killers" and eternally under the judgment of God.

This older view has continued within many Christian communities, and history has witnessed the pogroms of Russia, the antisemitic policies of Eastern Europe, the Dreyfus Affair in France, the genocidal activities of the Nazis and their allies, the antisemitism of the Ku Klux Klan in the US, and continued antisemitism being promoted by right-wing nationalist groups in Europe and elsewhere into the twenty-first century. However, with the emergence of "Christian Zionism," something new was being added to this complex outlook, something to compete with the mentality of pogroms and massacres. This could arguably often have a rather manipulative approach towards Jews (and Israel) and could—and can—appear to be as much about using Jews, as supporting them, in order to accelerate hoped-for Christian eschatological timetables. It has been argued that, in the sixteenth century, the bitter antisemitism of the older Martin Luther was largely due to the fact that the Jews had not responded to the Reformation changes and converted to Christianity. In short, they had failed to play their part in the "end-times script" as it had been envisaged by Luther. What followed was anger and threats by the disappointed Protestant reformer, directed against the Jews, using language of which the Nazis would have been proud. Nevertheless, overall the more engaged attitudes towards Jews (as expressed by a number of Protestants) still stands in stark contrast to a history of discrimination, persecution, and slaughter.

CROMWELL AND THE JEWS

This eschatological focus on the Jews has had direct political impacts. For example, in the 1650s, Oliver Cromwell encouraged the return of Jews to England (expelled in 1291 under the antisemitic Edward I) as a direct result of this more favorable view of the Jewish community and the necessity to encourage conversion in order to hasten the second coming of Christ.[3]

This view also included economic calculations. Spanish and Portuguese Jews who had been expelled from Spain had settled in the Netherlands. Their financial and entrepreneurial skills assisted Amsterdam's development as a port city and in international trading. The Dutch were religious compatriots but economic rivals of the British, and Cromwell hoped that allowing Jewish immigration would assist the London-based economy.

Cromwell was also encouraged in this outlook by the influential rabbi, Menasseh ben Israel, who lived in Amsterdam. In October 1655, Cromwell submitted his proposals as a seven-point petition to the ruling Council of State. It called for Jews to be allowed to return to Britain. Not everyone was convinced by this reversal of policy. In December, the proposal faced opposition at the Whitehall Conference. Nevertheless, it was resolved that an unofficial readmission would be tolerated. It was rather half-hearted but still of great historic importance.

As a result, in 1656, Cromwell made a verbal promise, backed by the Council of State, which allowed Jews to return to Britain and which guaranteed their right to practice their religion without molestation. In response, a significant number of Jews took up this opportunity and relocated. However, it was not until 1858 that formal political emancipation was granted to Jews and they were eventually allowed free access to all levels of society and education. It is a notable example of how tolerance is not the same as warm acceptance and equal rights.

THE EMERGENCE OF "CHRISTIAN ZIONISM"

The idea of the Jews playing a key role in the lead-up to the second coming of Christ diminished with the Restoration of 1660 but continued to be debated among the Puritans of New England. In Britain, this Christian Zionism came to prominence again in the nineteenth century and accompanied the weakening of the Ottoman Empire and the importance of the "Eastern Question" in British imperial politics. It involved facilitating the return of the Jews to Palestine.

People as diverse as the Particular (Calvinist) Baptist preacher Charles Spurgeon (died 1892) and the evangelical Anglican and political

3. Whittock, *When God Was King*, 164.

reformer Lord Shaftesbury (died 1885) advocated it. Indeed, Anthony Ashley-Cooper, seventh earl of Shaftesbury (president of the London Society for Promoting Christianity Amongst the Jews) wrote to the UK's Prime Minister Aberdeen (prime minister 1852–55) in 1853, urging a Jewish homeland in Palestine as a means of stabilizing the region. It was not his first action regarding this idea. As early as 1839, Shaftesbury had published an article in the *Quarterly Review*, which constituted the first recorded proposal by a major politician to resettle Jews in Palestine.[4] Then again, in 1841, he wrote an article in the *Colonial Times* entitled: "Memorandum to Protestant Monarchs of Europe for the restoration of the Jews to Palestine."

Lord Shaftesbury was a premillennialist and believed in the imminent second coming of Christ. This made the matter of the Jews an urgent issue to be addressed. He played a major role in the emergence of mature Christian Zionism.[5] His letter to PM Aberdeen revealingly stated that what was then termed "Greater Syria" within the Ottoman Empire was "a country without a nation" in need of "a nation without a country." Furthermore, he added that the Jews are "the ancient and rightful lords of the soil."[6] In his diary he wrote: "There is a country without a nation; and God now in his wisdom and mercy, directs us to a nation without a country."[7]

This early use of the phrase "A land without a people for a people without a land" echoes the words of Alexander Keith (died 1880), who was another British proponent of the restoration of the Jews to Palestine as part of fulfillment of biblical prophecy. Neither seemed particularly aware of the people who were already occupying the land and whose ancestors had done so for many centuries. It was an intellectual, moral, and theological oversight that would run and run. And the modern conflict between Israeli and Palestinian (Muslim and minority Christian) is a result of the fact that while there was "a people without a land," there most definitely was not "a land without a people."

It was in such an outlook that theological beliefs and imperial geopolitics became inextricably entwined; an interaction still apparent in the

---

4. Masalha, *Zionist Bible*, 83.
5. Larsen, *Company of the Preachers*, 463.
6. Hyamson, "British Projects," 140.
7. See: Garfinkle, "On the Origin," 539–50.

Middle Eastern policies of Donald Trump and the political agenda of the US evangelical right in the twenty-first century.

This "Jewish Restoration" approach, as seen in the UK in the nineteenth and early twentieth centuries, combined a wish to save Jews from Russian pogroms but, at the same time, avoided immigration into the UK. It was rooted in an aversion to immigration of foreigners (which often signposted antisemitism on the part of UK politicians but certainly signposted it as existing among many of their constituents) with an apparently warm attitude towards the Jews—as long as they settled somewhere else. This led to support for the idea by the young Winston Churchill. It eventually produced the historic Balfour Declaration of 1917, promising a homeland in Palestine for the Jews, which was firmly rooted in Christian Zionist beliefs as well as in imperial ambitions and the needs of the First World War to gain Jewish support for the Allied cause.

"JEWISH ZIONISM" AS AN ENGINE OF SECULAR GEOPOLITICAL CHANGE

As we have seen, politically active and influential "Christian Zionists" intermittently engaged with the idea of the restoration of Jews to Palestine between 1655 and 1917. However, the primary driver of geopolitical change in the Middle East came from within the Jewish community itself.

As we saw in chapter 6, in the sixteenth and seventeenth centuries several self-proclaimed "messiahs" appeared within Jewish communities across Europe and promoted the idea of a return to Palestine. This was as eschatologically motivated as the "Christian Zionism" that emerged towards the end of this period. Both movements saw a Jewish return to "the land" as being part of end-times events and presaging divine intervention that would transform the world order. However, what later emerged as "Jewish Zionism" in the nineteenth century (constituting what many would regard as the definitive form of the ideal) was rooted more in secular aspirations for security and safety than apocalyptic change.[8] This stands in sharp contrast to the millenarianism that drove the formation of "Christian Zionism."

Following the failure of Jewish eschatological activities in the sixteenth and seventeenth centuries, the *Haskala* (Jewish Enlightenment) movement developed in the late eighteenth century. This encouraged

---

8. Brasher, "Millennialism in Contemporary Israeli Politics," 69–70.

Jews to assimilate into Western (secular) culture.[9] It is notable that by the early nineteenth century the belief in a return of Jews to the Palestinian homeland was kept alive almost entirely by Christian millenarians who continued the outlook first associated with Oliver Cromwell. However, despite the efforts of the promoters of *Haskala*, most of the Jews in Eastern Europe (for example in Poland and western Russia) did not assimilate into gentile societies. At the same time, they became the object of vicious antisemitic tsarist pogroms. In response the Russian society known as *Hovevei Zion/Ziyyon* (Lovers of Zion) movement was formed that promoted the idea of the settlement of Jewish farmers and artisans in Palestine.[10] Herein lay the roots of modern "Jewish Zionism."

In 1897, Theodor Herzl convened the first Zionist Congress at Basel, in Switzerland. This drew up the Basel Program that declared that "Zionism strives to create for the Jewish people a home in Palestine secured by public law."[11] Herzl was an Austrian journalist who personally regarded assimilation as the most desirable option but who concluded that, in view of the depth of antisemitism, it was virtually impossible to realize. Only a national homeland, he believed, could provide security for the Jews.

At first the center of the movement was in Vienna where the weekly *Die Welt* (The World) was published. In addition, Zionist congresses met there yearly until 1901. After that they met every two years. In 1904, the leadership of the movement moved from Vienna to Cologne, and then relocated again to Berlin.

Failing to find support for Zionism among Ottoman officials, the movement increasingly looked to Britain. In response, the British government offered 6,000 square miles (15,500 square km) of Uganda for settlement in 1903.[12] Here was land but not in the right place.

At first Zionism did not attract a strong following. Before 1914, only a minority of European Jews subscribed to it (most of them were Russian, although the leadership was Austrian and German in the main). However, pogroms and restrictive legislation in the Russian Empire accelerated support for the movement and caused growing numbers of young Russian Jews to emigrate to Palestine. By the outbreak of the First World War in 1914, there were about 90,000 Jews living in Palestine. Of these,

9. Feiner, *Jewish Enlightenment*.
10. Campos, *Ottoman Brothers*, 219.
11. Medoff and Waxman, *Historical Dictionary of Zionism*, 233.
12. See: Rovner, *In the Shadow of Zion*, 52.

about 13,000 settlers lived in forty-three Jewish agricultural settlements as agricultural pioneers.[13]

During the First World War, Chaim Weizmann and Nahum Sokolow (both rooted in the Russian Jewish community), worked with the British government, leading to the Balfour Declaration in November 1917. The declaration became part of Britain's League of Nations mandate over Palestine from 1922, when it took over administration from the defeated Ottomans.

In March 1925, the Jewish population in Palestine was officially estimated at 108,000. By 1933, it had risen to about 238,000 or 20 percent of the population.[14] It began to accelerate after Hitler came to power in 1933. As it did so, the Arab population (which feared that Palestine would become a Jewish state) began a trenchant resistance to both Zionism and the British. Violence escalated. From 1936 to 1939, a major Arab uprising in Palestine led to the British restricting Jewish immigration. This occurred in 1939, the year that the start of warfare began the most terrible persecution of Jews in world history. These new restrictions were opposed by Zionist underground groups. Zionist "freedom fighters" (or "terrorists," depending on who assessed them) included the "Stern Gang" and the "*Irgun Zvai Leumi*." In addition to bombings and assassinations, these groups also organized illegal Jewish immigration to Palestine.

After 1945, and following the Nazi Holocaust, many European Jews saw their only hope of future safety lying in migration to Palestine. The British could not manage the resulting conflict between Jewish communities and the indigenous Arab population. Violence spiraled. The matter was given to the newly created United Nations, which in 1947 proposed a partition of the land along religious/ethnic lines. Jerusalem would be an international city.[15]

The creation of the state of Israel in May 1948 led to an invasion by neighboring Arab countries (the Arab-Israeli War, 1948–49) intent on snuffing out the new nation. It was not to be. The Arab invasions were successfully resisted by the Jewish Israeli forces. When an armistice was signed in 1949, Israel was larger than the territory originally allotted to it under the United Nations partition plan of 1947. It was a staggering and historic achievement, and the Middle East had been dramatically

---

13. Stefon, *Judaism*, 151.
14. Stefon, *Judaism*, 151.
15. *Jerusalem: The Future of the Holy City for Three Monotheisms*, 147.

reconfigured. In time the US became the protector of Israel and the USSR of the Arab states opposing the new nation. Cold War politics were being drawn into the end-times equation.

As a result of the conflict, since 1948 approximately 800,000 Arabs have fled or have been expelled (a feature often glossed over) from the area that became Israel.[16] A geopolitical earthquake has transformed the "political landscape" of the Middle East. But to what extent is it an "apocalyptic earthquake?"

ZIONISM AS AN ESCHATOLOGICAL MOVEMENT?

Zionism is not intrinsically an eschatological movement. For many who believe in it—in the past as now—it offers primarily earthly means by which Jewish lives, beliefs, liberty, and property can be secured in a hostile world. While it entailed a return to the biblical homeland this did not inevitably mean a commitment to apocalyptic expectations of what would come next. Indeed, from the outset, rabbis in Eastern Europe condemned the movement, "concerned that the Zionist millennial vision was an attempt to preempt the Messiah."[17] As a result, many rabbinical leaders rejected the Balfour Declaration of 1917.[18]

Consequently, Zionism is not intrinsically millenarian. Many of the original settlers were secular Jews—many of socialist ideology—who viewed their mission as nationally transformative but not a trigger that would cause the "day of the Lord" to occur. Indeed, the Israel of 1948 has, consequently, been described as "a socialist democratic state."[19]

In addition, much of modern Judaism (especially among Liberal and Reformed Jews) often tends to focus on belief in an ultimately redeemed world, without insisting on a personal Messiah. Some modern writers consider the activism of Jews in secular reforming and revolutionary movements as a secularized version of traditional Jewish beliefs in the Messiah and global transformation. And the traditional Orthodox view has been to eschew activities that might be interpreted as seeking to accelerate the pace of the apocalypse.

---

16. Stefon, *Judaism*, 151.
17. Brasher, "Millennialism in Contemporary Israeli Politics," 70.
18. Brasher, "Millennialism in Contemporary Israeli Politics," 70.
19. Brasher, "Millennialism in Contemporary Israeli Politics," 70.

Despite this, aspects of modern Jewish Zionism arguably include semimessianic or semimillenarian features. After all, the establishment of the state of Israel after 2,000 years of statelessness appears miraculous and a fulfillment of biblical prophetic promises. Among more Orthodox Jews the belief in the literal future appearance of the Messiah remains a fervent article of faith. In the context of this, it is not difficult to see why the conflicts that have centered on Israel since 1948 have (for some in this community, as for evangelical Christians) come to be viewed through an apocalyptic lens, even if they were initially reluctant to subscribe to a millenarian form of Zionism.

Viewed through such a lens, compromise with Arabs within or outside the borders of Israel is viewed as undermining a divine mandate. Indeed, expansion of territory becomes more than a simple security strategy. Instead, it becomes an integral part of restoring *Eretz Yisra'el* in a way reminiscent of the empire of Solomon in the Old Testament.

Many religious Jews, particularly (but not exclusively) within the ultra-Orthodox community, have come to view the role of Israel in eschatological terms. Indeed, some subscribe to "catastrophic messianism," whereby the secular Israeli state is the precursor to the re-creation of the fully restored ideal nation of Israel due to the actions of the Messiah.[20] Since the year 2000 (the start of the second *intifada*) there has been a creation of common ground between the minority of the Israeli community who can be described as "Jewish messianists," and the settler movement and other right-wing nationalists.

In the twenty-first century, a revitalization of the more religious concept among "Jewish messianists" and ultranationalists in Israel has accompanied a reenergizing of these beliefs among (especially US) Christian evangelicals. This has amplified its impact. For these Christians, the establishment of the state of Israel is interpreted as the direct fulfillment of Old Testament prophecy.[21] This belief has impacted modern politics in many ways. Most obvious is the support of the US evangelical right for Israel. Almost all Old Testament prophecy assumes the presence of a Jewish community in the Middle East.[22] While New Testament prophecy is much less geographically specific, some parts of it have been read in the same way.

20. Court, *Approaching the Apocalypse*, 193.
21. For example, Fruchtenbaum, "Israel in Prophecy," 155.
22. Whittock, *End Times, Again?*, 156.

The establishment of the state of Israel is, for many evangelical Christians, the event that has started the "end-times clock" running. Jesus' image of a fig tree's leaves signaling the coming of summer being like the signs indicating the imminent last days (Matt 24:32–33) is often taken as a reference to the restoration of Israel.[23] His reference to "this generation" not passing away until all is accomplished (Matt 24:34) was once taken by modern prophecy students as a generation starting in 1948. That interpretation is now rarely referred to, as a biblical generation would have ended in the mid-1990s.[24] However, the belief that Israel is a fulfillment of prophecy is well established.

The Israeli capture of the whole of Jerusalem in the 1967 Six-Day War was regarded as a direct fulfillment of prophecy, since now Israel was both in "the land" and in control of the ancient capital city, which features so prominently in prophecy.[25] Leading US evangelicals, post-1945, have strongly argued for Israel playing a major part in God's plans in the time immediately preceding the second coming.[26] In recent years this has developed into political influence within the US that is unprecedented and a direct influence on US foreign policy.

This alliance between the US evangelical right and right-wing Israeli nationalists has led to an increasingly hard line being adopted regarding Palestinian aspirations, Israeli settlement in the West Bank, and territorial concessions for peace. Indeed, many "Jewish messianists" and Christian evangelicals would view such concessions as being directly contrary to the will of God. With the second coming viewed as imminent, long-term peacemaking has little appeal.

As time has gone on, this evangelical support has expressed itself in many ways, but one of the most controversial is support for the rebuilding of a Jewish temple on the Temple Mount in Jerusalem. Since this would require the demolition of the Islamic buildings of the Dome of the Rock, the Al-Aqsa Mosque, the Dome of the Chain, and other structures, the conflagration this would cause is difficult to exaggerate.[27] Since the 1980s these hopes for the rebuilding brought together conservative evangelicals in the US, and a small minority drawn from Jewish messianist temple

---

23. Whittock, *End Times, Again?*, 157.
24. Whittock, *End Times, Again?*, 157.
25. Fruchtenbaum, "Israel in Prophecy," 157.
26. Ariel, "Radical Millennial Movements," 679.
27. Ariel, "Radical Millennial Movements," 679.

builder groups,[28] such as the "Temple Mount Faithful," and the "Movement for the Establishment of the Temple." In the mid-1980s, the Israeli security services caught several Jewish and Jewish-Christian groups who were planning to blow up the Islamic sites on the Temple Mount.[29]

The contested Zionisms are now more in agreement than at any time in the past. A coalition of Jewish and Christian fundamentalists and nationalists have radically contributed to this.[30] The decided shift to the right in both contemporary Israeli and US politics—accompanied by a corresponding decline in prospects of an Israeli-Palestinian peace settlement—means that the potential for catastrophic conflagration has consequently increased exponentially.

---

28. Ariel, "Radical Millennial Movements," 679–80.
29. Ariel, "Radical Millennial Movements," 682–83.
30. See: Inbari, *Jewish Fundamentalism*.

CHAPTER 15

The View from the East
Orthodoxy, Putin, and Russian Millenarianism

MUCH OF THE MODERN populist Christian use of millenarian ideas has originated among evangelicals in the US and in English-speaking countries influenced by US culture (both theologically and politically). As a result, much of the end-times talking in the twenty-first century has been done with—as it were—an American accent. However, the US and those global communities influenced by US evangelical end-times beliefs are not alone in these beliefs in, or manipulation of, "apocalyptic politics." This is becoming increasingly obvious.

In Russia, the Orthodox Church has its own deep-rooted version of these beliefs, and these are (in the post-Soviet era) influencing the nature of Putin's Russia. This includes challenging the West and "liberal democratic values"; expanding Russian influence in ex-Soviet republics; branding criticism of the regime as being antagonistic to the values of "Holy Russia"; and opposing many features of modern society (such as LGBTQ rights).

A BRIEF INTRODUCTION TO THE RUSSIAN ORTHODOX CHURCH (ROC)

The Russian Orthodox Church is one of the largest *autocephalous* (ecclesiastically independent) Eastern Orthodox churches, with a membership estimated at over 90 million.[1] It dates from the tenth century when Christianity was introduced to the state of "Kyiv/Kiev Rus" (in modern Ukraine) by Greek missionaries from Byzantium (Constantinople).[2]

Until as late as 1448, the Russian Orthodox Church was headed by the "metropolitans of Kiev" (since 1328 they had been based in Moscow). In 1448, the Russian bishops first elected their own metropolitan without reference to the authority of Constantinople, and from this point the Russian church was autocephalous. In 1589, the metropolitan of Moscow was elevated to the position of patriarch. This elevation occurred with the approval of Constantinople. Moscow then stood fifth in line of honor after the patriarchs of Constantinople, Alexandria, Antioch, and Jerusalem. In 1721, Tsar Peter I (known as "the Great") abolished the patriarchate of Moscow and replaced it with the Holy Governing Synod. This was modeled after the synods of the Lutheran churches in Sweden and Prussia and increased state control over the community.

Many believers—both "Old Believers" who resisted seventeenth-century changes in liturgy and practices and Orthodox who accepted them—thought Peter the Great was the antichrist. This was due to a combination of his personal lifestyle and his cruelty; his mocking of the church; his actions to control church government; and his campaign of Westernization.[3] The last point (with its eschatological distrust of non-Russian influences that were—and are—often judged "anti-Christian") has continued to be a feature of end-times thinking in Russia and can be witnessed in modern claims about the alleged threat posed by modern Western influence.

In 1917, after the fall of the tsar, a council of the Russian Orthodox Church re-established the patriarchate. At the same time, the church experienced severe persecution at the hands of the Soviet regime. To many Orthodox believers the Soviet measures (closing churches, arresting priests, collectivizing agriculture) represented "the last desperate acts of the antichrist before his doom."[4] "Heavenly Letters" (allegedly written by the Virgin Mary or by Christ) circulated, urging peasants to leave the collective farms,[5] in defiance of the anti-Christian end-times regime. On

---

1. Editors of Encyclopaedia Britannica, "Russian Orthodox Church," lines 4–5.
2. For an examination of the history of this church, see: Kent, *A Concise History*.
3. Clay, "Apocalypticism in Eastern Europe," 635.
4. Clay, "Apocalypticism in Eastern Europe," 643.
5. Clay, "Apocalypticism in Eastern Europe," 643.

their part, the Soviet authorities promulgated a humanistic form of the millennium, in which they assumed that communism and science would transform human existence. It was a veritable battle for the soul of Russia.

This Soviet persecution relaxed somewhat during the Second World War (called the Great Patriotic War in the USSR); and some unofficial messages circulated among believers claiming that the end of the world was approaching. In the late 1950s, calculations were made by some believers, claiming that the Soviet regime would end in 1960, as the culmination of the forty-two months (interpreted as years) of the rule of antichrist stated in Revelation.[6] This did not occur, and persecution increased again in the 1960s and 1970s and extended into the mid-1980s, until it was ended by Gorbachev.

The collapse of the Soviet Union in 1991 led to a resurgence in influence of the Orthodox Church and a growing alliance between it and Russian nationalists. This has continued to the present day. In this, eschatological beliefs that once served as buttresses of resistance to the state (in the Soviet period) are now deployed as legitimizations of the current state and are a reemergence of the belief in Moscow as the "Third Rome" (see below).[7]

In the Russia of Vladimir Putin (president of the Russian Federation since 2000), the regime has frequently referenced the Russian Orthodox Church as representing an essential feature of Russian identity. This approach rapidly emerged in his first decade in power,[8] and has accelerated since. It should be remembered that more than 14 million people (or about 10 percent of the population) identify as Muslim in the Russia Federation,[9] but Putin has frequently sought to present Russia as a unified—and Orthodox—community. In return, the church has framed the Kremlin as the defender of Russian culture and of Russians living outside Russia.

In early 2022—following the Orthodox Christmas Day (7 January 2022) service at the Cathedral of Christ the Savior in Moscow—Patriarch Kirill commented on the unrest in Kazakhstan, which had resulted in troops from the Russian-led Collective Security Treaty Organization (CSTO) entering the country. His words were revealing: "We all know

6. Clay, "Apocalypticism in Eastern Europe," 643.
7. Clay, "Apocalypticism in Eastern Europe," 645.
8. See: Garrard and Garrard, *Russian Orthodoxy Resurgent*.
9. Fradkin, "Co-optation of Islam in Russia," lines 1–2.

that the most difficult events are taking place on the territory of our once-united huge country . . . It is on the territory of historical Russia."[10] Kazakhstan—though once part of the USSR—was never part of "historical Russia," although it does contain a Russian minority and Moscow has a history of claiming parts of northern Kazakhstan. Despite this latter point, most Russia-watchers concluded that Kirill's comments went well beyond the Kremlin's intentions in this CSTO intervention.[11] Russia is, arguably, not planning to annex parts of Kazakhstan in the foreseeable future. However, what Kirill's words seemed to indicate was a willingness to anticipate what the nationalist aims of the Putin regime *may be* or *may become*.[12] In this he was, arguably, aligning with existing Putinist policies that look to extend Kremlin power and influence in neighboring states that include Russian minorities; and he appeared to be signaling the ROC leadership's willingness to support an acceleration of this Russian expansionism. The events in Ukraine after February 2022 (as we shall shortly see) bear this out to an extraordinary degree.

However, this has not prevented the state from coming down hard when ordinary believers have been critical of the government. In addition, the church's internal divisions mean it stands at something of a disadvantage vis-à-vis the regime.[13] The nature of authoritarianism in modern Russia is that all institutions are subservient to the agenda of the Kremlin and will be brought into line if necessary. As a result, although the ROC plays an important part within the national culture promoted by Putin, its influence and autonomy are severely limited. It does not decide, or overtly influence, the direction of government policy; rather it follows the flow decided from the political center.

In October 2018, the Russian Orthodox Church cut its ties with the Ecumenical Patriarchate of Constantinople. This was after the patriarch there (the honorary primate of all Eastern Orthodoxy) approved the independence of the Orthodox Church of Ukraine. This move—which formally took effect in January 2019—removed it from the authority of the Russian Orthodox Church based in Moscow. This was denounced in Moscow as being a result of US and papal influence. Prior to this change, the Ukrainian Orthodox population had made up about 20 percent of

---

10. Galeotti, "In Moscow's Shadows," 33:00–33:14.
11. Galeotti, "In Moscow's Shadows."
12. Galeotti, "In Moscow's Shadows."
13. See: Papkova, *Orthodox Church*.

all the Orthodox believers under Moscow's patriarchate, so its loss was highly significant, practically as well as symbolically. Russia annexed Crimea from Ukraine in 2014, but it lost spiritual authority over the nation in 2019.[14]

The Russian invasion of Ukraine in February 2022 was driven by a nationalist desire to crush Ukrainian independence (and thwart any Ukrainian aims of joining NATO and the EU). However, while a *spiritual dimension*—forcing Ukraine back into the Russian Orthodox community—was not a decisive factor in causing the traumatic invasion, the attack was consistent with the concepts of "Holy Russia" and "Russia as the Third Rome" so central to both Russian Orthodox nationalism and Putin's framing of Russian nationhood. The decision to attempt to impose the will of the Kremlin on the whole of Ukraine (which occupies a key place within the deep story of ancient Russian nationhood and the establishment of orthodoxy north of the Black Sea) cannot be fully understood without taking this into account.

However, before we examine the apocalyptic dimensions of this, it will be helpful to sketch out something of the traditional Orthodox approach to eschatology.

THE ORTHODOX APOCALYPSE

Orthodoxy shares the eschatological heritage that is common to the global Christian church. However, as we have seen in the differences between Catholicism and Protestantism, this does not mean that there is unity of understanding regarding these beliefs.

In sharp difference to most modern Protestant evangelical outlooks, there is no belief in the rapture (Christians being removed from the earth before the great tribulation, which precedes Christ's return). And, it should be noted, there is little evidence of this belief being held by many Christians before the mid-nineteenth century.[15] In Orthodox thinking (as indeed in most Christian thought prior to the 1840s):

> When Jesus returns at the Second Coming, that will be the Last Day, the Great Judgment, the General Resurrection, and the Universal Transfiguration of Creation by the Holy Spirit all at

---

14. Sherwood, "Ukraine," lines 12–13.
15. Whittock, *End Times, Again?*, 145.

once. These events will not be separated into separate chronological events.[16]

In addition, most Orthodox would reject the literalist reading of the book of Revelation (and biblical prophecy generally) that is now a given among Protestant fundamentalists and many evangelicals (these terms not being synonymous). It would reject what might be called a "plain reading" of the text.[17] Overall, there is no definitive Orthodox dogma or doctrinal statement about the precise events of the end times.[18] Historically, Russian "Old Believers" thought that the millennium was not a future event but instead referred to the first thousand years of church history before, in their view, the Roman Catholic Church fell into heresy.[19] Despite having broken away from the Orthodox mainstream, this view of the Eastern Church as representing true belief was also a feature of the mainstream and remains influential.

However, while this is in stark contrast with much that emanates from the US, the end times continue to play a major part in Orthodox thinking and outlook. Orthodoxy looks to a future second coming and cosmic transformation but is less inclined to timetable it and more likely to see it as the culmination of an ongoing conflict with antichrist that characterizes the human condition (rather than representing a discrete future person and period). Within this process, Christians will continue to witness to their faith and face the constant struggle of living in a fallen world as they await the return of Christ. As we have seen, there is no rescue-rapture that lifts the church away from the suffering of the world. And, as Christians await the return of Jesus, "The New Jerusalem is even now descending."[20]

However, this has not prevented members of the Orthodox Church from interpreting specific events as being of end-time significance. As we have seen, the official position of a church does not prevent individual members (or even leaders) from espousing beliefs that are more concrete and determinative than one might expect from official faith statements. This is certainly occurring in areas of modern Russia.

16. Tobias, "Orthodox End of the World," lines 52–54.
17. Tobias, "Orthodox End of the World," lines 59–73.
18. Tobias, "Orthodox End of the World," lines 74–78.
19. Clay, "Apocalypticism in Eastern Europe," 639.
20. Tobias, "Orthodox End of the World," line 93.

For example, post-Soviet Russia, in the 1990s, witnessed a resurgence of millenarian beliefs that claimed to pit "The Third Rome against the Third Temple."[21] This was rooted in a Russian antisemitic tradition infamously seen in the *Protocols of the Elders of Zion*. Dating from 1903, those who distributed it then, and now, claim that it is evidence of a Jewish conspiracy to dominate the world. In fact, it is a work of antisemitic fiction and the "conspiracy" and its alleged leaders, the "Elders of Zion," never existed.[22] In the modern manifestation of this radicalized nationalist racism, Moscow is termed the "Third Rome" (after Rome and Constantinople). In contrast, the "Third Temple" is a reference to Judaism, which is claimed to be in opposition to Russian national interests and intent on global domination. The reemergence of this conspiracy theory is the latest manifestation of this belief and presents it in terms of an end-times conflict that is now (allegedly) occurring. This is not a unique example of such eschatological ideologies in Russia.

Since the year 2000, an alliance of right-wing Russian nationalists and the most conservative within the Orthodox Church has resulted in hard-line nationalist policy and actions being described in almost apocalyptic terms. When Putin was preparing to return as Russian president in 2012 (having been prime minister for four years, to circumvent constitutional limits on consecutive periods as president), Patriarch Kirill—head of the Russian Orthodox Church—described the Putin era as "a miracle of God."[23] Since then, Putin (professing a deep Orthodox faith) has increasingly positioned himself as a defender of traditional Orthodox Christian values in a world of turbulence and challenge. While this is not in itself apocalyptic, it has prepared the way for more extreme positions to be espoused by others and, in time, by Putin himself.

Some of the most conservative within the church have responded in kind to Putin's support and have sought to justify his increasingly authoritarian regime by drawing on religious beliefs earlier associated with Ivan Ilyin (a Russian fascist philosopher whose writings have had something of a revival in Putin's Russia). Reviewing this situation in 2019, one Russia expert commented that the Putinist/Orthodox alliance orientates itself around the view that "Russia is a unique and separate Christian

---

21. Hagemeister, "Third Rome against the Third Temple," 423–42.

22. United States Holocaust Memorial Museum, "Protocols of the Elders of Zion," lines 1–16.

23. Khodarkovsky, "Putin's Dream of Godliness," line 60–61.

civilization whose responsibilities are only to God."[24] This is, in effect, the "Third Rome" ideology that we referred to earlier. That has proved to be fertile ground from which semimillenarian attitudes can emerge.

The matter has become more pronounced as external aggression has increased. In 2015, Putin justified his recent annexation (in 2014) of Crimea from Ukraine by asserting that Crimea has "sacred meaning for Russia, like the Temple Mount for Jews and Muslims," and furthermore, that Crimea is "the spiritual source of the formation of the multifaceted but monolithic Russian nation." He added: "It was on this spiritual soil that our ancestors first and forever recognized their nationhood."[25] A fusion of nationalism and Orthodoxy has clearly occurred, along with a very particular interpretation of the arc of Russian history. Others have responded to this outlook using similar terminology but taking it further.

In 2014, as Russian-backed rebels sought to establish a separate political identity in the eastern Ukrainian region of the Donbas, one priest claimed that Ukrainian forces and those supporting them in the West were seeking "The establishment of planetary Satanic rule." Furthermore, he claimed, "What's occurring here is the very beginning of a global war. Not for resources or territory, that's secondary. This is a war for the destruction of true Christianity, Orthodoxy." He castigated the West in apocalyptic terms: "They are intentionally hastening the reign of antichrist." In contrast, he asserted, the Russian militia member, seeking to wrest the Donbas from Ukrainian control, "is also a monastic, but wages not an inner war with the spirits of evil, but an outer one."[26] It is clear, from other evidence, that this was far from a lone voice, and the outlook is extensive among the most extreme nationalists within the Russian Orthodox community. Since the beginning of the invasion of Ukraine, this rhetoric has escalated.

The process of political, religious, and apocalyptic synthesis that has developed under late Putinism has been succinctly described:

> Putin's regime is desperately searching for an ideology in the dark corners of Russian history and theology. The fact that this ideology depends on creating a nationalist and anti-Western

---

24. Khodarkovsky, "Putin's Dream of Godliness," lines 79–81.
25. Coyer, "Putin's Holy War," lines 118–23.
26. Coyer, "Putin's Holy War," lines 179–88.

rhetoric alongside a vision of an Orthodox Christian Holy Russia should give anyone pause for serious concern.[27]

In the Donbas, the violence that this engendered between 2014 and 2022 has extended to Christians who are not members of the Russian Orthodox Church. That a number of the Protestant congregations there have connections with the West has led to them being charged with being not truly Russian in a context where only the Russian Orthodox Church is presented as the valid representation of true Russian faith and spirituality. Jews too have fled from the rebels.[28]

It should be emphasized that, as we have seen, this nationalist construct and outlook also involves distinctly apocalyptic aspects that seek to root current nationalist policy in the deep history of Christian millenarianism, as well as of Russian orthodoxy.

The invasion of Ukraine—while primarily driven by Russian nationalist geopolitics in the post-Cold-War world—was also rooted in the spiritual outlook that has just been examined. The geopolitics of apocalyptic nationalism are in the mix.

A PUTIN-ERA PROPHET OF EXTREME APOCALYPTIC NATIONALISM?

Alexander Dugin (born 1962) has been highly influential regarding the need, as Russian nationalists would put it, for Mother Russia to fulfill its prophetic destiny. This involves overthrowing the present cultural order of things, including human rights and perceived "political correctness." This is rooted in a peculiarly Russian combination of Holy Russia nationalism and millenarianism. Dugin is a Russian philosopher and activist, and a founder of the Russian Geopolitical School and the Eurasian Movement.

He has combined political ideology with eschatology. This, it has been argued, is rooted in belief in "sacred history" and a "world plot" and an "eternal enemy" behind it, which is clearly derived from the Christian concept of the antichrist. It promotes the need for a conservative revolution. It has been argued that such constructions invariably lead to esoteric and conspiratorial antisemitism and that this ideology is geared to

---

27. Khodarkovsky, "Putin's Dream of Godliness," lines 113–17.
28. Coyer, "Putin's Holy War," lines 189–239.

an "occult metaphysical war" between Christianity and Judaism.[29] This, it has been argued, is an example of the nationalist and antisemitic version of eschatology referred to earlier.[30]

This is part of what has been described as a messianic and "paradigmatic" view of the role of the Russian state. This holds that out of a succession of "Times of Troubles" (a Russian phrase recalling a political crisis that occurred between 1598 and 1613), the Russian state emerges stronger, both spiritually and geopolitically. This ideology is rooted in the concept of a resurgent Russia, in opposition to the US, asserting its own unique spiritual and cultural identity. This has involved support for direct Russian intervention in Ukraine and, thus, confrontation with the West. It is claimed that this will accompany the creation of a revitalized Russian Orthodox national community and the end to Russian spiritual decay.[31] One can see why a number of commentators have viewed this ideology as a peculiarly Russian-nationalist millenarianism in its values and outlook. And in its apocalyptic vision of conflict between Russians and minorities and outside powers.

In the 1990s, Dugin was highly influential. In 1997, he published *The Foundations of Geopolitics*, containing an expansionist view of Russia that was applauded by hardline nationalists. The book arose from his fortnightly lectures at the military General Staff Academy under General Igor Rodionov (defense minister, 1996–97). In a nutshell, the book argued for reconstituting the old Soviet empire, then aligning with Japan, Germany, and Iran to eject US and liberal influence from Europe.[32] Georgia would be dismembered; Ukraine and Finland annexed; Azerbaijan given to Iran in exchange for a "Moscow-Tehran axis"; and Serbia, Romania, Bulgaria, and Greece would join Russia to constitute an Orthodox "Third Rome."[33]

To many observers, it was a vision rooted in how Russia likes to regard its sacred role in history, combined with apocalyptic mysticism and ruthless national ambition, while also drawing on worldviews closely associated with fascism in the twentieth century. It was also totally impractical. As well as assigning a role that was far beyond Russia militarily and politically, there was much about the book, its ideology and its

---

29. See: Shnirelman, "Alexander Dugin: Building a Bridge," 194–221.
30. Shnirelman, "Alexander Dugin: Between Eschatology," 443–60.
31. See: Shlapentokh, "Time of Troubles."
32. Clover, "Unlikely Origins," lines 119–31.
33. Clover, "Unlikely Origins," lines 183–89.

presentation that was (in the opinion of many analysts) reminiscent of the geopolitical outlook of Nazism.[34] This outlook arguably spread rapidly through the Russian far right, and influenced the thinking of many[35] because it appealed to their perception of national humiliation and the desire to reassert Russian greatness.

The rise of Putin to supreme power after 2000 caused Dugin to focus on him as the leader who might be the one to put into practice the kind of national transformation he argued for. However, Dugin came to be disappointed with (what he considered) the lack of appetite in the Putin regime for such apocalyptic conflict. The annexation of Crimea in 2014 did not immediately turn into a transformational and climactic battle. After that, some commentators reported that he had fallen out of favor with the Kremlin and appeared increasingly disenchanted with a lack of sufficient radicalism exhibited by the Putin regime.[36] However, the traumatic events of 2022 reveal that the Kremlin under Putin *does* draw inspiration from a deep well of violent radicalism.

RUSSIAN APOCALYPTIC POLITICS FOLLOWING THE ATTACK ON UKRAINE

In an extraordinary conversation (in March 2022) between Alexander Dugin and Yekaterina Sazhneva, columnist at the daily *Moskovsky Komsomolets* (*MK*), Dugin revealed the extent to which he saw the war against Ukraine in apocalyptic terms.[37] It should be noted that *MK* is now Russia's highest circulation daily. Its general political orientation has been described as "pro-Kremlin, but it also features critical coverage."[38] Since the invasion of Ukraine, it has been deemed significant enough a publication for its editor-in-chief to be targeted with EU sanctions.[39] Consequently, this is not a conversation hidden away in some dark corner of the internet.

It was clear from the report that Dugin sees the war (the "Special Military Operation" in official Russian parlance) as being a watershed

34. Clover, "Unlikely Origins," lines 132–42.
35. See: Clover, *Black Wind, White Snow*.
36. See: Shlapentokh, "Time of Troubles."
37. Dugin, "Russian Peace."
38. "Moskovskij Komsomolets," lines 1–3.
39. "EU introduces sanctions," lines 4–5.

moment in the modern history of Russia, which has seen Putin (previously the rational-opportunist that Dugin terms the "lunar Putin") transformed into an enthusiastic proponent of apocalyptic imperialism (what Dugin terms the "solar Putin").[40] Consequently, Putin is now, for Dugin, the one bringing "deliverance" to the Russian people and is, Dugin insists, a "man of destiny."[41]

Putin's coming is described in almost messianic terms. Dugin quoted the French writer and journalist Jean Parvulesco (died 2010) who had, we are told, predicted that a great Russian leader would arise who would "establish an imperial eschatological will over the land, from the Atlantic to the Pacific."[42] For Dugin, "Truth and God are on our [Russia's] side. We are fighting the absolute Evil embodied in Western civilization."[43]

When twenty-first-century conflicts are described in these terms, the possibility of nuclear catastrophe is very real. Addressing this possibility, Dugin frankly stated:

> It would be very right, very responsible, very Russian, to consider what is happening today in the apocalyptic dimension and to do everything possible to ensure that the inevitable consequences [nuclear war] do not come to pass. And if it is impossible to avoid what is destined to happen, it is important to be on the right side at the moment of the End of the World. On our [Russia's] side.[44]

Dugin did not go so far as to claim that the prophecies in the New Testament book of Revelation are about to be fulfilled, but he displayed remarkable sangfroid when confronted with the question of whether they might be. The interviewer had previously asked him: "As John's Revelation suggests, Pestilence (coronavirus) is followed by War, followed by Famine and Death. Are the horsemen of the Apocalypse coming?"[45] Dugin's reply suggested that his twin beliefs in the inevitability of the apocalypse and the defense of Russian identity were inextricably combined.

His ideology represents an intense apocalyptic nationalism. In this, pursuit of Russia's interests are coterminous with the defense of

---

40. Dugin, "Russian Peace," lines 1–9.
41. Dugin, "Russian Peace," line 203.
42. Dugin, "Russian Peace," lines 205–9.
43. Dugin, "Russian Peace," lines 239–40.
44. Dugin, "Russian Peace," lines 287–90.
45. Dugin, "Russian Peace," lines 276–77.

Christianity. Such a view can countenance global nuclear destruction in defense of this Orthodox Russian nationalism. This is a view that emerges clearly from his comments. In short, as he put it, "Christianity is the Russian Orthodox Church, and no one else." With such a radicalized apocalyptic mindset he could claim that "We [Russia] are conducting an eschatological military operation, a special operation on the vertical plane between Light and Darkness, in an end-time situation." In contrast, "The West is the party of Darkness by all its signs and symbols."[46] It could have come straight from the book of Revelation but with the words "Russia" and "the West" inserted at key points in the eschatological narrative.

The Apocalyptic Outlook Goes Mainstream

On its own, this interview could be viewed as the unrepresentative statements of an end-times prophet who has found his extreme views suddenly vindicated by the turn of events since February 2022 and the accelerating radicalism of Putin and his war in Ukraine. However, the news platform on which it was expressed reveals something far more significant than this. It indicates the way in which such radicalized apocalyptic statements are now within the mainstream of Russian discourse and outlook. Apocalyptic nationalism is, consequently, at the forefront of the narrative as the war has escalated. This is revealed in the fact that Putin, once the cold and rationalist operator, now speaks what one might term fluent *Duginese*. Musing on whether the president reads his writings, Dugin posited that the answer is that they both "read the same writings, written in golden letters on the sky of Russian history."[47]

The fact that apocalyptic nationalism is fast becoming the norm in Russia is reinforced from a wide range of sources. In April 2022—six weeks into the Russian invasion of Ukraine—Patriarch Kirill stated his belief that "It is the Orthodox faith, living and acting in the Orthodox church—this is the force that holds back (the antichrist)."[48] While not referring explicitly to the war in Ukraine, the implication seemed clear: Russian actions are part of an eschatological struggle against the forces of darkness (i.e., the West and decadent liberalism). Those opposing the current Russian regime, its war in Ukraine, and the stance of the

---

46. Dugin, "Russian Peace," lines 301–5.
47. Dugin, "Russian Peace," lines 313–14.
48. Hobson, "Russian Patriarch Says," lines 27–29.

Orthodox Church as represented by Kirill were, this implied, end-times agents of the antichrist.

There is a striking consistency in the way that current apocalyptic Russia nationalism is framed and what it holds in common with other far-right movements and conspiracy theories. In a later piece (published in May 2022) Dugin referred to "artificial pandemics and biological weapons" (the COVID-19 pandemic one assumes) as one of the ways that "liberal global elites" seek to implement the "total extermination" of those who oppose them.[49] Furthermore, he described the Ukrainian state, against which the Russian "special military operation" was deployed, as encompassing "Nazism, liberal values and gay pride parades."[50] The words could have been spoken by Kirill in his characterizing of the "antichrist West."

Furthermore, in the world proposed by the liberals, as Dugin sees it, "all humans will intermingle, creating a planetary civil society, one world" and "artificial intelligence will dominate humanity; people will become first genderless and then 'immortal'; they will live in cyberspace and their consciousness and memory will be stored on cloud servers. New generations will be created in a test tube or printed by a 3D printer."[51] According to this outlook, liberal values dehumanize people and, by implication, it is only the kind of worldview he espouses (as exemplified in the *Russkiy Mir*, Russia World) that offers hope for human survival. In the references to the threat allegedly posed by dehumanizing one-world rule, this echoes themes that are frequently espoused by eschatological conspiracy theorists and opponents of democratic liberal values. One can easily see how such a worldview morphs into a war of civilizations and is closely tied to an end-of-the-world-view, which brings us to the nuclear threat.

The Nuclear Dimension

In late April 2022—and following Russian testing of a new intercontinental ballistic missile—one political commentator remarked how, for Kirill, "the Russian nuclear shield was protecting Russia not just in a geopolitical sense but also, in spiritual terms, from the western way of life."[52]

49. Dugin, "Clash of Realism and Liberalism," lines 39–41.
50. Dugin, "Clash of Realism and Liberalism," line 69.
51. Dugin, "Clash of Realism and Liberalism," lines 42–48.
52. Jenkins, "Russian Nuclear Orthodoxy," lines 41–42.

In such an outlook, ideological and societal challenges to conservative Russian values—and the thwarting of Russian nationalist actions—can be framed as being as dangerous as weapons of mass destruction. And in such a context, a non-nuclear action by enemies could arguably be met by a nuclear reaction by Russia.

Igor Korotchenko, editor-in-chief of Russia's *National Defense Magazine*, told RIA news agency that the missile's launch was a signal to the West of Russia's ability to deal out "crushing retribution that will put an end to the history of any country that has encroached on the security of Russia and its people."[53] That would be alarming at any time, but in a period of escalating tension—with official Russian news outlets framing the current situation as an existential threat facing Russia—such language gives cause for real alarm. It is entirely in line with Putin's use of nuclear threats against those nations who oppose Russian acts of aggression that have been stated both before and during the conflict in Ukraine. For such extreme Russian nationalists, the defense of the *Russkiy Mir* (Russia World) outweighs all other global considerations, including global survival. This view was reflected in late February 2022, when the Russian news channel's anchor, Dmitry Kiselyov, commented—regarding the sanctions being applied by the US and European countries—that if there is no Russia, then why do we need the world?[54] Such an extreme outlook has the potential to short-circuit the very thinking that has held back nuclear war since 1945: "Mutually Assured Destruction" (MAD). The rhetoric has ramped up since then, and it accompanies the kind of weaponized eschatology articulated by Patriarch Kirill.

This has been described as "nuclear orthodoxy."[55] It implies that, "To ensure Russia is fit for the Second Coming, spiritual preparation is insufficient. Russia must be militarily and politically strong, or else it will succumb to influences that will undermine its Orthodox culture, and thereby its ability to prepare for the return of Christ."[56] This is where political and military policy meets the apocalypse. In this process, extreme Russian nationalism and extreme versions of Russian Orthodoxy have become more closely entwined than at any time since Putin became president. It was in this context that Pope Francis told Italy's *Corriere Della Sera*

---

53. Whittock, "Return of the Nuclear Threat?," lines 29–32.
54. Whittock, "Return of the Nuclear Threat?," lines 69–71.
55. Jenkins, "Russian Nuclear Orthodoxy," line 47.
56. Jenkins, "Russian Nuclear Orthodoxy," line 55–57.

newspaper that Kirill, "cannot become Putin's altar boy."[57] However, to many observers it appears that he has.

A NEW CHAPTER IN APOCALYPTIC POLITICS

It is clear that ultranationalist apocalyptic trends in Russian thought have been amplified by the attack on Ukraine in 2022. These ideas have injected increased radicalism into the turbulent cocktail of Russian right-wing thinking. At one time they appeared subservient to the overall agenda of the regime; regarded as sometimes useful but never independently significant.

In the period from 2000 until 2022, this Russian subservience of apocalyptic ideology to the will of the Kremlin could be contrasted with the far-reaching and ongoing end-times influence of the evangelical right within the US conservative political establishment. This could be explained by the fact that the Russian Federation is an authoritarian state, with the influence of pressure groups tightly controlled and votes and the media carefully managed. In that sense, the world's most powerful democracy (the US) appeared more open to the political influence of radicalized apocalyptic politics than Russia.

That changed in 2022. The invasion of Ukraine has hugely accelerated radicalized apocalyptic rhetoric in Russia. An increasing convergence has occurred, involving the most extreme Orthodox and political spokespeople (the latter including Putin himself in his nuclear threats). Dugin no longer seems a sidelined prophet of eschatological Russian nationalism. Ukrainian resistance, Russian military setbacks, global sanctions, and a movement among non-NATO states to apply for protection under the NATO umbrella, have been accompanied by the ratcheting up of nationalist language from Russia, including the use of apocalyptic justifications and threats. It seems that a new chapter has started in the history of global apocalyptic politics.

---

57. Reuters, "Russian Orthodox Church Scolds Pope Francis," lines 4–5.

CHAPTER 16

Apocalyptic Politics in Iran, and ISIS

AS WE HAVE SEEN in an earlier chapter, end-times beliefs play a major part in Islam. While Sunni and Shia Muslims have profound disagreements over the matter, apocalyptic belief continues to be a common feature among many otherwise-divided Islamic communities.

Of itself, this does not inevitably lead to radicalized outcomes. As with Judaism and Christianity, it is quite possible to hold such beliefs without them leading to the adoption of a politically radicalized agenda. This undoubtedly applies to the majority of believers. Nevertheless, there is much evidence to suggest that it can and does have such an effect for a minority. When this occurs, the outcomes can be extreme.

THE RISK OF AN IRANIAN SHIA APOCALYPSE

Apocalyptic beliefs are often associated with Shia Islam. Within Shia Iran, millenarianism is a factor driving opposition to the state of Israel, attacks on non-Shia Muslim states, and the drive to gain Iranian nuclear capability. These ideas are a dynamic ingredient in the explosive politics of the Iranian clerical elites and the powerful Iranian "Islamic Revolutionary Guard Corps" (IRGC).

In Iran, the original goal of the 1979 Islamic Revolution was utopian. It aimed to create an ideal society through the imposition of Islamic law and a theocratic government. Over the decades since then, while the regime has entrenched itself in power, it has failed to create a situation in which its vision is accepted by all Iranians. Indeed, over the past two decades its legitimacy has been questioned and its effectiveness challenged. Despite these occurrences the Islamic theocratic regime remains in power and its protectors in the IRGC are more powerful than ever.

However, it can be argued that the current "apocalyptic politics in Iran originates from the failure of the Islamic Republic's initial vision."[1] In the face of opposition, and in an often-hostile world, the regime has arguably switched from utopian to apocalyptic rhetoric as a means of energizing mass support. This has, no doubt, for many in the leadership, also served to (consciously or unconsciously) explain away the problems faced/caused by the regime. After all, in an end-times struggle opposition is to be expected. Such a vision of struggle, it has been argued by some commentators, is a product of the fact that "the Islamic Republic does not satisfy any strata of society, whether religious or secular" and has, in consequence, sought to create "a new world of [apocalyptic] meaning" in order to motivate and satisfy Iranian citizens.[2]

This apocalyptic vision is rooted in the Shia "Twelver" belief that looks for the future appearance of the *Mahdi* (or the Hidden Imam) to establish a world order and government that is in line with Shia beliefs and practices. It is significant that this increased apocalyptic strategy by the Iranian regime has been accompanied by the appearance of a number of people in Iran claiming to be the *Mahdi*. It is also significant that behavior by the regime has increased tension in the Gulf and the region generally. Iranian strategies of arming and supplying militias and other allies in Lebanon, Syria, and Iraq have had the complex effect of both increasing Iranian regional power and influence via these proxies and at the same time increasing tension between Iran and Israel (and its ally, the US) and Sunni Muslim states. In a negative feedback loop, a growing sense of isolation and internal opposition to its policies has further entrenched the regime's refusal to respond to calls for reform and democratization at home and have made it easier for it to see the world through an apocalyptic lens.

At the same time, the drive for nuclear capability (often claimed as a defensive necessity in a hostile world) has only increased hostility towards Iran from those who fear its acquisition of such weapons. Alongside this, the extreme statements that have periodically emanated from

---

1. Khalaji, *Agenda Iran*, vii.
2. Khalaji, *Agenda Iran*, vii.

Tehran towards Israel (and towards its Sunni neighbors) have only made those states more determined than ever to ensure that Iran never achieves this military nuclear capability. All of this has ratcheted up tension and increased the likelihood of conflict. But conflict is arguably hardwired into the ideology of the regime as it seeks to legitimize its position as a Shia republic.

This is because within Shia beliefs there is an apocalyptic tradition (believed by some) that associates the return of the Hidden Imam with considerable bloodshed. The tradition asserts that when the *Mahdi* appears, there will be two kinds of death: the "red death" and the "white death." Each of these will account for a third of the human population.[3] The "red death" will be caused by the sword of the *Mahdi*. The "white death" will be caused by plague. Only a third of the population of the world will survive.[4] In some hadiths, it is stated that the *Mahdi* himself will kill two-thirds of the world's population. In this he "will clean the earth from nonbelievers and deniers [of Islam]" and, in so doing, "he will continue to kill the enemies of God until God is satisfied."[5] Furthermore, the *Mahdi* "will order his twelve thousand solders to kill anyone who does not believe in your religion [i.e., Islam]."[6]

In addition, the expectations regarding Islamic relations with Jews in the end times is complex in the hadith tradition accepted within Shia communities. One hadith states that the *Mahdi* will *conquer* Jerusalem, another that he will *destroy* it.[7] While one hadith states that most Jews will convert to Islam in the last days, others state that Jews will be killed.[8] It is, therefore, not surprising to find eliminationist views regarding Israel being expressed by some of the most extreme Iranian leaders. These views regarding the destruction of Israel are often related to events that are expected to occur in preparation for the revealing of the Hidden Imam.

In 2007, then-president Mahmoud Ahmadinejad declared that "the countdown for the fall of the Zionist regime" had started, because "justice and the pioneer of justice [the Hidden Imam] is on his way."[9] In this out-

---

3. Khalaji, *Agenda Iran*, 4.
4. Sadr, *Al-Mahdi*, 195–96; Khalaji, *Agenda Iran*, 4.
5. Majlisi, *Behar al-Anwar*, 52:283; Isfahani, *Yati Ala*, 659; Khalaji, *Agenda Iran*, 4.
6. Isfahani, *Yati Ala*, 659; Khalaji, *Agenda Iran*, 4.
7. Khalaji, *Agenda Iran*, 4.
8. Khalaji, *Agenda Iran*, 4.
9. Khalaji, *Agenda Iran*, 24.

look, the most radical—and exterminatory—views expressed within Iran have roots in a contested and extreme ideology that claims it is based on aspects of the Shia hadith. Within this area of modern Iranian ideology, what can only be described as radicalized antisemitism claims that it is justified through appeal to apocalyptic traditions. It must, however, be stated that most modern Islamic scholars do not accept the validity of such an outlook regarding the Jews. However, many of the more radicalized do, and that is alarming.

For example, Muhammad Ali Ramin, who organized political support for Ahmadinejad in 2005, was not alone among extreme Iranian politicians in his opinion (expressed in 2006) that "they [Jews] were [across history] the source for such deadly diseases as the plague and typhus. This is because the Jews are very filthy people."[10] This attitude was unsurprisingly linked to Holocaust denial by this same Iranian spokesperson.[11]

The Ahmadinejad presidency (2005–13) was a time when extreme end-times and messianic rhetoric was very closely intermingled with policy.[12] And it was clearly meant by the president and his most ardent supporters. However, this outlook was certainly not confined to this particularly intense period. In the anti-Israel, anti-US, anti-Saudi, regional-power-enhancing nexus of Iranian foreign policy objectives, the aspect of Iranian foreign policy against Israel taps a deep well of belief that views "the Iran-Israel equation through the ideological and apocalyptic prism within the theological context of the End Times prophecies."[13] This is an explosive and volatile situation. Western commentators who do not give sufficient weight to this in assessing Iranian actions (usually due to seeing events through a secular agenda) are missing a major feature within the mix of factors driving Iranian actions. Indeed, it has been commented that "their [radical Iranian] interpretations of reality as well as the actions they undertake based on such interpretations are perfectly rational in their own minds when weighed against their beliefs."[14] While not constituting the only driving force, "considering the apocalyptic belief inherent

---

10. "Iranian Presidential Advisor," lines 14–15.
11. Khalaji, *Agenda Iran*, 25.
12. Mohammadi, *Political Islam*, 158.
13. Zaman, "Iran's Unscrupulous Role," 280.
14. Lubrano, "Iran, Hezbollah, and the End of Times," lines 135–36.

in Shia Islamist ideology constitutes a key factor in grasping the rationale behind the Islamic Republic's moves."[15]

While mainline Shia tradition insists that only prayer and obedience to Allah and Islamic principles can speed the appearance of the *Mahdi*, there is also a tradition that states that world chaos will accompany this event.[16] One can see, therefore, why some who subscribe to this are unconcerned when modern conflicts appear to be spiralling out of control. One can find similar perspectives among the most extreme members of the Christian evangelical right in the US. Apocalyptic outlooks rarely counsel peace, reconciliation, and caution. All too often they are accompanied by acceptance—even promotion—of conflict and turbulence.

This has serious implications for assessing the potential threat posed by Iranian nuclear capability. Iran's attempts to develop nuclear weapons and a ballistic missile delivery system has ratcheted up tension in an already-volatile Middle East. President Obama attempted to slow down this nuclear escalation with the 2015 Joint Comprehensive Plan of Action (JCPOA). It was a strategy much condemned by the Israeli administration and by Republicans in the US. Consequently, in 2018, President Trump pulled out of the JCPOA and imposed heavy financial sanctions on Iran's leadership, its military, and its oil exports. By November 2021, Iran had amassed a stockpile of enriched uranium many times larger than permitted, including material enriched to just below the level needed for a bomb. The Biden administration stated in May 2021 that the US would rejoin the JCPOA and lift current sanctions if Iran reverses its breaches. The long-term future of the JCPOA is uncertain.

While many analysts consider Iranian nuclear ambitions through the lens of conventional pragmatic geopolitics, they would be wise not to ignore the "wild card" of apocalyptic ideology. This is particularly the case regarding Iranian clerical attitudes towards the Shia theology of "Twelverism"—the anticipated appearance of the Hidden Imam—and its ramifications in the nuclear debate. It remains a belief that is hugely influential among the Iranian leadership. In August 2019, senior Iranian Ayatollah Mohammad Mehdi Mirbagheri stated that "In order for the Hidden Imam to reappear we must engage in widespread fighting with the West."[17] Earlier, in July 2019, Iran's Supreme Leader Khamenei

15. Lubrano, "Iran, Hezbollah, and the End of Times," lines 150–52.
16. Khalaji, *Agenda Iran*, 26.
17. Gilbert, "Is the Iranian Apocalypse Really Coming?," line 35.

affirmed that "The return of this holy land [Israel] to the World of Islam is not a strange and unattainable matter." He declared that Lebanese Hezbollah leader Sayyed Nasrallah's (Iran's most influential religious and political emissary in Lebanon) stated goal of praying at the Al-Aqsa Mosque (in Jerusalem) was "an absolutely practical and achievable aspiration for us."[18] Such a scenario is impossible to imagine short of a literal Armageddon in the Middle East.

In addition, there is persuasive evidence that a particularly radicalized form of the "Twelver" ideology is prevalent within the leadership of the IRGC.[19] This is hardly surprising, given that they are the armed protectors of the Iranian Revolution and the ruling ideology. Furthermore, they spearhead the most aggressive and expansionist aspects of Iranian foreign policy.[20] This includes the nuclear program, since "the Revolutionary Guard controls both the ballistic missile and satellite launch capability, the technology for which doubles as a delivery system."[21] The last will and testament of Major General Hassan Moghadam—a pioneer in Iranian missile development, killed in an explosion at a Revolutionary Guard base outside Tehran in 2011—included the wished-for epitaph: "The man who enabled Israel's destruction."[22] The combination of apocalyptic ideology and nuclear technology poses a massive threat to Israel and the region.

That the potential targets are non-Muslims (i.e., infidels) or those not accepted to be "true Muslims" means that for the most extreme Islamists any scruples about targeting noncombatants with weapons of mass destruction do not apply. The unpredictability of this threat is arguably increased by the fact that many of those making these decisions are frequently not drawn from centers of Islamic jurisprudence but are those elevated to political influence due to the turbulence that has created and maintained the hold on power of those who control Iran. This makes their actions harder to predict and less bound by traditional Islamic interpretations. In short, radical situations have produced their own cadres who reinforce the radicalism of the regime. And much of this radicalism is expressed in apocalyptic terms.

18. Gilbert, "Is the Iranian Apocalypse Really Coming?," lines 48–49.
19. Gilbert, "Is the Iranian Apocalypse Really Coming?," lines 57–58.
20. See: Silinsky, *Empire of Terror*.
21. Rubin, "Iran's Revolutionary Guards," lines 40–41.
22. Rubin, "Iran's Revolutionary Guards," lines 19–20.

The position was well expressed in late August 2019 by Saeed Ghasseminejad, an Iranian scholar now living in the US:

> I think the Islamic Republic of Iran and its leadership's apocalyptic vision can explain a good part of what Tehran is doing in the region. And ignoring it leads to misinterpretation of Tehran's decisions. While I do not believe the apocalyptic ideology is the only force behind the regime's decision-making process, I think it plays a significant role in how the Supreme Leader and the IRGC see the world.[23]

While not every Middle Eastern commentator would go as far as the September 2021 assertion that Iranian foreign policy aims to "advance a Khamenei-led Iranian apocalyptic death cult,"[24] it would certainly be unwise to ignore the extreme end-times beliefs that are playing a significant part in this policy.

THE APOCALYPTIC CALIPHATE OF ISIS

As we have seen in an earlier chapter, the belief in the "end of days" is central to Sunni Islam too. Not surprisingly, this has been a major feature in the ideology of the most extreme Islamist groups who consider themselves key actors in end-times events. Indeed, when ISIS established their short-lived, bloody "caliphate" in Syria/Iraq (2014–19) they did so believing in the imminent day of judgment and the end of the current world order. This was a central part of their ideology and propaganda.[25] In this emphasis they differed from a number of other Islamist and *jihadist* movements, including *al-Qaeda*. To ISIS, the imminent appearance of prophet *Isa*, in the company of one called the *Imam Mahdi*, to defeat *Al-Masih ad-Dajjal* (the false messiah, an equivalent of the Christian figure of antichrist) was interpreted as a war against the West in which ISIS would play a decisive part. This would culminate in the conquest of "Rome," which suggests a conquest of Europe. It should be noted that ISIS-affiliated groups in Libya, Afghanistan, and elsewhere still emphasize this, despite the final defeat and collapse of the original ISIS caliphate in 2019.

23. Gilbert, "Is the Iranian Apocalypse Really Coming?," lines 69–72.
24. Cooper and Moore. "US Afghanistan Withdrawal Aided Iran," lines 17–18.
25. See: Ostřanský, *Jihadist Preachers of the End Times*.

The group that later became infamous as the "Islamic State" originated in 1999. In this early period, it pledged allegiance to *al-Qaeda* (the group responsible for the 9/11 attacks, along with a number of other attacks against US and Western targets). Following the US-led invasion of Iraq in 2003, the Islamic State of Iraq (ISI) joined the Iraqi insurgency against US and other Western forces. While they suffered heavy casualties from US counter-insurgency measures after 2006 and in conflicts between Sunni tribes and *al-Qaeda* in Iraq, they benefitted from the US military withdrawal in 2011 and from the way that the Shia-dominated government in Baghdad repressed the Sunni minority, as Sunni politicians were arrested for supporting terrorism, Sunni army officers were demoted, and Sunni tribal militias were disbanded. In this context, ISI presented themselves as the protectors of the Sunni population and greatly benefitted from the support this garnered for them, including from those who brought military expertise into the group.

ISI further benefitted from the chaos into which Iraq and then Syria fell in the decade after this and succeeded in attracting significant support from radicalized Islamists (both in the Middle East and in the West). In June 2014, the group proclaimed itself to be a worldwide caliphate and began referring to itself as the Islamic State (*ad-Dawlah al-Islamiyah*; or IS). It was also variously known as the Islamic State of Iraq and the Levant (ISIL), as the Islamic State of Iraq and Syria (ISIS), or known as the latter by its Arabic acronym: *Daesh*. It should be noted that many Muslims objected to its use of the title "Islamic State" since they did not accept its self-proclaimed role as a leading force within the worldwide Islamic community.

As a caliphate, Islamic State claimed total authority (both religious and political) over all Muslims in the world. In June 2014, ISIS published a document in which it claimed that it had traced the family tree of its leader, Abu Bakr al-Baghdadi (then to be known as Caliph Ibrahim), back to Muhammad. This, it was claimed, gave him authority over all Muslims.

ISIS saw itself as having a divinely ordained mission to lead Islam in an apocalyptic conflict that would be part of the end times. Its aim was world domination. By December 2015, the group held power in a very large area, which extended from western Iraq to eastern Syria. Between about 8 and 12 million people lived in this territory, where the group enforced its own puritanical interpretation of *sharia* law. At the same time, it began the systematic annihilation or enslavement of all those who were members of non-Islamic groups, or who were regarded as not being true members of Islam (even if they described themselves as Muslims). It carried out widespread and horrific atrocities, and other human rights abuses, and became infamous in its use of social media to publicize these acts and call for assistance from those abroad who had been radicalized by its online activities.

This active online and social media presence has been a key aspect of the ISIS radicalization program and it continues to impact many young Muslims both in the Middle East and in western Europe today. Ancient apocalyptic beliefs were, and are, combined with modern information technology and communication methods. In the same way, the radicalized members of US Christian apocalyptic groups have used 4chan, 8chan, Facebook, Twitter, etc. in their efforts to create an alternative worldview and to control (distort) the narrative regarding events. Both movements are reminders that, in the third decade of the twenty-first century, many end-times activists have made a remarkable (and alarming) use of modern technology.

Military action against the Islamic State originally involved an international coalition led by the US, which started in the middle of 2016. Russian involvement followed, focused on Syria and in support of the Assad regime. In July 2017, ISIS lost control of its largest city, Mosul, to the Iraqi army. This was followed by the loss of its political capital, Raqqa, to the Syrian Democratic Forces. By the end of 2017, it had lost about 98 percent of the territory that it had once controlled and, in Iraq at least, it could no longer operate openly.[26] This was an astonishing reversal from a situation, just three years earlier, when it had held about one-third of Iraqi territory. By 2019, the caliphate had been destroyed, with its last pockets of territory in Syria being lost to its opponents.

Despite this, new ISIS affiliates continue to operate, most recently in Afghanistan where the group there is in conflict with the Taliban (rulers of the country since the rapid US withdrawal in the summer of 2021). As a result, its apocalyptic ideology has not vanished.

ISIS AND THE END TIMES

The radicalism of the Islamic State was rooted both in its extreme interpretations of Islam and in its confident assertions of its own role within

26. Rowan, "ISIS after the Caliphate," line 5.

apocalyptic events that were, in its view, preceding the imminent end of the current world order. This is a major difference between ISIS and other Islamist and *jihadist* movements (most notably *al-Qaeda*). Indeed, the group's emphasis on eschatology and apocalypticism is one of its defining features.

It has been noted that "References to the End Times fill Islamic State propaganda."[27] This has been one of its major attractions to foreign fighters who believe they have joined in an apocalyptic, world-changing (cosmos-changing) conflict. The chaos that had engulfed large areas of the Middle East in the years following the US-led invasion of Iraq in 2003 only added to the idea that the end of days was at hand.

For such—usually young—people, the idea of travelling to Syria to join the group involved them in a mission that they considered to be fulfilling Qur'anic and hadith prophecies and expectations. It was a heady cocktail of end-times expectations that often accompanied deep dissatisfaction with the societal context in which they lived; raised them above the populations and influences that they rebelled against; and (in the way ISIS interpreted morality) freed them from the usual moral norms.

In such a context, suicide bombing was engrained, along with willingness to face martyrdom in other ways. Death produced no fear in such a mindset. And, once in Syria or Iraq, recourse to extreme and imaginatively enacted violence was not only allowed—it was actively encouraged. At the same time, this puritanical violence was accompanied by activities that allowed the unfettered working out of male power and control (such as the sexual enslavement of Yazidi women and girls) because those targeted were slated as infidels and so unworthy of compassion or being accorded any personal human rights. It was an ideology that dwarfed the atrocities that had been committed at Münster in the 1530s, although both were committed by men who felt themselves imbued with messianic-inspired authority while being unconstrained by behavioral controls.

While earlier Islamists shared the same confidence in the rightness of their cause and assurance of rewards in heaven for martyrdom, the apocalyptic ideology integral to ISIS was in stark contrast to the early strategies of Bin Laden and *al-Qaeda*, who had decided "It was better to recruit by calling to arms against corruption and tyranny than against the

---

27. McCants, *ISIS Apocalypse*, 147.

antichrist. Today, though, the apocalyptic recruiting pitch makes more sense than before."[28]

There is evidence that as far back as 2006, ISI (as it was then called) regarded one of its leaders as being the *Mahdi* (he was later killed in US operations in 2010). The group thought that its actions would prompt divine intervention.[29] Between 2010 and 2014, the group—coming out of a period of severe setbacks—appears to have reformulated and relaunched its apocalyptic ideology.[30] In this more-developed form its ideology presented "the caliphate as a prophetic mechanism to purify the Muslim world and defeat crusader and Shi'ite apostate forces."[31] Its headquarters at Raqqa was portrayed as the new Medina. Here its charitable programs were accompanied by beheadings, crucifixions, stonings, amputations, and floggings. Morality police enforced its strict version of Islamic law. Having set itself the task (or seeing itself set the task by Allah) of creating a purified Islamic community in preparation for the apocalypse, Shia mosques and shrines in the areas under its control were destroyed, Christians were killed or expelled, and Yazidis (considered to be pagans) were enslaved or killed. And gays were hurled to their deaths from tall buildings.

Through this, ISIS believed that it was restoring *tawid* (unity) among Muslims; purging the community of *shirk* (polytheism), apostates, and infidels (Western forces and Christians); battling with Zionism; and rebuilding the true *ummah* (world community of Muslims). In its own words it saw itself as "Smashing the Borders of the *Tawaghit*" (non-Muslim creations). By this it meant that it was demolishing the national borders (particularly those of Syria/Iraq) created by the (in its view "crusader") Western powers after the First World War.[32] As it did so, political and religious authority was being brought together under Caliph Ibrahim. Despite being "People of the Book," many Christians suffered martyrdom at the hands of ISIS militants (and by their affiliates elsewhere), who described them as "people of the cross," and allies of

28. McCants, *ISIS Apocalypse*, 147.
29. Celso, *Islamic State*, 57; Moorcraft, *Dying for the Truth*, 269.
30. Celso, "Islamic State (IS)," 4.
31. Celso, "Islamic State (IS)," 4.
32. Judis, "Middle East That France and Britain Drew," lines 1–8.

the "crusaders."[33] These militants had ambitions of conquering "Rome" (Western Europe).[34]

It is noteworthy that ISIS were not the only ones who viewed the chaos and carnage as signs of the end times. Many of their opponents—Shia and Alawites—saw the upheaval and suffering as signs of the impending appearance of the Hidden Imam. In this way, the bitterly opposed forces of the Sunni *jihadists* and the Shia "Twelver" militias both interpreted the chaos in apocalyptic terms. In this context, Shia militias in Syria and Iraq regarded their fight against Islamic State militants as "an eschatological struggle to purify the world of diabolical forces."[35]

Despite the defeat of ISIS in its original location, this has not meant the end of this apocalyptic group. ISIS-affiliated groups exist in North Africa and Afghanistan. Other allied groups continue to pursue its terrorist agenda in other parts of the world. The apocalyptic violence associated with the Islamic State remains a threat to many communities and a magnet to the angry and disaffected.

At the same time, the tensions around Iran, its foreign policy, and its nuclear ambitions remain. The regime is entrenched and resistant to internal change. the Middle East remains highly volatile, and a great deal of this volatility is rooted in end-times ideologies that may influence the potential use of twenty-first-century technologies (such as nuclear capability).

From the perspectives of both extreme Sunni and extreme Shia groups, the end of days remains a goal to be sought through recourse to, or threat of, violence and destabilizing policies. Although they are not alone in carrying out actions that have brought tension, turbulence, and chaos to the region, it is undoubtedly true that these apocalyptic actors have made major contributions to the ongoing instability of the Middle East—and continue to do so.

---

33. Whittock and Whittock, *Story of the Cross*, 141.
34. Celso, "Islamic State (IS)," 10.
35. Celso, "Islamic State (IS)," 8.

CHAPTER 17

"One Nation—*Deeply Divided*—Under God"

Apocalyptic Politics and the Modern US

MANY APOCALYPTIC INFLUENCES fed into the political outlook of the "conservative right" in the US as it emerged as a major political player in the 1990s and into the twenty-first century.

This chapter explores the way in which apocalyptic outlooks have shaped the political influence of religious ideas within the Republican Party (under Reagan, two Bush presidencies, and particularly connected with Donald Trump). This involves both the mainstream "religious right" and the more politically radical adherents of "Christian reconstructionism."

THE US "EVANGELICAL RIGHT": RADICALIZED END-TIMES ACTORS IN THE "CULTURE WARS"?

Mainstream leaders of the Christian evangelical right come from a tradition deeply imbued with apocalyptic outlooks. However, it should be noted here that the focus in this chapter is more on the political expression of these outlooks than on their theological base. These ideas are today represented by leaders in groupings in the US such as the Southern Baptist Convention and the Assemblies of God, to name two influential bodies.

Technically, there is no such group as the "evangelical right." It is not a denomination, and no groups formally gather under such a collective title. However, it certainly exists.[1] Today, several terms are used to describe the phenomenon: the "Christian right," the "new Christian right," the "religious right,"[2] and "socially conservative evangelicals."[3]

Their common characteristics are a conservative (often literalist) interpretation of the Bible; a conservative approach to social issues such as sexuality, gender identity, and abortion; and right-wing ideology regarding state intervention in society, racial issues (though rarely explicitly expressed as such), environmental protection and fossil fuels, foreign (particularly Middle Eastern) policy, and gun control. It is that third strand that is so distinctive and characteristic of the US evangelical movement. It has arguably become "the right (at times the far-right) at prayer."

This third strand can be contrasted with evangelicals in the UK. In many ways those in the UK are influenced by developments in theology, worship, and practice in the US. However, this is not the case regarding homogeneity of political views. Research in the UK reveals that self-defined evangelicals appear to be significantly internationalist in their outlook and voting behavior.[4] Illustrative of this is the fact that a small majority of UK evangelicals voted "Remain" in the 2016 EU Referendum.[5] This would be unimaginable in the US. The history of the US explains why this difference exists.

The racial history of the US has influenced the outlook of a group that has many members in the southern states, and this has fed into a sense of anxiety regarding the US as a multiracial society (even when many of the black population were historically Christian before the ending of slavery). Consequently, much of what follows refers to *white* evangelicals. This background has encouraged a distrust of federal government and "liberal" interventions in society. In the early twentieth century the evangelical block divided over the matter of "fundamentalism" (belief in the literal historical accuracy of every word of the Bible). This added to an underlying sense of a "culture war" against aspects of modernity, science,

1. Roberts and Whittock, *Trump and the Puritans*, 85–86.
2. See: Wacker, "Christian Right."
3. See: Pulliam, "Phrase 'Religious Right' Misused."
4. See: Smith and Woodhead, "Religion and Brexit."
5. See: Chitwood, "British Evangelicals Brace for Brexit"; Smith and Woodhead "Religion and Brexit."

and critical thinking. From 1910 onward, the US evangelical movement was dominated by fundamentalists.

In the 1940s, 1950s, and 1960s, anxieties about the perceived threat of communism and changing patterns of social behavior caused many evangelicals to gravitate towards the Republican Party as a way of defending what they would have described as the "Protestant-based moral order."[6] During the 1960s, the mood music of the US changed (both literally and figuratively) as it did across much of the Western world. In this period of flux, the threat of secularization came to be seen by US evangelical Protestants as the biggest threat to their understanding of Christian values. Also, during the 1960s, the southern Democrat section of voters (including many evangelicals) shifted position. Fear of the Civil Rights Movement among southern blacks, as well as opposition to the counterculture emerging across the US, caused these "Dixiecrats" to move towards the Republican Party. The evangelical right was being formed. "To those unhappy with the trajectory of American society, government was presented as a major source of these problems."[7]

These changes meant that an increasing polarization was occurring so that theologically conservative evangelical Christians increasingly identified with a raft of politically conservative issues (opposition to racial integration, abortion, nontraditional sexual behavior, and federal "interference") that were associated with the Republican Party. In time this also came to include opposition to gun control and environmentalism. This created a synthesis of theologically and socially conservative principles with ones that came straight from right-wing and nationalist ideology. In time the fusion became such that the strands cannot now be disentangled.

This had a major impact on the political tone of end-times beliefs in the US. In its origins the movement's biblical stance included a literalist interpretation of prophetic texts. The Cold War then led to an interpretation of prophetic texts in line with US and Western outlooks. Views on the Middle East reflected literalist views on the re-establishment of Israel and a future Armageddon combined with, and influenced by, the political geography of the Cold War that pitted Israel and the US against a combination of Arab states and the USSR. When combined with the concept of the pre-tribulation "rapture" (a belief with few adherents

---

6. Williams, *God's Own Party*, 3.
7. Roberts and Whittock, *Trump and the Puritans*, 91.

before the mid-nineteenth century but, thereafter, very popular with US evangelicals),[8] this idea of a cataclysmic future became firmly embedded in the religious outlook of the US right. It is rooted in what is termed "premillennialism," the belief that Christ will return to earth at the end of a period of global crisis, sinfulness, and divine judgment (the "great tribulation") and will then begin a millennium of rule on the earth.[9]

The rightward shift accelerated due to America's internal "culture wars" of the late twentieth century. The power and influence of the religious right increased considerably during the presidency of George H. W. Bush (1989–93). The determination of evangelicals to dominate the Republican Party was exacerbated by the years of the Clinton presidency (1993–2001). George W. Bush's electoral success owed much to the widespread support he received from *white* evangelical voters. Then, in 2008, Barack Obama's success (a black president committed to proactive federal government initiatives on several fronts) was a sharp reversal of all that the evangelical right had been working on for over twenty years. The Obama presidency (2009–17) appeared to pose an existential threat.[10] As a result, in 2016 Donald Trump secured the votes of 81 percent of white evangelicals (approximately 33.7 million votes).[11] Trump appeared to speak to the "deep story" of these voters, living in a bewildering nation and world that was changing around them and in which they increasingly felt marginalized.[12] At the same time, the global community became more turbulent with the rise of China and an increasingly fractious Russia. Climate change only added to anxieties, before being met with denial and antagonism regarding government "interference" from the right. This was accompanied by an eschatological dismissal of the threat due to the claimed imminence of the second coming from many evangelicals. It might even be viewed, if accepted as occurring, as an end-times judgment.

This "applied eschatology" clearly influenced Trump's decisions to move the US embassy to Jerusalem (announced in 2018) and to support Israeli sovereignty over the Golan Heights (announced in 2019). Both

---

8. Whittock, *End Times, Again?*, 145.
9. Whittock, *End Times, Again?*, 64, 67.
10. Roberts and Whittock, *Trump and the Puritans*, 100.
11. Roberts and Whittock, *Trump and the Puritans*, 18.
12. Roberts and Whittock, *Trump and the Puritans*, ch. 5.

"were designed to appeal to American evangelical Christians."[13] Polling in the US in 2017 revealed that 80 percent of evangelicals believed that the creation of Israel in 1948 was a fulfillment of biblical prophecy that will bring about Christ's second coming.[14]

In addition, Trump's decision to leave the Paris climate agreement in 2017 (the decision was implemented in 2020) "sat easily with a group that contains many who deny the reality of climate change caused by human action, or do not consider it a threat that can be averted by human agency."[15]

Whatever one feels about these geopolitical and environmental issues, "it is undeniable that huge numbers of voters in the US see these decisions through an end-times lens."[16] Arguably the situation is becoming more extreme following Trump's defeat in the presidential election of 2020.

THE END-TIME BATTLEFIELDS IN THE 2020s

Several areas delineate what we might call the end-times political battlefields in the third decade of the twenty-first century. Central is the place of Israel and policy towards the Middle East. With regard to Middle Eastern policy, the evangelical wing of US Protestant churches offers robust support for the state of Israel. This is so clearly articulated that it is now termed "Christian Zionism."

Distrust of transnational organizations are another area of conflict. Whether it is the United Nations or the European Union, a particular approach to end-times analysis within the US presents these as inimical to US interests and freedom of action and spiritualizes this with undercurrents of accusations that these are aspects of an emerging one-world-government that will be utilized by antichrist.

The COVID-19 pandemic illustrates how right-wing and libertarian ideas can become imbued with apocalyptic tones. What began as a debate over public health measures and restrictions—designed to slow the spread of infection and save lives—has morphed into anti-vaxx movements that, as well as including those who oppose federal restrictions for

13. Whittock, "What Happens?," lines 34–35.
14. Whittock, *End Times, Again?*, 10.
15. Whittock, "What Happens?," lines 38–41.
16. Whittock, "What Happens?," lines 42–43.

libertarian reasons and those disseminating extreme conspiracy theories, also includes many who see the pandemic through an end-times lens.[17] In 2020, for example, it was claimed to be the fulfillment of prophecy in Revelation (the breaking of the "fourth seal"). Stephen Flurry, host of the Trumpet Daily Radio Show, referred to it as the beginning of the fulfillment of Old and New Testament prophecies and asserted: "We know there's all kinds of imminent pestilence epidemics that are going to sweep across this world during the Great Tribulation."[18] He went on to say that "This is one of the Four Horsemen of the Apocalypse" and "this is prophesied to get worse, much worse."[19] This view of prophecy being fulfilled in the pandemic—and variations on it—are widespread on the internet and social media.[20] Examples can be found via the Twitter hashtag #*Jesusiscoming* and on a number of websites.[21] An internet search will find assertions that COVID-19 forms part of a range of end-times diseases that fulfill biblical prophecies. There are also frequent claims that the "unvaxxed" are acting in line with God's will, by refusing to comply with public health restrictions. There are many online platforms conveying these, or similar, views regarding the pandemic and its claimed place within an apocalyptic program.

For some, this easily segues into the very distinctive phenomena of US "survivalism" and gun ownership, in which weapons protect against the forces of antichrist. This is where the extreme edge of the evangelical movement morphs into the armed nationalist militias and those who stormed the Capitol in Washington, DC, on 6 January 2021.

Research suggests that this US Christian nationalism is encouraged by "cues" from influential elites that inflame perceived victimhood and anxieties regarding racial and religious identities, and encourage support for conspiratorial information sources. The religious aspect of the attack on the Capitol was particularly conditioned by white identity, perceived victimhood, support for the QAnon movement,[22] and, it can be strongly argued, apocalyptic beliefs.

17. Dein, "Covid-19 and the Apocalypse," lines 147–53.

18. Kettley, "Coronavirus," lines 13–15; Dein, "Covid-19 and the Apocalypse," lines 151–52.

19. Kettley, "Coronavirus," lines 22–23, 28.

20. See: Dein, "Covid-19 and the Apocalypse," lines 154–60.

21. Mcmaster, "Why Some People Think," lines 17–20.

22. See: Armaly et al., "Christian Nationalism and Political Violence."

Climate change has also become an end-times battleground. With COP26 grappling with the threat posed to the planet by climate change, Franklin Graham (son of Billy Graham) responded to UK Prime Minister Boris Johnson's warning that the world is at "one minute to midnight on the doomsday clock," with a tweet (on 2 November 2021) that stated:

> @BorisJohnson said we are "one minute to midnight" as it relates to climate change. I believe we're one minute to midnight —not regarding climate change, but on God's clock, when he will bring judgment on those who have rejected him & his son, Jesus Christ.[23]

He had expanded on the same theme on Facebook one day earlier. There he wrote:

> The G20 Summit's big focus was on climate change. If we have an unusually warm summer, they say climate change is to blame. If we have a harsh winter, it's due to climate change. If it's wetter than normal, it's climate change. If it's dryer than normal, climate change. Climate change is nothing new—the Bible records it over 4,000 years ago.[24]

As is so often the case with those who are deeply embedded in end-times speculation, this tends to encourage passivity in the face of global challenges. In the case of Graham, the Facebook post can only be read as denial regarding the current global crisis. It seems to totally disregard the massive amount of evidence that clearly indicates that human-caused global warming is a reality. And this refusal to accept the facts is intertwined with Graham's eschatology.

To be fair to Graham, he concluded this Facebook post with: "No man knows the day or the hour . . . " However, he then returned to the end-times speculation: "but I believe we are getting close."[25] And this, it seems, is the reason for dismissing the threat of climate change. Since the world has no future, there is no need to address this issue. When one compares this to pro-fossil fuel statements by members of the evangelical right one can see that politically weaponized theologies are operating within right-wing agendas.

---

23. Whittock, "Franklin Graham Is Speculating," lines 3–5.
24. Whittock, "Franklin Graham Is Speculating," lines 33–36.
25. Whittock, "Franklin Graham Is Speculating," lines 14–15.

QANON AND "THE STORM"

An explosive input into mainline apocalyptic right-wing politics has come from the phenomenon known as "QAnon." In October 2017, a "drop" (a.k.a. a post) appeared on 4chan from an anonymous account calling itself "Q Clearance Patriot." These posts later shifted to 8chan and then to 8kun. This is the infamous Q. Claiming to be a government insider with high security clearance, what followed was a huge number of cryptic drops that centered on the claim that Donald Trump was engaged in an existential conflict with a "deep state" international conspiracy of devil-worshipping pedophiles and cannibalistic child-murderers.

The Q drops claimed that the Trump-led resistance was leading to "The Storm," when the members of the cabal would be arrested by the military, with some being imprisoned at Guantánamo Bay, and others facing military tribunals and execution. In this crude and simplistic scenario—with no regard to due process, or legal constraints—one can read the wild fantasies of a core of angry people who have a dystopian view of society and a desire to impose themselves and their outlook on their nation. It represents a humanistic millenarian "realized eschatology," focused on an imminent judgment day that will be followed by a reordering of US society. One can see how this also appeals to many of those who already have a politically radicalized form of spiritual eschatology (within the US evangelical right).

There is no evidence whatsoever to support the belief that Q is a highly placed government insider, and many experts assert that the drops follow a familiar pattern of cryptic clues (to be "investigated' and "understood" by insiders) that is common to the extreme and unregulated world of 4chan, 8chan, 8kun, and similar dark-web online platforms.

At first these drops were followed and shared by a minority of far-right Trump supporters, drawn from those persuaded by Q's outlandish claims. However, the impact massively expanded in 2020 in the turbulent run-up to the US presidential election. It was then that the supporters of QAnon deluged social media with false information about COVID-19, the Black Lives Matter protests, and, of course, the presidential election that pitted their man against the evil cabal.

As it went mainstream it drew support from Republican politicians as well as from the Trump base. This was a key moment in the process of mainstreaming ideas that, prior to this, had existed mostly on the dark web. However, the ground had been prepared for it by a pre-existing inclination within the US far right to accept conspiracy theories (such as believing the Sandy Hook Elementary School massacre was a fraud) that had already leaked into wider society through extreme TV and radio reporting on right-wing media outlets.

It has been noted that in 2020 QAnon "expanded its reach to include health-conscious yoga moms, anti-lockdown libertarians and evangelical Christians."[26] In short, a wide range of people across US society have bought into Q. In December 2020, an NPR/Ipsos poll found that 37 percent of those polled were unsure whether the statement "A group of Satan-worshipping elites who run a child sex ring are trying to control our [US] politics and media" (the QAnon core belief) is true or false; while 17 percent believed it to be true.[27] Only 47 percent thought the statement false. In addition, 39 percent believed in a "deep state" that had undermined Trump. This view was held primarily by Republicans and FOX News viewers (a majority of those in both these subsets agreed with it). But 49 percent of white males and rural residents thought so as well.[28]

Since 2020, adherents have publicly adopted Q slogans, such as "Where We Go One, We Go All," and used the letter "Q" on badges and flags. These are unspecific enough for some political activists to use in order to promote the movement, but deny any direct allegiance to the QAnon phenomenon. But people hear and understand the "dog whistle." However, tens of thousands more have become quite open in their adherence to Q. This includes large numbers of white, end-times-focused evangelicals. In January 2021, research by the American Enterprise Institute's Survey Center on American Life found that of those inclined to believe QAnon, 27 percent were white evangelical Christians. When combined with identified political affiliation this stood at 31 percent of white evangelical Republicans. In short, there is "significant overlap between Q followers and evangelicals."[29] As we explored earlier, such an overlap is not surprising.

In the aftermath of Trump's defeat in November 2020, Q stopped posting. The last drop occurred on 8 December 2020.[30] However, the concepts promoted by Q are now mainstream in a context where Trump

26. Roose, "What Is QAnon?," lines 51–53.
27. "More Than 1 in 3 Americans," lines 25–28.
28. "More Than 1 in 3 Americans," lines 34, 36–40.
29. Rogers, "Why QAnon Has Attracted," lines 20–32, esp. 32.
30. Brewster, "'Q' Hasn't Posted In Six Months," line 8.

and huge numbers of his supporters continue to promote the idea that the 2020 presidential election was stolen, and that Biden's accession to the presidency in January 2021 was based on election fraud.

As we have seen, there is a strong crossover between those believing in QAnon and the community of end-times-focused white evangelicals. The two groups are not the same, of course, but many of them share key characteristics: a sense of impending catastrophe (Armageddon/"The Storm"); being a minority at odds with much of mainstream life, ideas, and culture; frustration, balanced by personal empowerment in holding a belief that is above scrutiny; distrust of mainstream media; belief in unseen forces directing society; being members of a homogenous, self-referencing, and self-reinforcing community; having right-wing (including far-right) views regarding society and politics; belief that being "in the right" can justify actions otherwise considered illegal; a belief in American exceptionalism and nationalism; racial anxieties in a changing world where their influence is declining; and a commitment to guns.

WHERE IS AMERICA HEADED?

The current situation in the US is one that suggests that the storming of the Capitol on 6 January 2021 was not the *culmination* of a process of radicalization. Instead, it was a manifestation of *ongoing* radicalized politics. Arguably, given what has occurred since then, the most far-reaching of its effects are only just beginning.[31]

Since then, the "Stop the Steal" campaign (regardless of the lack of evidence for electoral fraud in the 2020 presidential election) and QAnon conspiracy theories have continued their trajectory of becoming part of mainstream politics (despite the end of the Q drops). Also woven into this situation is an apocalyptic outlook that is prepared to countenance extreme measures in order to confront and defeat opponents.

A review of the situation, in January 2022, concluded that "White evangelical Christians believe that they are being illegitimately persecuted and are increasingly invested in the boundary between the perceived morally righteous and their enemies" and (with data showing people leaving the evangelical right in protest at its extreme political positions) "Those who remain are not only deeply loyal to a shared political project,

---

31. Gatehouse, "Coming Storm."

but less likely to encounter internal checks on radical ideas."[32] In short, radicalization is intensifying.

In the US the future actions of the proponents of the most extreme end-times beliefs are becoming harder to predict according to the usual norms and values of democratic modern society. For over fifty-five years, those US evangelical communities influenced by the values of the Christian reconstructionist Chalcedon Foundation (founded in 1965) have espoused the establishment of a society based on a "biblical worldview." In 2017, this was described as "a society that rejects democratic principles, including the notion that governmental authority derives from the consent of the governed, and that is opposed to the values of egalitarianism, pluralism, and tolerance."[33] This is combined with the aim of "undermining a commitment to a religiously neutral public sphere in favor of a view of religious freedom that cannot coexist with various freedoms, religious and otherwise, with which it does not agree,"[34] and has connected "libertarian, patriot, neoconfederate, and extreme gun rights groups."[35] The intensity of such radicalization has dramatically increased since this was written in 2017. Reconstructionism would involve *theonomy*: government implementing Old Testament laws (there being no warrant or structure for such an imposition in the New Testament), such as the death penalty for adultery, idolatry, and many more.

While what is sometimes termed a "dominionist" reordering of society around an end-times ideology is common to both reconstructionism and evangelicalism, what is intriguing is that reconstructionism is, in its origins and its applications, postmillennialist (Christ will return *after* a golden age governed by Christian principles has been established), whereas almost all modern evangelicals are premillennialists (human society will degenerate and *then* Christ will return and *establish* the millennium).[36] Consequently, the influence of reconstructionism within evangelicalism (arguably a significant one) appears something of a puzzle.

Partly this illustrates how "'small packages' of ideas" can be shared between faith communities without signing up to the whole of another

---

32. Braunstein, "Backlash against Rightwing Evangelicals," lines 69–75.
33. Ingersoll, "Christian Reconstruction Movement," lines 383–85.
34. Ingersoll, "Christian Reconstruction Movement," lines 406–8.
35. Ingersoll, "Christian Reconstruction Movement," lines 424–25.
36. See: Ingersoll, *Building God's Kingdom*, ch. 1.

(rival) ideological framework.[37] Consequently, the ideas of reconstructionism have reach that is out of proportion to the size of the core group from which they originate. In this sense, reconstructionism, from the study of one community in the Pacific Northwest in September 2021, was described as a "numerically small but influentially growing movement,"[38] and one that "projects its soft power very deliberately and very effectively."[39] This might well be taken as a comment on the impact of the movement as a whole.

More fundamentally, it illustrates a common desire to impose a set of values (held by a shrinking minority) onto a much wider and pluralistic society. For classic reconstructionists, this will lead to a Christian (basically theocratic) golden age established by Christian influence. In contrast, for evangelicals this is more likely to be envisaged as imposition of "godly rule" on a recalcitrant society (and opposing the burgeoning power of antichrist) in an end-times struggle that will *soon* be ended by the return of Christ. Either way, the apocalypse is the end point that justifies such radical, arguably inherently coercive, plans to bring US society into line with the beliefs of a minority of its citizens.

When combined with accelerating right-wing populism, all of this has huge implications for the future of US politics and society. The "end times" are increasingly becoming "now times," and the potential for radical, even violent, strategies designed to speed its coming is increasing.

---

37. Whittock, "Baptist Roots," 321; Ingersoll, *Building God's Kingdom*, ch. 1.

38. Ward, "Understanding the Christian Reconstructionist Movement," lines 9–10; see: Gribben, *Survival and Resistance in Evangelical America*.

39. Ward, "Understanding the Christian Reconstructionist Movement," lines 60–61; see: Gribben, *Survival and Resistance in Evangelical America*.

Afterword
The Nature of Political Apocalypse

OVER THE COURSE of 2,000 years, end-times beliefs have taken many forms across different cultures in different time periods. These have led to many different political outcomes designed to either actively hasten the coming end times, vigorously enact their expected characteristics in the present, or create a social situation in preparation for events outside of the control of those taking part in these activities. While passivity is a feature of some apocalyptic movements, most of them actively engage with events in order to partake in the expected process of change and transformation. While contexts and beliefs differ hugely, several characteristics stand out that unite many of these movements.

COMMON FEATURES ACROSS MANY APOCALYPTIC GROUPS

Times of stress and turbulence are a major cause of apocalyptic activity. When present certainties seem shaken, many people are more prepared to consider an ultimate "shaking" of the whole order of things to be possible. Indeed, they may consider such a "shaking" to be imminent. Such times of stress may be human induced, as in conquest and conflict, or caused by natural factors such as disease, climatic change, or other environmental stresses.

Marginalization, powerlessness, or a sense of reduced influence (whether demographically caused or due to other political, social, or economic factors) often lies behind many of the movements. When personal power to influence events seems slight, looking towards divine (or externally driven) intervention often becomes a feature of such groups.

The Ghost Dance movement was a reaction to the destruction of Native American culture when military resistance had failed to arrest or reverse it. Xhosa Cattle-Killers reacted against intrusive colonialism, a characteristic shared with many other African apocalyptic movements. Medieval Jewish groups felt personally powerless in the face of external aggression, as had many of their compatriots before them; but prophetic texts seemed to promise success to radical resistance. The South African "Israelites" acted in the context of deteriorating economic and social conditions for the black community.

A reaction against forms of modernity may be a characteristic where these features are bewildering, unsettling, or threaten the position (demographically, culturally, economically) of a particular group. This can cause a readjustment of previous adherence to political norms if it is felt that these no longer deliver power and influence. The behavior of extreme members of the evangelical right in the US could be cited as an example of this phenomenon in the twenty-first century, when democracy may be sacrificed if radical actions are considered to be in line with what is viewed as the eschatological flow of events.

The presence of a messianic leader is not a prerequisite of such outbursts, but often accompanies them. Such a messianic leader offers a person who is considered to have received revelatory guidance sufficient to read the "signs of the times," and who acts as spokesperson for God or spiritual forces outside the normal human experience. At times such a leader may present themselves as embodiments of figures foretold in prophecy (the *Mahdi*, or one of the figures in Revelation). Or they may attempt to co-opt and adapt existing messianic figures, as in extreme German anabaptist activities. At other times they will begin the movement *de novo*, claiming a new insight that explains current circumstances and promises a way forward, often through a time of trial (for example Alice Lakwena, Kinjikitile Ngwale, Onyango Dunde).

These leaders often borrow features from different religious traditions that are then given apparent coherence by the messianic leader. Claiming absolute authority over members, the movement is, in effect, a cult. In addition to the leaders just cited, the modern world has also seen the impact of "doomsday cults" with political ambitions that are centered on "messianic figures," such as Asahara Shoko (executed 2018) whose AUM cult followers released sarin nerve gas on the Tokyo subway in 1995, killing thirteen people and injuring about 5,500. Apocalyptic violence is often directed by one who claims an insight into the mind of God and the ability to read the "signs" in such a way as to justify the extreme violence that they direct.

Establishing an "alien other" is often a feature. Within Christian and Islamic apocalyptic groups this usually means associating an enemy with the forces of antichrist or *Dajjaal*. In the secularized millenarianism of the Nazis, the "alien other" was the Jews and others regarded as racially inferior. For extreme Russian nationalists, the enemy is the West and liberal values. Such an "identification" can both serve to "explain" opposition or problems being faced by associating it with an objectified enemy and bind together the "in-group."

The sense of approaching the end times through struggle has also produced movements that actively promote conflict. This may be to test the perceived purity of followers; bring down existing structures; or enhance the power of a leader, who alone appears to provide stability in the middle of upheaval. Nazism is an obvious example.

Suspension of social norms and behavior is also often apparent. This may be presented as proof that those taking part in this breaking of the norms have been liberated from such constraints. ISIS behavior in Syria would be an example. It may be promoted as necessary to undermine current behavioral and social structures. It may be used to initiate members by making them break with, or even commit atrocities against, family and neighbors. The behavior of the Lord's Resistance Army and the horrors its child soldiers were forced to commit can be cited here. At the same time, this also binds new members to the movement by a shared part in the violence. The traumatization caused to those who act as perpetrators can also make them easier to dominate and use as "killing machines." At times it appears to offer an ideological justification for violent or sexual excess by those who gain gratification from this, but wish to cloak their behavior with self-referenced "legitimacy." The Anabaptists at Münster could be cited here, but are by no means unique.

The use of powerful imagery and metaphors to express complex matters and bind together those "in the know" often occurs. This can be found across all the movements and helps explain their "populist" character. At the same time, the claimed ability to interpret complex prophetic imagery is often a feature. One can see this in the way different Christian groups have claimed to have the key to unlock the meaning of the book of Revelation, or to compute sacred numerology to reveal the future. Or how Islamist groups have claimed they possess the only legitimate interpretation of verses in the Qur'an, or in the hadith traditions.

While some groups exist as a way back to what is perceived as a purer and simpler form of a belief or ideology, many others reveal a distinct syncretism in which millenarian ideas are borrowed, co-opted, and then deployed in order to justify actions. Syncretism (often co-opting Christian or Islamic motifs and blending them with indigenous traditions) can clearly be seen in several African, Asian, and Indigenous American movements. This often occurred as part of resistance to Western imperialism, while borrowing from beliefs brought by that imperial expansion. An example, with massive effects, was the Taiping movement in China with its co-opting of Christian messianic terminology.

What is clear from this is that, with the apocalyptic tradition deeply rooted in the three Abrahamic religions, it has influenced a wide range of global cultures even when those cultures have not adopted the entirety of the Abrahamic religious tradition in question. Other world religions also exhibit millenarian eschatological features, but the linear view of history central to the Abrahamic faiths has caused them to appear with great frequency in the justifications for apocalyptic radicalism by activist groups convinced the end time is at hand.

In addition, the concept of eschatological change (interwoven with messianic and millenarian expectations) has influenced such a wide range of communities that it seems to be an ideology that resonates with a deep need in human nature. Clearly, cultures whose cosmic time-scale is less linear are not so prone to this. However, they too can experience inputs from other faith communities (usually Abrahamic ones) leading to syncretism of the new with existing indigenous beliefs. Alternatively, such an indigenous community may identify some point in the cyclical cosmic cycle as occurring in the here-and-now. In which case the apocalyptic viewpoint can come into play.

What is certainly true is that forms of millenarian beliefs—giving rise to often-radicalized political responses—are still highly influential across the globe in the twenty-first century. Far from being a secular age, many modern movements still draw on this deep well-spring of belief in impending cataclysm, from which the elect will emerge victorious. Whether those espousing this belief think that they will simply *inherit* their status in the new millennium, or actively *implement* it, apocalyptic politics remain a potent force today within the cocktail of factors that drive radical action at times of turbulence. For many, the "end times" are very much "now times." And this has direct political effects on the modern world, as in the past.

Bibliography

Abdel Haleem, M. A. S., trans. *The Qur'an*. Oxford: Oxford University Press, 2010.
Adas, Michael. *Prophets of Rebellion: Millenarian Protest Movements against the European Colonial Order*. Chapel Hill: University of North Carolina Press, 2012.
Ai, Shu. "Envision of the Land-after-Death and Expectations for 'This Life': Translation and Reconfiguration of 'Kingdom of Heaven' in Taiping Rebellion Movement." *Journal of Languages, Texts, and Society* 4 (2020) 84–105.
al-Din Zarabozo, Jamaal. "The Major Signs of the Day of Judgment (Part 1 of 7): The Minor Signs." *The Religion of Islam*, August 13, 2007. https://www.islamreligion.com/articles/613/viewall/major-signs-of-day-of-judgment/.
"Alice Lakwena and the Holy Spirit Movement." *The East African*, March 31, 2012. https://www.theeastafrican.co.ke/tea/magazine/alice-lakwena-and-the-holy-spirit-movement-1308008.
"Alice Lakwena's Holy Spirit Movement." https://www.globalsecurity.org/military/world/para/hsm.htm.
Allen, Tim. "Understanding Alice: Uganda's Holy Spirit Movement in Context." *Africa* 61.3 (July 1991) 370–99.
Anderson, Eugene N. *The East Asian World-System: Climate and Dynastic Change*. New York: Springer, 2019.
Ariel, Yaakov. "Radical Millennial Movements in Contemporary Judaism in Israel." In *The Oxford Handbook of Millennialism*, edited by Catherine Wessinger, 667–87. Oxford: Oxford University Press, 2011.
Armaly, Miles T., et al. "Christian Nationalism and Political Violence: Victimhood, Racial Identity, Conspiracy, and Support for the Capitol Attacks." *Political Behavior* 44 (January 2022) 937–60. https://link.springer.com/article/10.1007/s11109-021-09758-y.
Barnai, Jacob. "Some Social Aspects of the Polemics between Sabbatians and Their Opponents." In *Millenarianism and Messianism in Early Modern European Culture, Volume I, Jewish Messianism in the Early Modern World*, edited by Matt D. Goldish and Richard H. Popkin, 1:77–90. 4 vols. Dordrecht, Netherlands: Springer, 2001.
Basit, Asif M. "Loyalty to the British Raj." *Al Hakam*, December 7, 2018. https://www.alhakam.org/loyalty-to-the-british-raj/.
Benz, Wolfgang. *A Concise History of the Third Reich*. Translated by Thomas Dunlap. Berkeley: University of California Press, 2007.
Bercovitch, Sacvan. *The American Jeremiad*. Madison: University of Wisconsin Press, 1978.

———. *The Puritan Origins of the American Self*. New Haven: Yale University Press, 1975.
Beverton, Alys. "Maji Maji Uprising (1905–1907)." *Blackpast*, June 21, 2019. https://www.blackpast.org/global-african-history/maji-maji-uprising-1905-1907/
"Black Hebrew Israelites." *Anti-Defamation League*, December 11, 2019. https://www.adl.org/resources/backgrounders/black-hebrew-israelites
Boyer, Paul. "Millennialism." In *The Encyclopedia of Politics and Religion: Volume I*, edited by Robert Wuthnow et al., 1:516–21. 2 vols. London: Routledge, 1998.
———. *When Time Shall Be No More: Prophecy Belief in Modern American Culture*. Cambridge, MA: Belknap, 1992.
Brasher, Brenda E. "Millennialism in Contemporary Israeli Politics." In *Expecting the End: Millennialism in Social and Historical Context*, edited by Crawford Gribben and Kenneth G. C. Newport, 67–78. Waco, TX: Baylor University Press, 2006.
Braunstein, Ruth. "The Backlash against Rightwing Evangelicals Is Reshaping American Politics and Faith." *The Guardian*, January 25, 2022. https://www.theguardian.com/commentisfree/2022/jan/25/the-backlash-against-rightwing-evangelicals-is-reshaping-american-politics-and-faith.
Brewster, Jack. "'Q' Hasn't Posted in Six Months—But Some QAnon Followers Still Keep the Faith." *Forbes*, June 8, 2021. https://www.forbes.com/sites/jackbrewster/2021/06/08/q-hasnt-posted-in-6-months-but-some-qanon-followers-still-keep-the-faith/?sh=3596ba736071
Brighton, Mark Andrew. *The Sicarii in Josephus's Judean War: Rhetorical Analysis and Historical Observations*. Atlanta: Society of Biblical Literature, 2009.
Brown, Dee. *Bury My Heart at Wounded Knee*. London: Pan, 1972.
Brown, Jonathan A. C. *Misquoting Muhammad: The Challenge and Choices of Interpreting the Prophet's Legacy*. London: Oneworld, 2014.
Campos, Michelle. *Ottoman Brothers: Muslims, Christians, and Jews in Early Twentieth-Century Palestine*. Palo Alto, CA: Stanford University Press, 2010.
Carrington, Philip. *The Early Christian Church: Volume 1, The First Christian Church*. 2 vols. Cambridge: Cambridge University Press, 2011.
Celso, Anthony. *The Islamic State: A Comparative History of Jihadist Warfare*. Lanham, MD: Lexington, 2018.
———. "The Islamic State (IS) and the Sudanese 'Mahdiyyah': A Comparative Analysis of Two Apocalyptic Jihadist States." www.psa.ac.uk/sites/default/files/conference/papers/2015/IS%20and%20the%20Sudanese%20Caliphate.docx2_.pdf.
Chalklin, Christopher. *The Rise of the English Town, 1650–1850*. Cambridge: Cambridge University Press, 2001.
Chesneaux, Jean. *Peasant Revolts in China, 1840–1949*. Translated by C. A. Curwen. New York: Norton, 1973.
Chitwood, Ken. "British Evangelicals Brace for Brexit." *Christianity Today*, December 13, 2019. https://www.christianitytoday.com/news/2019/december/british-evangelicals-brexit-deadline-boris-johnson-vote.html.
Churchill, Bernardita Reyes. "History of the Philippine Revolution: The Katipunan Revolution." https://ncca.gov.ph/about-ncca-3/subcommissions/subcommission-on-cultural-heritagesch/historical-research/history-of-the-philippine-revolution/
Clay, J. Eugene. "Apocalypticism in Eastern Europe." In *The Continuum History of Apocalypticism*, edited by Bernard McGinn et al., 628–48. New York: Continuum, 2003.

Clodfelter, Micheal. *Warfare and Armed Conflicts: A Statistical Reference to Casualty and Other Figures.* Jefferson, NC: Mcfarland, 2002.

Clover, Charles. *Black Wind, White Snow: The Rise of Russia's New Nationalism.* New Haven: Yale University Press, 2016.

———. "The Unlikely Origins of Russia's Manifest Destiny." *Foreign Policy*, July 27, 2016. https://foreignpolicy.com/2016/07/27/geopolitics-russia-mackinder-eurasia-heartland-dugin-ukraine-eurasianism-manifest-destiny-putin/.

Cohn, Norman. *The Pursuit of the Millennium.* St. Albans, UK: Paladin, 1970.

Collins, John Joseph. *The Apocalyptic Imagination: An Introduction to Jewish Apocalyptic Literature.* Grand Rapids: Eerdmans, 2016.

———. "Millenarianism in Ancient Judaism." *Critical Dictionary of Apocalyptic and Millenarian Movements*, January 15, 2021. www.cdamm.org/articles/ancient-judaism.

Combés, Isabelle. "Las batallas de Kuruyuki: Variaciones sobre una derrota chiriguana." *Bulletin de l'Institut Francais d'Etudes Andines* 34.2 (2005) 221–33.

Cook, David. *Contemporary Muslim Apocalyptic Literature.* Syracuse, NY: Syracuse University Press, 2005.

Cooper, Abraham, and Johnnie Moore. "US Afghanistan Withdrawal Aided Iran in Its Apocalyptic Mideast Vision." *The Medialine*, September 14, 2021. https://themedialine.org/news/opinion/us-afghanistan-withdrawal-aided-iran-in-its-apocalyptic-mideast-vision/.

Court, John M. *Approaching the Apocalypse: A Short History of Christian Millenarianism.* London: Taurus, 2008.

Coyer, Paul. "Putin's Holy War and the Disintegration of the 'Russian World.'" *Forbes*, June 4, 2015. https://www.forbes.com/sites/paulcoyer/2015/06/04/putins-holy-war-and-the-disintegration-of-the-russian-world/?sh=51619ca285b4.

Dass, Nirmal. *The Deeds of the Franks and Other Jerusalem-bound Pilgrims: The Earliest Chronicle of the First Crusades.* Lanham, MD: Rowman & Littlefield, 2011.

Dastmalchian, Amir. "Islam." In *The Palgrave Handbook of the Afterlife*, edited by Benjamin Matheson and Yujin Nagasawa, 153–76. London: Palgrave Macmillan, 2017.

Dein, Simon. "Covid-19 and the Apocalypse: Religious and Secular Perspectives." *Journal of Religion and Health* 60.1 (2021) 5–15. https://www.ncbi.nlm.nih.gov/pmc/articles/PMC7598223/.

Dewhirst, Jonathan. "The Satiru Uprising, Nigeria, 1906." *Britain's Small Forgotten Wars*, May 2020. http://www.britainssmallwars.co.uk/the-satiru-uprising-nigeria-1906.html.

Diacon, Todd A. "Contestado Rebellion." https://www.encyclopedia.com/humanities/encyclopedias-almanacs-transcripts-and-maps/contestado-rebellion.

Dugin, Alexander. "The Clash of Realism and Liberalism." *The Postil Magazine*, May 1, 2022. https://www.thepostil.com/the-clash-of-realism-and-liberalism/.

———. "The Russian Peace: A Conversation with Alexander Dugin." *The Postil Magazine*, April 1, 2022. https://www.thepostil.com/the-russian-peace-a-conversation-with-alexander-dugin/.

Duka, Cecilio D. *Struggle for Freedom: A Textbook on Philippine History.* Manila: REX, 2008.

Editors of Encyclopaedia Britannica. "Mujahideen, Islam." *Encyclopaedia Britannica.* https://www.britannica.com/topic/mujahideen-Islam.

———. "Qing Dynasty." *Encyclopaedia Britannica*. https://www.britannica.com/topic/Qing-dynasty.

———. "Rizalist Cult." *Encyclopaedia Britannica*. https://www.britannica.com/topic/Rizalist-cult.

———. "Russian Orthodox Church." *Encyclopaedia Britannica*. https://www.britannica.com/topic/Russian-Orthodox-Church.

Elliott, Emory. "The Legacy of Puritanism." *National Humanities Center*. http://nationalhumanitiescenter.org/tserve/eighteen/ekeyinfo/legacy.htm.

Esler, Philip F. "Social-Scientific Approaches to Apocalyptic Literature." In *The Oxford Handbook of Apocalyptic Literature*, edited by John J. Collins, 123–44. Oxford: Oxford University Press, 2014.

"EU Introduces Sanctions against Leadership of TASS, VGTRK, Moskovsky Komsomolets." *APA*, April 9, 2022. https://apa.az/en/cis-countries/eu-introduces-sanctions-against-leadership-of-tass-vgtrk-moskovsky-komsomolets-373023.

Evans, Craig A. *Jesus and His Contemporaries: Comparative Studies*. Leiden: Brill, 2001.

Evans, Richard J. *The Third Reich at War*. London: Penguin, 2009.

Fadlalla, Mohamed H. *Short History of Sudan*. Bloomington, IN: iUniverse, 2004.

Feiner, Shmuel. *The Jewish Enlightenment*. Translated by Chaya Naor. Philadelphia: University of Pennsylvania Press, 2004.

Fern, Susan, and Susan Sorek. *The Jews against Rome: War in Palestine AD 66–73*. London: Bloomsbury Academic, 2008.

Firestone, Reuven. *Holy War in Judaism: The Fall and Rise of a Controversial Idea*. New York: Oxford University Press, 2012.

Fischer, Claude S. *Made in America: A Social History of American Culture and Character*. Chicago: University of Chicago Press, 2010.

———. "Pilgrims, Puritans, and the Ideology That Is Their American Legacy." *Berkeley Blog*, November 24, 2010. https://blogs.berkeley.edu/2010/11/24/pilgrims-puritans-and-their-american-legacy/.

Fradkin, Rebecca. "The Co-optation of Islam in Russia." *Hudson Institute*, February 7, 2020. https://www.hudson.org/research/15699-the-co-optation-of-islam-in-russia.

France, Richard Thomas. *The Gospel According to Matthew: An Introduction and Commentary*. Grand Rapids: Eerdmans, 1985.

Fraser, Antonia. *Cromwell: Our Chief of Men*. London: Granada, 1973.

Friedländer, Saul. *The Years of Extermination: Nazi Germany and the Jews, 1939–1945*. London: Phoenix, 2008.

Fruchtenbaum, Arnold. "Israel in Prophecy." In *The Popular Encyclopedia of Bible Prophecy*, edited by Tim LaHaye and Ed Hindson, 153–58. Eugene, OR: Harvest House, 2004.

Furnish, Timothy R. *Holiest Wars: Islamic Mahdis, Their Jihads, and Osama Bin Laden*. Westport, CT: Praeger, 2005.

Galeotti, Mark. "In Moscow's Shadows: Kazakhstan, through the Russian Lens." *Apple Podcasts*. Episode 55. 39:16. https://podcasts.apple.com/gb/podcast/in-moscows-shadows/id1510124746?i=1000547323593.

Gallagher, Eugene V., and Herman Tull. "Millenarianism I. Christianity." In *Encyclopedia of the Bible and Its Reception, vol. 19, Midrash and Aggadah–Mourning*, edited by Constance M. Furey et al., 19:159–61. 20 vols. Berlin: de Gruyter, 2021.

Garfinkle, Adam M. "On the Origin, Meaning, Use and Abuse of a Phrase." *Middle Eastern Studies* 27.4 (October 1991) 539–50.
Garrard, John, and Carol Garrard. *Russian Orthodoxy Resurgent: Faith and Power in the New Russia*. Princeton: Princeton University Press, 2008.
Gatehouse, Gabriel. "The Coming Storm: Welcome to the Future." *BBC Sounds*, January 4, 2022. Episode 7. 37:35. https://www.bbc.co.uk/sounds/play/p0bchs4q.
Geitner, Lorin C. "End-Times in the East: Eschatology in Hinduism and Jainism." *Sacred History Magazine* (September 2006) 1–4. https://ssrn.com/abstract=908997.
Gellately, Robert. *Lenin, Stalin and Hitler: The Age of Social Catastrophe*. London: Cape, 2007.
Gerlach, Christian. "The Wannsee Conference, the Fate of German Jews, and Hitler's Decision in Principle to Exterminate All European Jews." In *The Holocaust: Origins, Implementation, Aftermath*, edited by Omer Bartov, 106–61. Abingdon, UK: Routledge, 2000.
Germano, David. *Embodying the Dharma: Buddhist Relic Veneration in Asia*. Albany: State University of New York Press, 2012.
Gilbert, Lela. "Is the Iranian Apocalypse Really Coming?" *Religion Unplugged*, August 26, 2019. https://religionunplugged.com/news/2019/8/26/watch-out-for-the-iranian-apocalypse.
Glenn, Cameron, et al. "Timeline: The Rise, Spread, and Fall of the Islamic State." *Wilson Center*, October 28, 2019. https://www.wilsoncenter.org/article/timeline-the-rise-spread-and-fall-the-islamic-state.
Goldish, Matt. "Introduction." In *Millenarianism and Messianism in Early Modern European Culture, Volume I, Jewish Messianism in the Early Modern World*, edited by Matt D. Goldish and Richard H. Popkin, 1:xv–xix. 4 vols. Dordrecht, Netherlands: Springer, 2001.
Goodman, Martin. *The Ruling Class of Judaea: The Origins of the Jewish Revolt against Rome, AD 66–70*. Cambridge: Cambridge University Press, 1993.
Gottheil, Richard, et al. "Esdras, Books of." *Jewish Encyclopedia*. https://jewishencyclopedia.com/articles/5969-ezra-apocryphal-books-of.
Gradie, Charlotte M. *The Tepehuan Revolt of 1616: Militarism, Evangelism, and Colonialism in Seventeenth-Century Nueva Vizcaya*. Salt Lake City: University of Utah Press, 2000.
Grant, R. G. "Third Battle of Nanjing." *Encyclopaedia Britannica*. https://www.britannica.com/event/Third-Battle-of-Nanjing.
Greaves, Richard L. *Glimpses of Glory: John Bunyan and English Dissent*. Stanford, CA: Stanford University Press, 2002.
Gribben, Crawford. *Survival and Resistance in Evangelical America: Christian Reconstruction in the Pacific Northwest*. Oxford: Oxford University Press, 2021.
Grossman, James, and Albert J. Raboteau. "Black Migration, Religion, and Civic Life." In *Immigration and Religion in America: Comparative and Historical Perspectives*, edited by Richard Alba et al., 304–18. New York: New York University Press, 2009.
Guerrero, Milagros C. "The Colorum Uprisings: 1924–1931." *Asian Studies* 5.1 (1967) 65–78.
Günther, Sebastian. "Eschatology and the Qur'an." In *The Oxford Handbook of Qur'anic Studies*, edited by Mustafa Shah and Muhammad Abdel Haleem. Oxford: Oxford Academic, 2020. DOI: 10.1093/oxfordhb/9780199698646.013.11.

Hackett, Rosalind. "Millennial and Apocalyptic Movements in Africa." In *The Oxford Handbook of Millennialism*, edited by Catherine Wessinger, 385–419. Oxford: Oxford University Press, 2011.

Hagemeister, Michael. "The Third Rome against the Third Temple: Apocalypticism and Conspiracism in Post-Soviet Russia." In *Handbook of Conspiracy Theory and Contemporary Religion*, edited by Asbjørn Dyrendal et al., 423–42. Leiden: Brill, 2018.

Hearn, Maxwell K. "The Qing Dynasty (1644–1911)." *The Metropolitan Museum of Art*, October 2003. https://www.metmuseum.org/toah/hd/qing_1/hd_qing_1.htm.

Hengel, Martin. *The Zealots*. Translated by David Smith. Edinburgh: T. & T. Clark, 1989.

Hilberg, Raul. *The Destruction of the European Jews, vol 3*, 3 vols. Rev. ed. New York: Holmes and Meier, 1985.

Hill, Christopher, and Edmund Dell. *The Good Old Cause: The English Revolution of 1640–1660*. New York: Kelly, 1969.

History.com Editors. "Rastafarianism." *History.com*, May 31, 2017. https://www.history.com/topics/religion/history-of-rastafarianism.

———. "Taiping Rebellion." *History.com*, February 22, 2018. https://www.history.com/topics/china/taiping-rebellion.

"Hitler Quotes." https://ptfaculty.gordonstate.edu/jmallory/index_files/page0508.htm.

Ho, Ping-ti. *Studies on the Population of China, 1368–1953*. Cambridge: Harvard University Press, 1959.

Hobson, Peter. "Russian Patriarch Says Orthodox Faithful Are Holding Back the Antichrist." *Reuters*, April 7, 2022. https://www.reuters.com/world/europe/russian-patriarch-says-orthodox-faithful-are-holding-back-antichrist-2022-04-07/.

The Holy Bible, New Revised Standard Version (Anglicised Edition). Oxford: Oxford University Press, 1995.

Hooper, Richard J. *End of Days: Predictions of the End from Ancient Sources*. Sedona, AZ: Sanctuary, 2011.

Hull, Isabel. *Absolute Destruction: Military Culture and the Practices of War in Imperial Germany*. Ithaca, NY: Cornell University Press, 2005.

———. "Military Culture and the Production of 'Final Solutions' in the Colonies: The Example of Wilhelminian Germany." In *The Specter of Genocide: Mass Murder in Historical Perspective*, edited by Robert Gellately and Ben Kiernan, 141–62. Cambridge: Cambridge University Press, 2003.

Hyamson, Albert. "British Projects for the Restoration of Jews to Palestine." *Publications of the American Jewish Historical Society* 26 (1918) 127–64.

Ileto, Reynaldo Clemeña. *Pasyon and Revolution: Popular Movements in the Philippines, 1840–1910*. Quezon City: Ateneo de Manila University Press, 1979.

Iliffe, John. *A Modern History of Tanganyika*. Cambridge: Cambridge University Press, 1979.

Inbari, Motti. *Jewish Fundamentalism and the Temple Mount: Who Will Build the Third Temple?* Translated by Shaul Vardi. Albany: State University of New York Press, 2009.

Ingersoll, Julie J. *Building God's Kingdom: Inside the World of Christian Reconstruction*. Oxford: Oxford University Press, 2015.

———. "The Christian Reconstruction Movement in U.S. Politics." *Oxford Academic*, January 10, 2017. https://www.oxfordhandbooks.com/view/10.1093/oxfordhb/9780199935420.001.0001/oxfordhb-9780199935420-e-25

"Iranian Presidential Advisor Mohammad Ali Ramin: 'The Resolution of the Holocaust Issue Will End in the Destruction of Israel.'" *The Meir Amit Intelligence and Terrorism Information Center*, July 5, 2006. https://www.terrorism-info.org.il/en/19129/.

Isfahani, Dehsorkhi, et al. *Yati Ala al-Nas Zaman*. Qom, Iran Entesharat-e Mir Fattah, 2004.

Jenkins, Mark. "Russian Nuclear Orthodoxy." *Catholic Herald*, April 26, 2022. https://catholicherald.co.uk/russian-nuclear-orthodoxy/.

Jerusalem: The Future of The Holy City for Three Monotheisms, US Congress House Committee on Foreign Affairs, Hearings, July 28, 1971, Volume 5. Washington, DC: US Government Printing Office, 1971.

Johnson, Paul. *A History of Christianity*. New York: Athenium, 1976.

Judis, John B. "The Middle East That France and Britain Drew Is Finally Unravelling." *The New Republic*, June 26, 2014. www.newrepublic.com/article/118409/mideast-unravelling-and-theres-not-much-us-can-do.

Juergensmeyer, Mark. *Terror in the Mind of God: The Global Rise of Religious Violence*. Oakland: University of California Press, 2017.

Kaplan, Amy. *Our American Israel: The Story of an Entangled Alliance*. Cambridge: Harvard University Press, 2018.

Kent, Neil. *A Concise History of the Russian Orthodox Church*. Washington, DC: Academica, 2021.

Kershaw, Ian. *Hitler, 1889–1936: Hubris*. London: Penguin, 1999.

———. *Hitler, the Germans, and the Final Solution*. New Haven: Yale University Press, 2008.

Kettley, Sebastian. "Coronavirus: Fears Fourth Seal of Apocalypse Broken as Bible Warning of Pestilence Unfolds." *Express*, April 20, 2020. https://www.express.co.uk/news/weird/1244611/Coronavirus-fourth-seal-apocalypse-Bible-Book-of-Revelation-pestilence-coronavirus-news.

Keynes, Simon. "An Abbot, an Archbishop, and the Viking Raids of 1006–7 and 1009–12." *Anglo-Saxon England* 36 (2007) 151–220.

Khalaji, Mehdi. *Agenda Iran. Apocalyptic Politics: On the Rationality of Iranian Policy. Policy Focus #79*. Washington, DC: Washington Institute for Near East Policy, 2008.

Khodarkovsky, Michael. "Putin's Dream of Godliness: Holy Russia." *The New York Times*, January 22, 2019. https://www.nytimes.com/2019/01/22/opinion/putin-russia-orthodox-church.html.

Kiang, Clyde. *The Hakka Odyssey and Their Taiwan Homeland*. Salem, OH: Allegheny, 1992.

Kipling, Rudyard. "Fuzzy-Wuzzy." http://www.kiplingsociety.co.uk/poems_fuzzywuzzy.htm.

Kohler, Kaufmann, and Richard Gottheil. "Dönmeh." *Jewish Encyclopedia*. https://jewishencyclopedia.com/articles/5278-donmeh.

Landes, Richard. "Medieval and Reformation Millennialism." *Encyclopaedia Britannica*. https://www.britannica.com/topic/eschatology/Medieval-and-Reformation-millennialism.

———. "The Views of Augustine." *Encyclopaedia Britannica*. https://www.britannica.com/topic/eschatology/Renewed-interest-in-eschatology.

Langer, Erick D. *Expecting Pears from an Elm Tree*. Durham, NC: Duke University Press, 2009.

Larsen, David L. *Company of the Preachers*. Grand Rapids: Kregel, 1998.

Larson, Warren Fredrick. "Jesus in Islam and Christianity: Discussing the Similarities and the Differences." *Missiology* 36.3 (July 2008) 327–41.

Lassner, J. "Abu Isa Esfahani." *Encyclopaedia Iranica*. https://www.iranicaonline.org/articles/abu-isa-esfahani-founder-of-the-isawiya-an-obscure-jewish-sect-in-islamic-times.

Latteri, Natalie E. "A Dialogue on Disaster: Antichrists in Jewish and Christian Apocalypses and Their Medieval Recensions." *Quidditas* 38 (2017) 61–82.

Lawee, Eric. "The Messianism of Isaac Abarbanel, 'Father of the [Jewish] Messianic Movements of the Sixteenth and Seventeenth Centuries.'" In *Millenarianism and Messianism in Early Modern European Culture, Volume I, Jewish Messianism in the Early Modern World*, edited by Matt D. Goldish and Richard H. Popkin, 1:1–40. 4 vols. Dordrecht, Netherlands: Springer, 2001.

Lenowitz, Harry. "The Charlatan at the Gottes Haus in Offenbach." In *Millenarianism and Messianism in Early Modern European Culture, Volume I, Jewish Messianism in the Early Modern World*, edited by Matt D. Goldish and Richard H. Popkin, 189–202. Dordrecht, Netherlands: Springer, 2001.

Lipschutz, Mark R., and R. Kent Rasmussen. *Dictionary of African Historical Biography*. Berkeley: University of California Press, 1989.

Lubrano, Mauro. "Iran, Hezbollah, and the End of Times: Ideology in Context." *The Foreign Analyst*, January 19, 2018. http://theforeignanalyst.com/iran-hezbollah-and-the-end-of-times-ideology-in-context/.

"The Maji Maji Rebellion." *Violence in Twentieth-Century Africa* (blog). https://scholarblogs.emory.edu/violenceinafrica/sample-page/the-maji-maji-rebellion-2/.

Majlisi, Muhammad Baqer. *Behar al-Anwar fi Dorrar-e Akhbar al-Aima al-Athar*. Tehran: Al-Maktabah al-Islamyah, 1993.

Masalha, Nur. *The Zionist Bible: Biblical Precedent, Colonialism and the Erasure of Memory*. London: Routledge, 2014.

Maxon, Robert M. *Conflict and Accommodation in Western Kenya: The Gusii and the British, 1907–1963*. Madison, NJ: Fairleigh Dickinson University Press, 1989.

McCants, William Faizi. *The ISIS Apocalypse: The History, Strategy, and Doomsday Vision of the Islamic State*. New York: St. Martin's, 2015.

Mcmaster, Geoff. "Why Some People Think COVID-19 Heralds the Apocalypse." *The University of Alberta*, April 24, 2020. https://www.ualberta.ca/folio/2020/04/why-some-people-think-covid-19-heralds-the-apocalypse.html.

Medoff, Rafael, and Chaim I. Waxman. *Historical Dictionary of Zionism*. Lanham, MD: Scarecrow, 2008.

Meyer-Fong, Tobie. *What Remains: Coming to Terms with Civil War in 19th Century China*. Redwood City, CA: Stanford University Press, 2013.

Michaelis, M. "'Jewish Bolshevism' and Russo-German Relations in 1933: A Documentary Note." *Soviet Jewish Affairs* 1.2 (1971) 112–18.

Milani, Milad. "The Cultural Products of Global Sufism." In *Handbook of New Religions and Cultural Production*, edited by Carol Cusack and Alex Norman, 659–80. Brill Handbooks on Contemporary Religion 4. Leiden: Brill, 2012.

Miller, Michael T. *The Name of God in Jewish Thought: A Philosophical Analysis of Mystical Traditions from Apocalyptic to Kabbalah*. London: Routledge, 2016.

Mishkat al-Masabih. Translated by James Robson. Lahore, Pakistan: Sh. Muhammad Ashraf, 1981.
Mohammadi, Majid. *Political Islam in Post-Revolutionary Iran: Shi'i Ideologies in Islamist Discourse*. London: Bloomsbury, 2015.
Moorcraft, Paul L. *Dying for the Truth: The Concise History of Frontline War Reporting*. Barnsley, UK: Pen and Sword Military, 2016.
Mor, Menahem. *The Second Jewish Revolt: The Bar Kokhba War, 132–136 CE*. Leiden: Brill, 2016.
"More Than 1 in 3 Americans Believe a 'Deep State' Is Working to Undermine Trump." *Ipsos*, December 30, 2020. https://www.ipsos.com/en-us/news-polls/npr-misinformation-123020.
Morris, Brian. *Religion and Anthropology: A Critical Introduction*. Cambridge: Cambridge University Press, 2006.
"Moskovskij Komsomolets." *Euro Topics*. https://www.eurotopics.net/en/170195/moskovskij-komsomolets#.
Mounce, Robert H. *The Book of Revelation*. New International Commentary on the New Testament 27. Grand Rapids: Eerdmans, 1998.
Murrell, Nathaniel Samuel. "Introduction: The Rastafari Phenomenon." In *Chanting Down Babylon*, edited by Nathaniel Samuel Murrell et al., 1–22. Philadelphia: Temple University Press, 1998.
Nafissi, Mohammad. "Shiism and Politics." In *Routledge Handbook of Religion and Politics*, edited by Jeffrey Haynes, 111–27. Abingdon, UK: Routledge, 2009.
"Nation of Islam." *Southern Poverty Law Center*. https://www.splcenter.org/fighting-hate/extremist-files/group/nation-islam.
Neiman, Sophie. "The Enduring Harm Inflicted by the Lord's Resistance Army." *The New Humanitarian*, August 11, 2020. https://www.thenewhumanitarian.org/news-feature/2020/08/11/Kony-LRA-Uganda-Congo-CAR.
Nishikawa, Yukiko. *Human Security in Southeast Asia*. Abingdon, UK: Taylor & Francis, 2010.
Noakes, Jeremy, and Geoffrey Pridham. *Nazism 1919–1945, Volume Four: The German Home Front in World War II*. Exeter: University of Exeter Press, 1998.
Oegema, Gerbern S. *The Anointed and His People: Messianic Expectations from the Maccabees to Bar Kochba*. London: Bloomsbury Academic, 1998.
Oliver, Isaac W. "Jewish Apocalyptic Expectations during and after the Revolts against Rome." In *Winning Revolutions: The Psychosocial Dynamics of Revolts for Freedom, Fairness, and Rights, Volume I*, edited by J. Harold Ellens, 1:129–38. 3 vols. Santa Barbara, CA: ABC-CLIO, 2014.
Ostřanský, Bronislav. *The Jihadist Preachers of the End Times: ISIS Apocalyptic Propaganda*. Edinburgh: Edinburgh University Press, 2019.
Overy, Richard. *The Dictators: Hitler's Germany, Stalin's Russia*. London: Lane, 2004.
Pakenham, Thomas. *The Scramble for Africa: White Man's Conquest of the Dark Continent from 1876 to 1912*. London: HarperCollins, 1992.
Palafox, Quennie Ann J. "193rd Birth Anniversary of Apolinario Dela Cruz." *National Historical Commission of the Philippines*, September 6, 2012. https://nhcp.gov.ph/193rd-birth-anniversary-of-apolinario-dela-cruz/.
Papkova, Irina. *The Orthodox Church and Russian Politics*. Washington, DC: Woodrow Wilson Center, 2011.

Parrinder, Geoffrey. *World Religions, from Ancient History to the Present*. New York: Facts on File, 1983.

Peters, Frank. "People of the Book." *Oxford Bibliographies*, December 14, 2009. https://www.oxfordbibliographies.com/view/document/obo-9780195390155/obo-9780195390155-0059.xml.

Phillips, Andrew. *War, Religion and Empire: The Transformation of International Orders*. Cambridge: Cambridge University Press, 2010.

Pickens, George F. *African Christian God-Talk: Matthew Ajuoga's Johera Narrative*. Lanham, MD: University Press of America, 2004.

Popkin, Richard H. "Christian Interest and Concerns about Sabbatai Zevi." In *Millenarianism and Messianism in Early Modern European Culture, Volume I, Jewish Messianism in the Early Modern World*, edited by Matt D. Goldish and Richard H. Popkin, 1:91–106. 4 vols. Dordrecht, Netherlands: Springer, 2001.

———. "Introduction to the Millenarianism and Messianism Series." In *Millenarianism and Messianism in Early Modern European Culture, Volume I, Jewish Messianism in the Early Modern World*, edited by Matt D. Goldish and Richard H. Popkin, 1:vii–xiv. 4 vols. Dordrecht, Netherlands: Springer, 2001.

Porter, Stanley E. "Millenarian Thought in the First-Century Church." In *Christian Millenarianism: From the Early Church to Waco*, edited by Stephen Hunt, 62–76. London: Hurst, 2001.

Pulliam, Sarah. "Phrase 'Religious Right' Misused, Conservatives Say." *Christianity Today*, February 12, 2009. https://www.christianitytoday.com/ct/2009/februaryweb-only/106-42.0.html

Purcell, Victor. *The Boxer Uprising: A Background Study*. Cambridge: Cambridge University Press, 2010.

Raedts, Peter. "The Children's Crusade of 1213." *Journal of Medieval History* 3.4 (1977) 279–323.

"Rastafarian Beliefs." *BBC*, October 9, 2009. https://www.bbc.co.uk/religion/religions/rastafari/beliefs/beliefs_1.shtml.

Redles, David. "National Socialist Millennialism." In *The Oxford Handbook of Millennialism*, edited by Catherine Wessinger, 529–48. Oxford: Oxford University Press, 2011.

Reff, Daniel T. "The 'Predicament of Culture' and Spanish Missionary Accounts of the Tepehuan and Pueblo Revolts." *Ethnohistory* 42.1 (Winter 1995) 63–90.

Reuters. "Russian Orthodox Church Scolds Pope Francis after 'Putin's Altar Boy' Remark." *Premier Christian News*, May 5, 2022. https://premierchristian.news/en/news/article/russian-orthodox-church-scolds-pope-francis-after-putin-s-altar-boy-remark?_psrc=personyzeRelated.

Roach, Levi. *Æthelred the Unready*. New Haven: Yale University Press, 2017.

Roberts, Andrew. *The Storm of War*. London: Lane, 2009.

Roberts, James, and Martyn Whittock. *Trump and the Puritans: How the Evangelical Religious Right Put Donald Trump in the White House*. London: Biteback, 2020.

Robinson Waldman, Marilyn. "Eschatology: Islamic Eschatology." *Encyclopedia.com*. https://www.encyclopedia.com/environment/encyclopedias-almanacs-transcripts-and-maps/eschatology-islamic-eschatology.

Rogers, Kaleigh. "Why QAnon Has Attracted So Many White Evangelicals." *FiveThirtyEight*, March 4, 2021. https://fivethirtyeight.com/features/why-qanon-has-attracted-so-many-white-evangelicals/.

Romero, Simon. "Why New Mexico's 1680 Pueblo Revolt Is Echoing in 2020 Protests." *The New York Times*, September 27, 2020. https://www.nytimes.com/2020/09/27/us/pueblo-revolt-native-american-protests.html.

Roose, Kevin. "What Is QAnon, the Viral Pro-Trump Conspiracy Theory?" *The New York Times*, September 3, 2021. https://www.nytimes.com/article/what-is-qanon.html.

Rovner, Adam L. *In the Shadow of Zion: Promised Lands before Israel*. New York: New York University Press, 2014.

Rowan, Mattisan. "ISIS after the Caliphate." *Wilson Center*, November 28, 2017. https://www.wilsoncenter.org/article/isis-after-the-caliphate-0.

Rubenstein, Jay. *Armies of Heaven: The First Crusade and the Quest for Apocalypse*. New York: Basic, 2011.

Rubin, Michael. "Iran's Revolutionary Guards Keep Hinting at Nuclear Weapons Ambitions." *American Enterprise Institute*, January 9, 2021. https://www.aei.org/op-eds/irans-revolutionary-guards-keep-hinting-at-nuclear-weapons-ambitions/.

Sadr, Sayed Sadral-Din. *Al-Mahdi*. Edited by Sayed Baqir Khusroshani. Qom, Iran: Daftar-e Tablighate slami, 2000.

Schumacher, John N. "Syncretism in Philippine Catholicism: Its Historical Causes." *Philippine Studies* 32 (1984) 261–69.

Schwartz, Seth. *Imperialism and Jewish Society 200 B.C.E. to 640 C.E.* Princeton: Princeton University Press, 2009.

Scott, James C. *Decoding Subaltern Politics: Ideology, Disguise, and Resistance in Agrarian Politics*. London: Routledge, 2013.

Searcy, Kim. *The Formation of the Sudanese Mahdist State. Ceremony and Symbols of Authority: 1882–1898*. Leiden: Brill, 2010.

Setsuho, Ikehata. "The Millenarian Uprisings of Hesukristos in Philippine History." *Southeast Asia: History and Culture* 16 (1987) 3–36.

———. "Popular Catholicism in the Nineteenth-century Philippines: The Case of the Cofradia de San Jose." In *Reading Southeast Asia*, edited by Takashi Shiraishi, 109–60. Ithaca, NY: Cornell University Press, 2018.

———. "Uprisings of Hesukristos in the Philippines." In *Millenarianism in Asian History*, edited by Ishii Yoneo, 143–74. Tokyo: Institute for the Study of Languages and Cultures of Asia and Africa, 1993.

Sheinfeld, Shayna. "The Decline of Second Temple Jewish Apocalypticism and the Rise of Rabbinic Judaism." In *Apocalypses in Context: Apocalyptic Current Through History*, edited by Kelly J. Murphy and Justin Jeffcoat Schedtler, 187–210. Minneapolis: Fortress, 2016.

Sherwood, Harriet. "Ukraine: New Orthodox Church Gains Independence from Moscow." *The Guardian*, January 5, 2019. https://www.theguardian.com/world/2019/jan/05/ukraine-new-orthodox-church-gains-independence-from-moscow.

Shichor, Yitzhak. "Crackdowns: Insurgency, Potential Insurgency and Counterinsurgency in Modern China." In *Insurgencies and Counterinsurgencies: National Styles and Strategic Cultures*, edited by Beatrice Heuser and Eitan Shamir, 95–112. Cambridge: Cambridge University Press, 2016.

Shlapentokh, Dmitry. "The Time of Troubles in Alexander Dugin's Narrative." *Cambridge University Press*, October 31, 2018. https://www.cambridge.org/

core/journals/european-review/article/time-of-troubles-in-alexander-dugins-narrative/CAF11EDE51F7C4016D541CD40A096C61.

Shnirelman, Victor. "Alexander Dugin: Between Eschatology, Esotericism, and Conspiracy Theory." In *Handbook of Conspiracy Theory and Contemporary Religion*, edited by Asbjørn Dyrendal et al., 443–60. Leiden: Brill, 2018.

———. "Alexander Dugin: Building a Bridge between Eschatology and Conspiracy." *State, Religion and Church in Russia and Worldwide* 34 (2016) 194–221.

Siegel, Bernard J. "The Contestado Rebellion, 1912–16: A Case Study in Brazilian Messianism and Regional Dynamics." *Journal of Anthropological Research* 33.2 (Summer 1977) 202–13.

Silberklang, David. "Roots of Nazi Ideology." *Yad Vashem*. https://www.yadvashem.org/education/educational-videos/video-toolbox/hevt-nazi-ideology.html#233.

Silinsky, Mark D. *Empire of Terror: Iran's Islamic Revolutionary Guard Corps*. Lincoln, NE: Potomac, 2021.

"Simon Ben Kosiba." *Livius.org*. https://www.livius.org/articles/religion/messiah/messianic-claimant-18-simon-ben-kosiba/.

Sivertsev, Alexei M. *Judaism and Imperial Ideology in Late Antiquity*. Cambridge: Cambridge University Press, 2011.

Smith, Greg, and Linda Woodhead. "Religion and Brexit: Populism and the Church of England." *Religion, State and Society* 46.3 (August 2018) 206–23.

Spence, Jonathan D. *God's Chinese Son: The Taiping Heavenly Kingdom of Hong Xiuquan*. New York: Norton, 1996.

"Spirits in Uganda." *International Museum of Women*. http://exhibitions.globalfundforwomen.org/exhibitions/women-power-and-politics/religion/spirits-uganda.

Stackelberg, Roderick. *The Routledge Companion to Nazi Germany*. Abingdon, UK: Routledge, 2007.

Stanton, Gerald B. "The Doctrine of Imminency: Is It Biblical?" In *The Return: Understanding Christ's Second Coming, and the End Times*, edited by Thomas Ice and Timothy J. Demy, 107–36. Grand Rapids: Kregel, 1999.

Stefon, Matt, ed. *Judaism: History, Belief, and Practice*. New York: Britannica Educational, 2012.

Stein, George H. *The Waffen SS: Hitler's Elite Guard at War, 1939–1945*. Ithaca, NY: Cornell University Press, 1966.

Stiansen, Endre, and Michael Kevane. "Introduction: Kordofan Invaded." In *Kordofan Invaded: Peripheral Incorporation and Social Transformation in Islamic Africa*, edited by Endre Stiansen and Michael Kevane, 1–45. Leiden: Brill, 1998.

Strachan, Hew. *The First World War in Africa*. Oxford: Oxford University Press, 2004.

Tabor, James D. "Ancient Jewish and Early Christian Millennialism." In *The Oxford Handbook of Millennialism*, edited by Catherine Wessinger, 252–66. Oxford: Oxford University Press, 2011.

"Tenskwatawa." *Ohio History Central*. https://ohiohistorycentral.org/w/Tenskwatawa.

Tobias, Jonathan. "The Orthodox End of the World." *Pravmir*, July 25, 2019. https://www.pravmir.com/the-orthodox-end-of-the-world/.

Torrey, Charles C. "Apocalypse." *Jewish Encyclopedia*. https://www.jewishencyclopedia.com/articles/1642-apocalypse.

Travis, Stephen H. "Eschatology." In *New Dictionary of Theology*, edited by Sinclair B. Ferguson and David F. Wright, 228–31. Leicester: Inter-Varsity, 1988.

Tuchman, Barbara W. *A Distant Mirror: The Calamitous 14th Century*. Harmondsworth, UK: Penguin, 1979.

Tucker, Spencer. *The Encyclopedia of the Spanish-American and Philippine-American Wars: A Political, Social, and Military History*. Santa Barbara, CA: ABC-CLIO, 2009.

"Uganda's Brutal Lord's Resistance Army, Past and Present." *France24*, May 6, 2021. https://www.france24.com/en/live-news/20210506-uganda-s-brutal-lord-s-resistance-army-past-and-present.

United Nations Security Council. "Lord's Resistance Army." https://www.un.org/securitycouncil/sanctions/2127/materials/summaries/entity/lord%E2%80%99s-resistance-army.

United States Holocaust Memorial Museum. "Protocols of the Elders of Zion." *Holocaust Encyclopedia*. https://encyclopedia.ushmm.org/content/en/article/protocols-of-the-elders-of-zion.

Urban, Hugh B. "Millenarian Elements in the Hindu Religious Traditions." In *The Oxford Handbook of Millennialism*, edited by Catherine Wessinger, 369–82. Oxford: Oxford University Press, 2011.

UShistory.org. "3d. Puritan Life." www.ushistory.org/us/3d.asp.

Vine, W. E. *An Expository Dictionary of New Testament Words*. Nashville: Nelson, 1983.

Wacker, Grant. "The Christian Right." *National Humanities Center*. http://nationalhumanitiescenter.org/tserve/twenty/tkeyinfo/chr_rght.htm

Warburg, Gabriel. *Islam, Sectarianism, and Politics in Sudan since the Mahdiyya*. Madison: University of Wisconsin Press, 2003.

Ward, Alex. "Understanding the Christian Reconstructionist Movement." *The Ethics & Religious Liberty Commission*, September 24, 2021. https://erlc.com/resource-library/articles/understanding-the-christian-reconstruction-movement/.

Wasserstrom, Steven. *Between Muslim and Jew*. Princeton: Princeton University Press, 1995.

White, Frances. "How Many Died in the Chinese Taiping Rebellion?" *History of War*, August 15, 2014. https://www.historyanswers.co.uk/history-of-war/how-many-died-in-the-chinese-taiping-rebellion/.

White, Matthew. *Atrocities: The 100 Deadliest Episodes in Human History*. New York: Norton, 2013.

Whittock, Martyn. "Baptist Roots: The Use of Models in Tracing Baptist Origins." *The Evangelical Quarterly* 57.4 (October 1985) 317–26.

———. *A Brief History of the Third Reich*. London: Robinson, 2011.

———. *The End Times, Again?: 2000 Years of the Use & Misuse of Biblical Prophecy*. Eugene, OR: Cascade, 2021.

———. "Franklin Graham Is Speculating in His End Times Tweet to Boris Johnson. No One Knows When Jesus Will Return." *Premier Christianity*, November 12, 2021. https://www.premierchristianity.com/opinion/franklin-graham-is-speculating-in-his-end-times-tweet-to-boris-johnson-no-one-knows-when-jesus-will-return/5706.article.

———. *The Reformation*. Oxford: Heinemann Educational, 1992.

———. "The Return of the Nuclear Threat?" *Christian Today*, April 26, 2022. https://www.christiantoday.com/article/the.return.of.the.nuclear.threat/138514.htm.

———. "What Happens When the 'End Times' Are Now?" *History News Network*, January 16, 2022. https://historynewsnetwork.org/article/182179

———. *When God Was King: Rebels and Radicals of the Civil War and Mayflower Generation*. Oxford: Lion Hudson, 2018.

Whittock, Martyn, and Esther Whittock. *Jesus: The Unauthorized Biography*. Oxford: Lion Hudson, 2021.

———. *The Story of the Cross*. Oxford: Lion Hudson, 2021.

Whittock, Martyn, and Hannah Whittock. *Norse Myths and Legends*. London: Robinson, 2017.

———. "Vikings: When the Hammer Met the Cross." *Church Times*, October 26, 2018. https://www.churchtimes.co.uk/articles/2018/26-october/features/features/vikings-when-the-hammer-met-the-cross.

Williams, Daniel K. *God's Own Party: The Making of the Christian Right*. Oxford: Oxford University Press, 2010.

Williams, David J. *Acts*. Understanding the Bible Commentary Series. Ada, MI: Baker, 2011.

Wright, Nicholas Thomas. *Jesus and the Victory of God*. London: SPCK, 2015.

Zaman, Shams uz. "Iran's Unscrupulous Role in the Arab Spring: A March Back to Authoritarianism?" In *The World Community and the Arab Spring*, edited by Cenap Çakmak and Ali Onur Özçelik, 275–300, London: Palgrave Macmillan, 2019.

Ziegler, Philip. *The Black Death*. Harmondsworth, UK: Penguin, 1982.

Zimmer, Heinrich. *Myths and Symbols in Indian Art and Civilization*. New York: Harper & Row, 1962.

www.ingramcontent.com/pod-product-compliance
Lightning Source LLC
Chambersburg PA
CBHW022016220426
43663CB00007B/1105